FORD MADOX FORD:
PROSE AND POLITICS

FORD MADOX FORD: PROSE AND POLITICS

ROBERT GREEN

CAMBRIDGE UNIVERSITY PRESS

CAMBRIDGE

LONDON   NEW YORK   NEW ROCHELLE

MELBOURNE   SYDNEY

Published by the Press Syndicate of the University of Cambridge
The Pitt Building, Trumpington Street, Cambridge CB2 1RP
32 East 57th Street, New York, NY 10022, USA
296 Beaconsfield Parade, Middle Park, Melbourne 3206, Australia

First published 1981

Printed in Great Britain by
Western Printing Services Ltd, Bristol

British Library Cataloguing in Publication Data
Green, Robert
Ford Madox Ford.
1. Ford, Ford Madox, b.1873 – Criticism and
interpretation
828′.9′1209   PR6011.O532/   80–41566
ISBN 0 521 23610 X

There is something more in Art than the surroundings in which it is produced and the psychological antecedents of the artist. The type and the school are explicable on that basis, but never the individuality, the specific quality which makes one what one is. This method leads one perforce to set little store by talent. The only significance of the masterpiece is as a historical document. It is the radically opposite standpoint to La Harpe's and to the old criticism. In the old days it was believed that Literature was an entirely individual matter, and that books dropped like thunderbolts from the skies. Now we have come to deny all will and all absolutes. The truth, I think, lies in the middle.

Flaubert, *Letter to Mme Roger des Genettes*

You cannot write about Euripides and ignore Athens.

Ford, *Henry James*

for Walter and Nina

CONTENTS

▬▬

Preface   *page* ix
Abbreviations   xiii

PART ONE   1891–1909   1

1   The early years   3
2   The 'Fifth Queen' trilogy: the politics of nostalgia   33

PART TWO   1910–1915   51

3   Georgian pessimism: sketches for *The Good Soldier*   53
4   *The Good Soldier*: the politics of agnosticism   80

PART THREE   1916–1928   111

5   The novelist of reconstruction   113
6   *Parade's End*   129

PART FOUR   1929–1939   169

7   Ford's last novels: 'the small producer'   171
8   The shape of an achievement   183

Notes   196
Bibliography   204
Index   215

PREFACE

The least necessary addition to criticism of Ford Madox Ford would be another study of his techniques, since this aspect of his work was the object of a great deal of attention in the sixties. At that time Ford critics were, by and large, 'formalist' in method, and, as a result, the 'Ford' who emerged from their studies was a reflection of the allegiance of these scholars – a consummate craftsman and manipulator of such modernist devices as 'time-shift' and *'progression d'effet'*. The present study acknowledges Ford's success in this direction, but proposes that, while he was undoubtedly an outstanding technician, Ford was also a man who wrote at a particular point in time and in particular places. The sixty-six years of his life, from 1873 to 1939, span a crucial period of European cultural and political history – the end of 'Victorianism'; conflict in South Africa and the First World War; the Russian Revolution; the rise of Fascism; the genesis of literary and artistic modernism. Instead of replicating earlier New Critical work on Ford, I shall be placing him within this historical context, looking at the ways in which he responded to the astonishingly rapid changes in European politics and culture. Thus I shall comment in some detail upon Ford's political beliefs – in the pre-war period, his antipathy to collectivism, and, after the war, the similarities between his views and those of C. H. Douglas and the Social Credit movement – and shall examine the connection between these beliefs and the techniques of his novels.

In thus establishing Ford as an historical figure, a man who lived through history and was himself a part of that

same history, I have been encouraged by some of the writer's
own comments and the approaches he himself employed as a
critic. His excellent chapter on Conrad in *Mightier than the
Sword*, for instance, treats his partner as a political novelist;
his discussion of the rise of the English novel, in the book of
that title, stresses the pressures of social and educational
change on the fiction of Defoe; and, like Lukács, he sees in
his two propaganda books how German culture is the product
of German history. None of these insights might be expected
from a man uninterested in political movements, a man only
concerned with the crafting of a novel. Commenting on the
rise of the Pre-Raphaelite Brotherhood in 1848, the 'Year of
Revolution', Ford remarks that 'the times. . .were ripe for
revolt, and, had the Pre-Raphaelites not come when they did,
their places would almost inevitably have been supplied by
other young men'. It was also Ford who wrote in *The March
of Literature* that 'Byron and Espronceda', the Romantic
Movement of the early nineteenth century, 'gave the impulse
to *Das Kapital*'. Ford was clearly aware of the intimacies
between art and politics.

This study also widens the focus of discussion of Ford in
another respect, as my title 'prose and politics' indicates.
I am interested in Ford as a writer of *prose*, and not just as a
novelist. He himself drew no firm line between 'fiction' and
memoir or autobiography, between the 'novel' and the essay
or volume of propaganda. Arguably, indeed, everything Ford
wrote should be considered as fiction, and it therefore seems
appropriate that the novels be treated alongside the rest of
his prose. As a result, more than usual attention will be paid
to such prose works as *Ancient Lights*, *The Critical Attitude*,
Henry James, the two volumes of war-propaganda, *Provence*
and *Great Trade Route*, partly for their own intrinsic interest
and partly for the illumination they cast on the novels of the
same period.

The conclusion of this study is that the orthodox critical
evaluation of Ford ought not to be overturned in any important respect. His major achieved works will undoubtedly

remain *The Good Soldier* and the war quartet, *Parade's End*,
with the 'Fifth Queen' trilogy a very distinguished example
of the historical novel. But evaluation is not the sole function
of literary criticism and the purpose of this study is, rather,
to provide a fresh context in which to situate those major
fictions. Our understanding of *The Good Soldier* is, I think,
enriched when we see it in relation to Ford's political pessimism just before the war. The novel *is* a great technical
accomplishment, yet it's also necessary to acknowledge that it
was written at a particular time and in particular, unrepeatable
circumstances. It did not, to adopt Flaubert's words, simply
drop from the early modernist skies like a thunderbolt. Similarly the magnificent *Parade's End* should be placed within
the era of 'reconstruction', as a major document in the endeavour to find imaginative forms for the post-Versailles world.

The organisation of this book follows from its fundamentally historicist approach. Discussion of Ford's works by
genre – so that all the historical novels, from the 'Fifth
Queen' trilogy, written just before the war, to the late *Little
Less Than Gods*, are treated in the same chapter – is appropriate for a formalist study, but would be less apt here.
Instead we shall examine Ford's works chronologically, discussing all the prose works of a particular period together.
The heart of the book is my discussion of the major novels,
with *Parade's End*, *The Good Soldier* and the Tudor trilogy
being given full treatment in long, single chapters. I have
arranged the rest of Ford's prose, fiction and non-fiction,
around these central chapters, in order, again, to try to place
the major texts within the context, both of Ford's other works
and of the relevant historical and cultural shifts. From each
of the four periods into which I have divided Ford's life I
have selected one less successful novel (*The Inheritors*, *A Call*,
The Marsden Case and *Vive Le Roy*) to exemplify Ford's
lesser fiction. Perfectly adequate commentaries already exist
on all Ford's second-rate novels, and it seemed unnecessary to
exhume them individually here.

One final, more personal, possibly impertinent comment

is perhaps in order at this point. All the secondary material published on Ford to date – the biographies by Mizener and MacShane; the magnificent annotated bibliography of Professor Harvey; and several volumes of criticism – is of American origin. The present study is the first full-length appreciation by an English critic of the English novelist, Ford Madox Ford. There are doubtless many reasons for my compatriots' apparent neglect of Ford, but now, forty years after his death, is not too early for the first English book to appear. I should be very happy if this book were to mark a small beginning to the process of Ford's revival in the country of his birth, as well as to confirm his stature for other admirers.

Some of the material in this book was originally published, in rather different form, in *English Literature in Transition*, *Modernist Studies* and *English Literary History*. I am grateful to their editors and publishers for permission to reprint this material.

The early stages of preparation were supported by a Doctoral Fellowship from the Canada Council. I have also benefited from the diligence and kindness of staff at the Libraries of the University of Southampton; the University of Manitoba; the Manchester and Southampton Public Libraries; and the University of Malawi, where the final draft was written. A number of readers drew my attention to errors of omission and commission in earlier drafts; in particular I want to thank Bernard Bergonzi, Malcolm Bradbury, John Goode and J. M. Robinson for their invaluable criticism. Meredith Robinson, a pioneer in Canadian criticism of Ford, also offered me the warmth of his encouragement and friendship at a very early stage of this enterprise. My wife Ernestine shared the burden of the several drafts with unfailing good humour, and commented on them with a sharp intelligence. Also useful were the reiterated reminders of our son, Richard, that mine is only 'a book about other books'.

Zomba, Malawi, 19 March 1980

ABBREVIATIONS

PRIMARY SOURCES

AL	*Ancient Lights and Certain New Reflections, Being the Memories of a Young Man*
AMCSU	*A Man Could Stand Up–*
BEN	*The Benefactor, A Tale of a Small Circle*
BSDG	*Between St Dennis and St George, A Sketch of Three Civilisations*
CA	*The Critical Attitude*
CALL	*A Call, The Tale of Two Passions*
COLLP	*Collected Poems*
CP	*The Cinque Ports, A Historical and Descriptive Record*
EE	*England and the English, An Interpretation*
EG	*An English Girl, A Romance*
EN	*The English Novel from the Earliest Days to the Death of Joseph Conrad*
ER	*The English Review*
FMB	*Ford Madox Brown, A Record of his Life and Work*
FQ	*The Fifth Queen, And How She Came to Court*
FQC	*The Fifth Queen Crowned*
GS	*The Good Soldier; A Tale of Passion*
GTR	*Great Trade Route*
HC	*The Heart of the Country, A Survey of a Modern Land*
HH	*Hans Holbein the Younger, A Critical Monograph*
HJ	*Henry James, A Critical Study*

HM	The 'Half-Moon', A Romance of the Old World and the New
INH	The Inheritors, An Extravagant Story
IWN	It was the Nightingale
JC	Joseph Conrad, A Personal Remembrance
LLG	A Little Less Than Gods, A Romance
LP	Last Post
LWBE	Ladies Whose Bright Eyes, A Romance
MA	Mr Apollo, A Just Possible Story
MBM	Mister Bosphorus and the Muses
MC	The Marsden Case, A Romance
MF	Mr Fleight
MOL	The March of Literature from Confucius to Modern Times
MTF	A Mirror to France
MTS	Mightier than the Sword, Memories and Criticisms
NC	The Nature of a Crime
NHD	The New Humpty-Dumpty
NMP	No More Parades
NP	New Poems
NYE	New York Essays
NYINA	New York is not America
OH	On Heaven and Poems Written on Active Service
PAN	The Panel, A Sheer Comedy
PE	Parade's End
POR	The Portrait
PRB	The Pre-Raphaelite Brotherhood, A Critical Monograph
PROV	Provence, From Minstrels to the Machine
PS	Privy Seal, His Last Venture
RA	The Rash Act
ROM	Romance, A Novel
ROS	Rossetti, A Critical Essay on his Art
RTY	Return to Yesterday
SDN	Some Do Not...
SL	The Soul of London, A Survey of a Modern City

SP	*The Spirit of the People, An Analysis of the English Mind*
TR	*Transatlantic Review*
TTR	*Thus to Revisit, Some Reminiscences*
VLR	*Vive Le Roy*
WBITA	*When Blood is their Argument, An Analysis of Prussian Culture*
WM	*Women and Men*
WWM	*When the Wicked Man*

SECONDARY SOURCES

Cassell	Richard A. Cassell, *Ford Madox Ford – A Study of his Novels* (Baltimore, 1961)
Gordon	Ambrose Gordon, Jr, *The Invisible Tent: The War Novels of Ford Madox Ford* (Austin, 1964)
Harvey	David Dow Harvey, *Ford Madox Ford 1873– 1939, A Bibliography of Works and Criticism* (Princeton, 1962)
Hoffmann	Charles G. Hoffmann, *Ford Madox Ford* (New York, 1967)
Huntley	H. Robert Huntley, *The Alien Protagonist of Ford Madox Ford* (Chapel Hill, 1970)
Lid	R. W. Lid, *Ford Madox Ford: The Essence of His Art* (Berkeley, 1964)
Meixner	John A. Meixner, *Ford Madox Ford's Novels – A Critical Study* (Minneapolis, 1962)
Mizener	Arthur Mizener, *The Saddest Story – A Biography of Ford Madox Ford* (New York, 1971)
Ohmann	Carol Ohmann, *Ford Madox Ford – From Apprentice to Craftsman* (Middletown, Connecticut, 1964)
Stang	Sondra J. Stang, *Ford Madox Ford* (New York, 1977)
Wiley	Paul L. Wiley, *Novelist of Three Worlds: Ford Madox Ford* (Syracuse, 1962)

PART ONE

1891–1909

Date	Novels	Prose	Poetry	Children's Books
1891				*The Brown Owl*
1892	*The Shifting of the Fire*			*The Feather*
1893			*Questions at the Well*	
1894				*The Queen Who Flew*
1895				
1896		*Ford Madox Brown*		
1897				
1898				
1899				
1900		*The Cinque Ports*	*Poems for Pictures*	
1901	*The Inheritors*			
1902		*Rossetti*		
1903	*Romance*			
1904			*The Face of the Night*	
1905	*The Benefactor*	*Hans Holbein* *The Soul of London*		
1906	*The Fifth Queen*	*The Heart of the Country*		*Christina's Fairy Book*
1907	*Privy Seal* *An English Girl*	*The Pre-Raphaelite Brotherhood* *The Spirit of the People*	*From Inland*	
1908	*The Fifth Queen Crowned* *Mr Apollo*	*The English Review*		
1909	*The 'Half-Moon'*	*The English Review*		

1

THE EARLY YEARS

I

Ford Madox Ford was born in December 1873 in Merton, near Wimbledon in South London, a far cry from those spacious rural 'seats', Groby and Branshaw, which he was to invent for the heroes of his best novels. His unremarkable birthplace – Merton is part of the suburban London celebrated in the verse of John Betjeman – is only the first of many instances where the facts of Ford's life failed to correspond to the novelist's subsequent inventions about his own noble past. The circumstances of his birth were respectable, but scarcely aristocratic.

Ford's father, Francis Hueffer, came from a line of prosperous Catholic printers in Munster. He had left Germany in 1869, possibly as a result of his atheistic views, to settle in London where he lived the life of a distinguished musicologist until his death in 1889. In 1872 he married Catherine, daughter of Ford Madox Brown the painter, and Ford was the eldest of their three children.[1] The marriage united two streams of artistic and intellectual innovation, the English Pre-Raphaelite movement and the new forces in European music and philosophy, for Francis Hueffer founded two magazines to popularise Schopenhauer and Wagner in England, just as his son was to establish *The English Review* and *Transatlantic Review* to advertise the innovative work of later generations. Ford was later to remark that he was 'brought up in the back rooms and nurseries of pre-Raphaelism' (*AL*, 106–7), and there is some evidence that his childhood among artists and musicians was oppressive. Certainly it did implant in him a lasting belief in the importance of art and, as a result of the uncomfortable brilliance of his Rossetti cousins, a suspicion of the competitiveness and rancour of artistic communities. His attitude to the Pre-Raphaelites in particular, and to Victorian culture in general, was to remain deeply ambivalent.

In 1881, at the age of seven, Ford was sent to a 'progressive' boarding-school in Folkestone run by a German couple. He remained at school in Kent until 1889 when his father's death enforced his removal to University College School, in Gower Street. Francis Hueffer died a poor man and the family finances became strained. In the following year Ford, now sixteen, left school, evidently ambitious to become a musician. As a young man in London in the nineties Ford came into contact with the socialism of William Morris and with the world of the political anarchists. He affected a black coat, with a cape slung over the shoulders which floated out behind him as he walked:

This cape had been Gabriel Rossetti's and had come down to him through his grandfather; it was over thirty years old. The jacket he wore under it was 'a water-tight German forester's pilot jacket', also secondhand, and under that was a fifteen-year-old blue-linen shirt of his grandfather's and a red-satin tie. This costume, he felt, was the proper wear for a young man of Pre-Raphaelite descent who sympathised with Morris' socialism; Morris' disciples, he noted, had much imitated Rossetti's cape. (*Mizener*, 16)

The youthful Ford was clearly modelling himself on the 'New Dandyism' of the nineties, mixed with a carefully eccentric devotion to the lovable shabbiness of his grandfather. The painter embodied for Ford the nobility and selflessness of the authentic artist, and Ford Madox Brown was to remain the strongest influence on his grandson until the meeting with Conrad in 1898.

With Brown's encouragement Ford published his first book, a fairy-story aptly entitled *The Brown Owl* (1891), and this was quickly followed by two volumes in a similar vein, *The Feather* (1892) and *The Queen Who Flew* (1894). Ford later dismissed these books as being 'about Princes and Princesses and magicians and such twaddle'. (*MTS*, 94) Yeats had founded the Irish National Literary Society in 1891, early evidence of the decade's 'Celtic Revival', and by choosing to write his earliest works as fairy-stories Ford was perhaps responding to the period's new interest in myth, folklore, magic and mysticism. It's more likely, though, that Ford, still only twenty, hadn't yet discovered his true subjects, for, as he later remarked, the novelist needed to 'live' before he began to write. (*NYINA*, 133)

The same inexperience marred *The Shifting of the Fire* (1892), Ford's first novel, published when he was eighteen. This was no more credible or realistic than the fairy-stories, 'almost entirely amateurish,' 'implausible and...absurd... written in a ludicrously elegant style'. (*Cassell*, 117; *Mizener*, 18) *The Shifting of the Fire* was derivative of Victorian fictional melodramas and the plot is reminiscent of a novel of the same type, Hardy's early *Desperate Remedies* (1871). The full flavour of Ford's archaic style can be appreciated in the extract cited by Arthur Mizener:

[The host] was fain to let them go to their rooms above. Here the air struck cold on entry, despite the fires which burned bravely, with crackling red embers, yet were they glad without more ado to doff their clothes in cold and shivering haste, thrusting themselves between the sheets...(*Mizener*, 18)

Both the archaic language and the inverted syntax are plainly derivative, and Conrad's comment in 1898 that the book was 'delightfully young' was more revealing of the liberality with which he was prepared to treat Ford at the start of their collaboration than of the novel's true merits.[2]

The Shifting of the Fire was the only novel Ford had published before his collaboration with Conrad, though he had drafted 'Seraphina', an early, unsatisfactory version of *Romance* (1903), in 1896–7. It's clear, then, that Ford had not yet developed any coherent ideas about fiction beyond the general belief in the value of art that was part of his Pre-Raphaelite heritage. *Ford Madox Brown* (1896) is a dutiful and professional biography of his grandfather, but it doesn't offer evidence that Ford had discovered any revolutionary views about language and art before the momentous meeting with Conrad in the autumn of 1898. At one point he described his grandfather's professional enemies as 'tares in the Brunonian wheat' and there are plenty of other examples of precious solemnity in the biography. Ford's early works, like his strange costume, were in truth deeply conventional and borrowed from the past.

Ford Madox Brown was written in Sussex where Ford had been living since his marriage in 1894, devoted to 'the Tory conservatism, the Pre-Raphaelite medievalism, and "the simple life" so fashionable among advanced intellectuals' of that period. (*Mizener*, 37) Conrad and Ford were introduced by Edward Garnett in September 1898 and it was at Conrad's suggestion that they soon started work on the revision of the unpublishable 'Seraphina'. Friends had advised Conrad to try to find an English collaborator to help him write more fluently and correctly. Ford was also useful to him in 1898 because he was at that time 'discouraged and floundering' and benefited from the younger man's psychological support. For his part, Ford greatly admired Conrad's gifts as a writer and, most importantly, Conrad inspired him with the settled purpose of becoming a novelist. The meeting and the years of close friendship around the turn of the century were the most influential events of Ford's life as a novelist. The collaboration gave Ford a sense of the discipline and architecture required of the novel that had been lacking from 'Seraphina' and *The Shifting of the Fire*. They were to work together, intermittently, until 1908.

Ford only brought to the partnership enthusiasm and a wholehearted, if as yet undirected, commitment to art's nobility, but Conrad had already laid the foundations of his career with *Almayer's Folly* (1895), *An Outcast of the Islands* (1896) and *The Nigger of the 'Narcissus'*, serialised by Henley in 1897. He had also, in the Preface published at the end of *The Nigger*, issued his own manifesto, a positive statement of the centrality of fiction. The Preface, one of the seminal documents of English modernism, asserts, above all, the importance of fiction as a genre and how it 'aspires to be art'.[3] Conrad wrote little here about the 'grammar' or 'architecture' of particular texts. Unlike the Preface to *What Maisie Knew*, it's not an account of the genesis of a single story. Instead Conrad accepts the larger task of justifying fiction's generic claim; it 'seeks the truth', it 'brings to light the truth' of human existence. The thinker, he acknowledged, does this by 'plung[ing] into ideas', the scientist by the investigation of facts. The novelist has the same aim, the discovery of truth, but he alone 'descends within himself' and 'finds the terms of his appeal':

He speaks to our capacity for delight and wonder, to the sense of mystery surrounding our lives; to our sense of pity, and beauty, and pain; to the latent feeling of fellowship with all creation – to the subtle but invincible conviction of solidarity that knits together the loneliness of innumerable hearts, to the solidarity in dreams, in joy, in sorrow, in aspirations, in illusions, in hope, in fear, which binds men to each other, which binds together all humanity – the dead to the living and the living to the unborn.[4]

Ideas, facts and theories are ephemeral and demolished anew by every generation. Only the discoveries of the artist, salvaged from his own depths, have a lasting validity. Conrad asserted, like Sidney and Shelley, the cognitive value of imaginative art.

In this respect indeed Conrad's Preface is very much a document of its time, a part of that widespread reaction against positivism, that revulsion from ideology and abstract thought, from 'the whole tendency to discuss human behaviour in terms of analogies drawn from natural science' which characterised European thought at the end of the nineteenth century.[5] The style bears the imprint of Pater, still enormously influential in the nineties, as Conrad proclaims that 'all art. . .appeals primarily to the senses, . . .its high desire [being] to reach the *secret spring* of responsive emotions'.[6] The sociologists and philosophers of that decade,

Conrad's 'thinkers', were similarly bent on 'displac[ing] the axis of social thought from the apparent and objectively verifiable to the only partially conscious area of unexplained motivation'.[7] Nevertheless, although we can place Conrad's Preface, with its stress on the emotional and subjective bases of art, alongside the work of Freud, Bergson and Durkheim, it's also important to remember that his main concern in the Preface was actually the liberation of art from any analogies with political or moral thought. The 'worker in prose', Conrad urged, has no business responding to the reader's demand 'to be edified, consoled, amused;...to be promptly improved, or encouraged, or frightened, or shocked, or charmed'.[8] Conrad thus distinguished the novelist's role from the thinker's; the novelist's business is 'before all, to make you *see*'. This is a phrase that Ford was constantly to repeat as the central aim of the novelist, the effort to make the reader 'see'. In emphasising the novelist's need to visualise, Conrad's Preface effectively dissociated the novel from any prescriptive function.

With this abandonment of explicit moral purposefulness Conrad 'joined the attack...upon the nineteenth century's seduction by abstractions, by the resounding appeal of moral terms or shibboleths that had lost their basis in conduct or sincerity'.[9] Ford, who had so recently endured a Pre-Raphaelite upbringing, must have warmed to this assertion of the novel's freedom from dogmatism. Association with Conrad provided Ford with an escape, guided and encouraged, from the moralistic bases of Victorian aestheticism that had been impressed on him by late-Victorian artists. The association was truly a 'rite of passage' for Ford, his introduction to artistic independence. In *Henry James* (1913) he was later to describe how, as a young man, he had been directed to notice the 'profound moral purpose' in that novelist, and how bewildered he had been not to discover any such high seriousness. (*HJ*, 45) In a similar vein, *Return to Yesterday* (1931) includes an episode in which Ford claims to have rebelled against his Victorian upbringing by reading comics in the cellar. (*RTY*, 84) Joseph Conrad's value to Ford, then, was that he provided the younger man's truancy with a *post facto* seal of respectability. He legitimised, as it were, the reading of comics. Conrad's manifesto and their conversations must have supported Ford's own Pre-Raphaelite belief in art's centrality, and at the same time removed any vestigial attraction in the Brotherhood's moral earnestness.

Ford became Conrad's 'secret sharer' and they devoted much of their energy over the next decade, until 1908 when they disagreed over *The English Review*, to forging a modernist poetics for the novel. They took as their models the great French realist novelists of the nineteenth century – Flaubert, Stendhal and Maupassant, with Turgenev included as being French in spirit and sympathy – and desired to graft onto the English novel some of the impersonal rigour and verbal conciseness of that group. In *The March of Literature* (1938) Ford invented an imaginary paragraph from *Vanity Fair* and then proceeded to rewrite it in the style of Flaubert, as 'impressionism'. Commenting on his two versions – and Ford was always an excellent exponent of 'Practical Criticism' – he remarked that in the second, impressionistic paragraph

the author is invisible and almost unnoticeable and. . .his attempt has been, above all, to make you see. It is presented rather than narrated because all that you get are the spectacle of the affair and the psychological reaction of one of the characters. . .Similarly, moral-drawing comment would take away from the vividness and entirely destroy the verisimilitude of the scene. . .the drawing of a moral is unnecessary; and the introduction of himself by the author in order to draw the moral would have the effect of completely destroying the reality of the scene for the reader. (*MOL*, 768–9)

Madame Bovary epitomised the visual clarity and authorial displacement of French realism. These were the two qualities that Ford and Conrad wished to import into English fiction.

In thus seeking, alongside James, to 'redeem the English novel for the intelligent world', Conrad and Ford were doing work that proved their early insight into the crucial lines of development of modernism.[10] 'In a real sense they were on to what would be the entire modern movement in prose fiction and poetry.'[11] And yet the seminal importance of their collaboration cannot be measured by the novels, *Romance* and *The Inheritors* (1901), they jointly wrote. These were unremarkable. The real demonstration of the theories in action was only provided by the novels they published independently, by *Lord Jim* (1900) and *Nostromo* (1904), and by Ford's much later *The Good Soldier* (1915) and *Parade's End* (1924–8). Here are the successful, influential applications of the collaborative theory, novels of indisputable stature and originality. Students of the partnership have often conjectured about the explanation for the mediocrity of the joint novels, and the possible influence of domestic and temperamental obstacles. Perhaps, however, the failure of the two writers to produce any major shared novels could have been anticipated by the very terms Conrad himself had employed in the 1897 Preface. In its second sentence this essay had defined art as a '*single-minded* attempt to render the highest kind of justice to the visible universe'.[12] 'Single-minded' here refers not only to the qualities of tenacity and stamina required of the novelist; it also implies the importance, fundamental to the whole Preface, Conrad attributed to the workings of the individual sensibility, the writer's descent within himself and exploration of 'that lonely region of stress and strife'.[13] Such a journey could scarcely be made in tandem: notions of loneliness and risk are central to Conrad's Preface and to his practice in *Lord Jim* and *Nostromo*.

These two novels, then, with *The Good Soldier* and *Parade's End*, constitute the permanent value of the theories forged around the turn of the century. The partnership was committed to 'the adequation of language to the thing perceived or the sensation undergone'; to the value of '*progression d'effet*', the importance of every phrase, sentence and episode in the novel's accumulating power; and to 'the principle of juxtaposition without copula of chapter with chapter. . .as the mainspring of poetic effect'.[14] None of these theories had been set out in Conrad's Preface, aside from an undeveloped allusion to the need for a novel to 'carry its justification in every line'.[15] It was only in the Conrad–Ford 'workshop' that the Preface was given flesh and means found to put into practice the aspirations voiced at the end of *The Nigger of the 'Narcissus'*.

There is now no serious doubt that Ford benefited immeasurably from his 'apprenticeship' with Conrad; nor, despite Jessie Conrad's celebrated dislike of Ford, that Conrad was given the strength to complete *Lord Jim* and *Nostromo*. Conrad's major fiction belongs to the period of, and immediately after, his partnership with Ford. In its short-term effects the collaboration might have seemed futile, for both *Romance* and *The Inheritors* were critical and commercial failures. Despite these set-backs, which were especially painful to Ford, he was now ready to embark alone on his career as a novelist. He was furnished, when he moved to London in 1904, with a totally serious commitment to fiction, as well as with a series of formal precepts. Indeed the period of the collaboration was Ford's formative years, and he was to remain devoted to the theories the two men had established for the remainder of his life. Different aspects of the theories were, it is true, to be emphasised at different times. Thus between 1909 and 1915 it was to be fiction's analogies with sculpture that Ford would choose to stress among the ideas of the Preface, whereas in the twenties and thirties he was to be more concerned with the novel's value as a contribution to what Conrad had called in 1897 'the latent feeling of fellowship with all creation'.[16] Fundamentally, though, Ford was to remain wedded to his 'impressionism' – his title and one that Conrad avoided – for the rest of his life. In his memorial volume, *Joseph Conrad* (1924), Ford was to remark that his friend 'prized fidelity, especially to adventurers, above all human virtues and saw very little of it in this world'. (*JC*, 61) Ford remained faithful to the adventurous Conrad throughout his life: in the concluding pages of his last book he quoted the first and last sentences of *Heart of*

Darkness as examples of fictional impressionism. (*MOL*, 767–71) Such was the abiding effect on Ford of the collaboration at the turn of the century.

The partnership with Joseph Conrad was undoubtedly the most decisive element in Ford's life as a novelist between 1898 and 1908, but it would be wrong to suggest that the search for an impressionist poetics of fiction was Ford's sole preoccupation during those years. He also responded to external forces, to the Boer War and the modernisation of England, and his novels were an attempt to render his impressions of such cultural changes, as well as an endeavour to rework the forms of fictional narrative. The following pages will be concerned with the relationship between Ford's political responses and his technical preoccupations.

II

'The opening of the twentieth century finds us all, to the dismay of the old-fashioned individualist, "thinking in communities".'[17] So wrote Beatrice and Sidney Webb in their influential essay, 'Lord Rosebery's Escape from Houndsditch', in September 1901, the year that also saw the publication of *The Inheritors*, the first fruit of a very different literary partnership. This novel was indeed designed as an attack on the very values – modernity, innovation, collective efficiency – the Webbs personified. The year before, in *The Cinque Ports*, a curious mixture of travelogue and jeremiad, Ford had bemoaned the passing of old traditions and their replacement by a bustling materialism. His view of the past in *The Cinque Ports*

when nothing hurried, nothing was passion-worn, nothing strove; when everyone was at peace with his neighbours, when the greatest of crimes was that of sitting up 'late o' nights' (*CP*, 215)

is sentimental and idealised, intended to counter what he saw as the reformists' contempt for 'the lessons of tradition'. (*CP*, 270) In the final lines of *The Cinque Ports* 'the hurry and turmoil' of the present, 'all these wheels, all this machinery' –

symptom of developments that had long been in train. The Boer War acted as a catalyst. To Ford it indicated the collapse of the old treasured forms. To the Social Imperialists, on the other hand, it only underlined the urgency of political renovation.

The Inheritors describes how Arthur Granger, an aristocratic and unsuccessful novelist priding himself on his noble ideals, betrays these for the sake of a girl who fails to return his love. Granger first meets the girl in Canterbury Cathedral. She is an agent sent from the Fourth Dimension and Granger discovers that her people are to invade and take over the three-dimensional earth, capturing power because of their lack of ethical scruple. The invaders are 'cold...clear-sighted and admirably courageous, and indubitably enemies of society'. (*INH*, 123) They also, like Swift's Houyhnhnms, have 'no feeling for art'. Ford's satirical targets here, his identification of the ruthless invaders, were the leading figures of the Social Imperialist movement – Chamberlain in particular, and also Rosebery, Beatrice Webb and Milner. His fear of the subversives' amorality was plainly a response to what he saw as the dangerous confidence of the Social Imperialists. 'The most unmistakable and common characteristic of the insurgents was their aggressive, even predatory, self-assurance', as one of their historians has remarked,[23] and it's the arrogant self-righteousness of the collectivists that comes across most clearly in Ford's novel. 'The old order' (personified by Granger – or, more exactly, by his image of himself as a man of altruism and firm principles – and by Churchill, the Foreign Secretary), 'changeth', to be succeeded by the Fourth Dimensionists, in alliance with renegade terrestrial politicians such as Gurnard/Chamberlain. Their first objective is to besmirch Churchill and they plan to make use of Granger's aristocratic pedigree. The Duc de Mersch (Leopold) has entangled the Government in a nefarious scheme for civilising Greenland's Eskimos, for 'letting the light in upon a dark spot of the earth' in a phrase that echoes the contemporaneous *Heart of Darkness*. (*INH*, 32) Granger too is implicated in the plot against Churchill for having 'puffed' Mersch, though secretly despising him.

Granger has fallen in love with the girl despite knowing of her part in the conspiracy against Churchill, whom he admires for his probity and adherence to earlier traditions of public life. He could easily have saved Churchill by denouncing the girl. Instead he places his love for her above political and literary ideals. Ironically it is the unprincipled Callan, a novelist Granger despises as a hack, who exposes Mersch/ Leopold's scheme, thereby discrediting Churchill for having supported it. In this way, through the exposure of an imperialist scandal, 'all the traditional ideals of honour, glory, conscience', personified by Churchill/Balfour, are shown to have been 'committed to the upholding of a gigantic and atrocious fraud'. (*INH*, 185) Granger fails to save the 'old order' because of his obsession for the girl. Yet at the end of the novel he is disappointed when she marries Gurnard, the Chancellor of the Exchequer, and his betrayals go unrewarded.

She remains. One recognises her hand in the trend of events. Well, it is not a very gay world. Gurnard, they say, is the type of the age – of its spirit. And they say that I, the Granger of Etchingham, am not on terms with my brother-in-law.

The novel ends limply, with a distant nod towards change and decay but no details of the new world.

Gurnard and the girl now embody the 'new order', an alliance of bought politicians and remorseless invaders, and Granger's view of the future of England is of

an immense machine – unconcerned, soulless, but all its parts made up of bodies of men: a great mill grinding out the dust of centuries; a great wine-press. (*INH*, 206)

Ford's nightmare of the State as a giant mechanism gorging individuals is strikingly similar to Lord Rosebery's demand for 'national efficiency' in March 1902, a few months after the appearance of *The Inheritors*. Rosebery called for

a condition of national fitness equal to the demands of our Empire – administrative, parliamentary, commercial, educational, physical, moral, naval, and military fitness – so that we should make the best of our admirable *raw material*.[24]

Rosebery's sandwiching of 'moral' vigour between physical and military capacity, the implication that moral strength was as quantifiable and as easily produced as strong bones or machine-guns, indicates the authoritarian militarist tendencies Ford was opposing. To Rosebery and the Social Imperialists individuals were, as Ford feared, merely the State's raw material, to be exploited to fuel the imperial engine. This 'mechanistic' view of society is countered in *The Inheritors* by the traditional 'organicism' of the Conservative Party, with its theory of a 'natural' state of society that would be destroyed by the intervention of bureaucratic government. The shadows of a fearful apocalypse darken *The Inheritors*, and they fall too over Wells' early fiction and Masterman's *Condition of England* (1909). Nevertheless, there's a strange disjunction between Ford's rhetorical, melodramatic account of the future as a terrifying 'wine-press' and the dull dystopia that emerges from the novel's characters and episodes. Ford's pessimism appears not to have engaged his full creative energies. *The Inheritors* is a curiously bland nightmare.

Nevertheless it plainly aspired to be a serious political novel, a major part of its aim certainly being to render 'the whole uneasy and shifting mood of Imperialism in its later phase'. (*Wiley*, 140) Moreover we have other evidence that Ford strongly condemned such imperialist atrocities as the Belgian exploitation of the Congo and the Boer War. (*SP*, 142–3; *Mizener*, 535) *The Inheritors* does exemplify, through de Mersch and his Greenland venture, this element in Ford's thinking at the turn of the century. It's also true that the novel's ominous title suggests that Ford had perceived that 'a weakening tradition of rule diverted to imperialism will be destroyed by the same methods that it has used to subjugate others'; that, in other words, the 'old order' of the novel, the Conservative establishment, contained within itself the seeds of its own destruction, by virtue of its foreign involvements.

Salisbury had indeed adopted an imperialist position as early
as 1886 but this kind of imperialism was 'synthetic and
artificial; it was an effort to create form in a formless world'.[25]
Ford's novel implied that the Conservatives' inability to resist
the collectivist pressures of Chamberlain was linked with
their involvement in such 'synthetic', late-Victorian imperialism. The Social Imperialism which Ford attacked consisted of
two broad groups, one stressing the social reform demanded
by the Webbs, the second, which included Milner and
Mackinder, emphasising the need to strengthen the Empire.
The full creed involved the connection between these two
aims, the interdependence of imperialism and social reform:
hence the title. The Conservative Party's imperialism thus
rendered it ill-equipped to counter the imperialism of
Chamberlain and the 'Limps'. The unanimity of the Government's commitment to the Boer War was, to Ford, important
mainly as evidence of its weakness as a buffer against social
reform, against 'levelling'. Other analyses of imperialism at
the beginning of the century – by Hobson, Lenin and
Luxemburg – were to stress its moral vulnerability and economic contradictions. Ford, however, attacked imperialism
primarily because it had the effect of debilitating the Conservative Party. The novel's anti-imperialism ran a poor
second to its criticism of domestic reforms. Chamberlain, not
Leopold, was, as Ford himself acknowledged, the real villain.
The Inheritors might perhaps have been a better novel had
Ford followed *Heart of Darkness* and given more weight to
Leopold's amorality, but the exposure of imperialist brutali-
ties, of which Conrad had some bitter, first-hand experience,
remains only of subsidiary interest in the novel. Conrad
indeed makes a brief appearance in *The Inheritors*, 'a
cadaverous, weather-worn, passion-worn individual, badger-
grey', called, anagrammatically, Radet – his second name was
Teodor – but the 'ethical implications of unmasking greed
that has disguised itself as philanthropy' remains only a
peripheral theme.[26]

Ford was later to call *The Inheritors* 'a thin collaboration

with no plot in particular', 'tremendously sentimental',
immature and adolescent, and although he wasn't always the
most reliable judge of his work, these remarks do seem
remarkably apt. (*JC*, 53, 141) Still undefined, however, is the
real explanation for the novel's weakness. Certainly the argument frequently advanced that it is marred by its 'style', its
impressionistic telescoping of events, is well founded. Yet
this is inadequate because it only serves to indicate the
symptoms of the problem and fails to reach the deeper
causes of the novel's limitations. The fundamental problem
may be located in the nature of the ideals which *The
Inheritors* was intended to buttress and their place in political life at the beginning of the century. These may have
persuaded Ford to choose a hero and a narrative form incapable of being the vehicle for an effective attack on Social
Imperialist forces.

Ominously *The Inheritors*' opening episode takes place in
Canterbury, close to those southern ports Ford had lovingly
described in 1900. In that book, *The Cinque Ports*, they had
symbolised the hallowed traditions of the past, towns that
had quaintly survived into the twentieth century, preserved
in their own memories but economically isolated from the
metropolis to the north. The political attitudes behind *The
Inheritors* are damagingly similar, fatally divorced from the
present and from Birmingham's Chamberlain, that 'representative of a new bourgeois briskness, efficiency and hard-
headed, business-like treatment of governmental problems'.[27]
By contrast, Churchill/Balfour, the model politician of the
old school and Gurnard's antagonist, is described as a 'forgotten medieval city' (*INH*, 164), just like Rye or Hythe. In
other words, the protagonists are mismatched, Gurnard/
Chamberlain being so much more vital than the effete, ineffective Churchill.

Furthermore, Granger himself, the novel's narrator and
central figure, has, like the Victorian painters portrayed in
Ford's art-criticism of this period, an 'intense contempt for
the political mind', despising politics because he preferred

'to take the world at its face value'. (*INH*, 68, 41) This is only
a feeble attempt to rationalise his own inertia, his failure to
save Churchill. Granger's inglorious career, then, seems to be
proposing that any connections between the writer and the
public world of finance and politics are inevitably damaging.
The writer ought to model his life upon the recluse's. The
world of the artist's imagination is somehow more real than
the existence he spurns, but which must furnish him with the
raw material of his art. All of which indicates the powerful
influence of Pater and late-Victorian aestheticism, but is
scarcely consonant with Ford's desire to write a political
novel. The willed isolation of the novel's hero is very different
from the policy of 'permeation' conducted by the Webbs,
their robust decision to work alongside even those politicians,
such as Lord Rosebery, for whom they had scant personal
affection or intellectual affinity. The forthrightness of Ford's
political views is hardly matched by the delicacy of his
aestheticism.

Despite its understanding of the self-righteousness and
ruthlessness of the new collectivist forces, its perception of
Social Imperialism's 'undertones of authoritarianism and
intolerance',[28] *The Inheritors* is finally, then, not a successful
novel. Sceptical, like Balfour, of the efficacy of political action
in countering the new militancy, Ford's ideals seem impotent
by the side of Chamberlain's dynamism. The novel's insubstantiality was indeed paralleled by the difficulties Balfour
experienced in meeting Chamberlain's challenge, and he was
powerless to prevent the latter from effectively taking control
in 1903, though he remained the Party's nominal leader. An
aristocratic fastidiousness was insufficient. Ford's stance in
The Inheritors was similar. The novel suggests that there was
no way of avoiding the exploitation of the Eskimos or fore-
stalling the Fourth Dimensionist *coup*.

Moreover, Ford's employment of an explicitly apolitical
artist as the novel's narrator marred the credibility of the
narrative. *The Inheritors* is over-compressed, too impressionistic and shadowy at precisely those points where the author's

attack on collectivism really demanded the specificity of
Nostromo. At one stage Ford has Granger comment, in connection with part of the Dimensionist intrigue,

> I forget, I say, the details, if I ever heard them; they concerned
> themselves with a dynastic revolution somewhere, a revolution
> that was to cause a slump all over the world, and that had been
> engineered in our Salon.

This tone of aristocratic superiority is characteristic of the
narrator's manner and it can only jeopardise our sense of the
novel's reality. A political novel must be articulate about
the mechanics of fraud and jobbery. But Ford chose as narrator the last person who could enlighten us about the details
of the Churchill conspiracy, a man who shared the view of
Ford's grandfather that the artist should 'stick to his last'.
(*AL*, 147) The vagueness of *The Inheritors*, the absence of
'solidity of specification' and its lordly superiority to the
circumstantial, may be contrasted with the enormous detail
that accompanied the proposals on Local Government or the
Poor Law Commission tabled by the Webbs. The necessity to
substantiate the political world in a novel with such ambitions
was compromised by Ford's delicate aversion to public
life and his flight into nostalgia as a counterbalance to the
'socialism of the Right, of order, social hierarchy, and bureaucratic control'.[29]

A similar point was made by the contemporary reviewer
who criticised the novel on the grounds that 'the political
and financial fraud with which so much destruction is
wrought is too small and insignificant to be commensurate
with the disastrous results demanded by the "superseders"'.[30]
Exactly: to have functioned effectively, the Greenland
scheme should have been established with the same centrality
and resonance as the 'silver' of *Nostromo* or *Heart of Darkness*' 'ivory'. However, as the novel develops, we can see that
Ford was less interested in the public effects of Granger's
treachery than in the psychology of the traitor. Hence at the
end of the novel we learn how Granger returned to his life as
an outcast, but the only description of the victorious new

order is in the form of metaphors – the machine, mill, and wine-press. The allusiveness of this formulation is inadequate if only because the momentum of the early chapters requires that we know and feel what the Dimensionists have gone to such pains to establish. In Ford's splendid war novels, the *Parade's End* quartet, the metaphor of an immense machine is embodied specifically and credibly in the war-machine of Flanders and is clearly mediated through the hero's experiences.

Ford's refusal to specify the 'new order' in *The Inheritors* tempts us to suspect that the defeat of the traditionalists may finally be of no great import. *The Inheritors* is a strangely unfeeling novel of which Granger's unconcern for the fate of all the small investors whose lives are destroyed in de Mersch's fall is typical:

I knew too that there were faces like that everywhere; everywhere, faces of panic-stricken little people of no more account than the dead in graveyards, just the material to make graveyards, nothing more; little people of absolutely no use but just to suffer horribly from this blow coming upon them from nowhere.

Ford nowhere dissociates himself from such callousness and Granger's apathy fatally establishes itself as the prevailing mood of the novel. It would appear, then, as if Ford shared his narrator's belief in the possibility of a man simply washing his hands of treachery and returning to the sanctuary of 'private life'; the belief that freedom exists outside society. This stands at the furthest extreme from the Webbs' 'permeation' of the political fabric, their decision to embark on a policy of wholesale proselytism in order to convert their enemies. *The Inheritors*, on the other hand, endorses Granger's view that freedom lies in the retreat from a hostile world rather than in any struggle to change it. The literary shortcomings of the novel can scarcely be separated off from the fragility of the political ideals espoused. As a novel it is weakened by the absence of any kind of fervour or evangelicism; it's just too bland.

One final but related point should be made about the

novel's form. Ford elected to narrate his *roman à clef* as a Wellsian fantasy of extra-terrestrial invaders. Clearly he had in mind *The Time Machine* (1895), in which time is the fourth dimension, yet there was really no pressure on Ford to adopt the mode of fantasy when his political point could have been made with equal force had the subversive girl been an earthly Fabian. The observation that the Wellsian apparatus entailed the sacrifice of verisimilitude sidesteps the interesting question of why Ford chose such a restricting narrative form for a novel intended as a *roman à clef*. It's difficult to believe ignorance of the Fabians led Ford to avoid a realistic mode. Perhaps, rather, it was his lordly aversion to the social reformers – a dislike recorded later in *The Soul of London* (1905) – that made him deeply unwilling to delineate the superseders with any specificity. (The girl herself is not even named.) Although Ford was to claim that *The Soul of London* wasn't a book of political propaganda, the essay provides much evidence of his commitment to the survival of Tory 'individualism' and of his fear that this quality was being obliterated by the reformers. 'We have lost', he lamented in 1905,

great figures, old buildings, all touch with history, much of Christian kindness, much of our fear of public opinion, much of our capacity for interest in our fellow men, much of our powers of abstract reasoning, much of our old faiths. (*SL*, 158)

Yet those who were destroying these graces were not named. Ford's claim that *The Soul of London* would 'render the actual' means that a maudlin impressionism is preferred to any kind of rational argument with his enemies. (*SL*, xiv) His withdrawal from any debate with those whom he feared would soon come to power – scathingly he dubbed them 'the theorists', forgetful of his and Conrad's fascination with the theory of *fiction* – may help explain Ford's choice of extra-terrestrial invaders to represent the militant insurgency of Social Imperialism.

As a result of this withdrawal from realism, Ford's commitment to individualism and the glorious traditions of the

Conservative past had to be expressed in a form that was schematic, futuristic and ill-equipped to deal with the nuances and tensions of personal choice. Science fiction was indeed a strange carrier for the aristocratic ideals of landed property and the Established Church. The historical novel, to which Ford turned for the 'Fifth Queen' trilogy of 1906–1908, offered a more promising form, giving him the opportunity for the analysis of character and the leisurely, tender portrayal of the past lacking in *The Inheritors*.

The Inheritors expresses Ford's dislike of what he saw as the crude mechanism of the Social Imperialists, yet in its place he could only offer an effete traditionalism. The Social Imperialists, the movement Wells called 'the revolt of the competent', had united their disparate forces from a fear that, otherwise, social change would be effected by the revolutionary Left. They 'saw themselves as the only plausible alternative, combining modernity and stability and able to handle both social change and social order'.[31] At this period Ford's 'modernity' was purely formal, confined to a concern with innovations in fiction, with literary renewal. This artistic radicalism, which had been developed in the 'workshop' with Conrad, was placed at the service, paradoxically, of social and political conservatism. In opposing those who were concerned with the modernisation of *political* structures, Ford only proffered nostalgia. Yet all, fundamentally, were looking for new structures, new ways of ordering the world. *The Inheritors* is another illustration of the gap at the beginning of the century between the literary radicalism of James, Ford and Conrad and the efforts of those who were laying the foundations of a modern corporate state. Ford's distrust of the latter is as striking as the absence from Beatrice Webb's autobiography of any record of the cultural revolution in Edwardian London. Ford was as dissatisfied with the Victorian novel as Webb was with the nineteenth-century Poor Law, yet their efforts at modernisation took them in quite different directions.

III

Ford was an enormously prolific writer in the first decade of the century, *The Inheritors* standing alongside eight other full-length novels, eight books of 'non-fiction' and several issues of *The English Review*. Novels, art-criticism, a 'Condition of England' trilogy, a book of local history: he must have appeared indefatigable, yet the very range and volume of his early work makes it difficult to hold in clear focus. The connecting thread was that all this work was a response to the collapse of the Victorian hegemony in both literature and politics. 'Victorianism' as a cultural concept had been alive in the early eighties, but was dead by the late nineties. That faith in 'the homogeneity of society and intellect, a synthesis of progressive politics and moral art', exemplified in the grand moral and formal design of *Middlemarch*, had collapsed, and

the ascendancy of the old literary order crumbled in much the same way and for much the same reasons as the ascendancy of the old political order.[32]

In response to these changes, the prevailing direction of Ford's work of this period was towards the past, towards an aristocratic but doomed conservatism. By contrast, the forces in English political and cultural life that were working against the preservation of individualism and the established traditions were characterised by their concern for the future. All those agitating for 'national efficiency' possessed very clear blue-prints of the new order that would replace the existing muddle – what Wells in *The New Machiavelli* (1911) called the chaos of Bromsteadism. This London suburb in which Remington, the novel's hero, grew up epitomised for Wells the wastefulness of Victorian England. In its place Remington and his Social Imperialist colleagues soon after the Boer War

projected an ideal state, an organized state as confident and powerful as modern science, as balanced and beautiful as a body, as beneficent as sunshine, the organized state that should end muddle for ever; it ruled all our ideas and gave form to all our ambitions.[33]

All the various members of this movement were indeed 'projectors', armed with their own vision of the new world. Collectivists of all shades and of all parties had a robustness of action and energy of vision to which Ford could only respond with nostalgic passivity.

The consequence of Ford's lack of any coherent vision of the future is that his novels of this period have fractured, implausible endings. Granger is left adrift and isolated at the conclusion of *The Inheritors*. Similarly, in *An English Girl* (1907), Don Kelleg, the hero, is pulled between an acknowledgement that social reform is urgent and the seductive attractions of a comfortable, propertied existence. His decision at the end to work for social justice is marred by Ford's inability to substantiate that choice with psychological and political credibility. Social reform is pallid and stunted because Ford lacked the imaginative ability to present it in compelling terms. *The Benefactor* (1905), again, suffers from the absence of a coherent resolution. Its hero, Moffat, has sacrificed his own happiness and the desires of the woman he loves for the sake of the self-denying ordinances of his class. The novel is a penetrating analysis of the connections between class, money and sexual frigidity among the middle class, yet its whole momentum and Ford's sympathetic portrayal of Clara, the Meredithian heroine, demands from Moffat some attempt at a reassessment of his sexual code. *The Benefactor* fails in the end to provide this because Ford in 1905 was unable to imagine any alternative to a code that the novel had demonstrated to be inadequate. *Romance*, too, is characterised by enervation and passivity. Here, at the age of twenty-five, Ford had attempted with Conrad to write the story of a very old man looking back, with 'the whisper of a nonagenarian', on his distant, active youth. (*JC*, 14) 'Looking back' was indeed the general direction of Ford's Edwardian fiction and it wasn't until the post-war *Parade's End* that he was able to create a fictional future of any substance or coherence. Among all these early novels, among all the attempts to defend individualism against the decade's growing collectivism, the 'Fifth Queen' trilogy is the most successful, because the conventions of the historical novel permitted Ford the licence to use the past creatively. In this trilogy Ford was to find a way of embodying his values that carried conviction just because it was set in the past. Nostalgia was no longer the handicap that it had been in *The Benefactor* and *The Inheritors*.

Ford's employment of this novel as a means of supporting Balfour had implied a measure of confidence in the Conservative Party's ability to counteract Chamberlain's pressures. More generally, too, it suggested that Ford had some hope that the two-party system could still be made to function effectively. But Balfour lost effective control in 1903, when the Chamberlain faction became the majority of the Unionist Party, and so the very party on which *The Inheritors* had earlier pinned its hopes was, from 1903 to 1912, committed to a Social Imperialist programme. Disillusioned, Ford became a member of the Liberal Club in 1905, but when he left in 1908 he was effectively without party allegiance. Just as the Conservative Remington in *The New Machiavelli* discovered that no party was able to satisfy his ideals, so too did Ford find himself out of sympathy with both major parties. When the Liberals came to power in 1906 with a 'Limp' majority in the Cabinet, Social Imperialism had become the guiding programme of both parties. The 'Fourth Dimensionists' had now in effect taken over the parliamentary system. For these reasons Ford's earlier *party* allegiance gave place after 1908 to an explicit *class* allegiance. He would now support the 'classes' against the 'masses'. The keynote of *Mr Apollo* (1908) is a new apprehension – also exemplified in *The Condition of England* (1909), written by his friend Masterman, the Liberal politician – of the vast, unknown, urban proletariat. *Mr Apollo* is a brittle, weak novel, but it does serve to reveal the fears that lay behind the establishment of *The English Review* in the same year. Frustrated with orthodox party politics, Ford was increasingly afraid of the growing antagonism between the rulers and the ruled.

In the same year Gide and five other French writers were founding the *Nouvelle Revue Française*, aimed at

a 'classicism' of thought and expression – 'a vindication of the conscious mind' through the exercise of 'a rigorous critical vigilance.'[34]

Ford started *The English Review* with rather similar convictions and ends, emphasising 'classicism' and high standards, while at the same time being as hospitable as *Nouvelle Revue* to formal experimentation. Both were organs of 'modernism'. *The English Review*, though, wasn't solely a literary magazine. It regularly carried political contributions of all shades. Ford himself proclaimed the *Review* had no party-bias, that it was uncommitted to either the Liberal government or the Conservative opposition, and this claim was undoubtedly sincere.[35] Nevertheless, its editorial assumptions did have a very real ideological bias, which in practice aligned the *Review* with the 'classes', the status quo, and against the 'masses', against reform. Ford's celebrated 'critical attitude' towards literature was in fact closely entwined with his political beliefs, though earlier criticism has tended to view it as solely an aesthetic code. The situation, as Ford saw it, was that public life was a whirlpool of opposing and contradictory theories, whose only effect was to exacerbate hostility between class and class. Antipathetic to any comprehensive, systemic analysis of social problems, such as the Webbs' Fabianism, and sceptical of the leftist radicalism of his friend Cunninghame Graham, Ford wanted to take the heat out of public life, replacing it with an attitude of aloof rationalism, above party and ideology. He felt that the Edwardian middle class, whether Liberal or Conservative, was threatened by a class war, and in these circumstances Ford envisaged the *Review* as a safety-valve. A neo-Augustan distrust of 'enthusiasm', in either literature or politics, which he shared with Balfour, led Ford to call for a spirit of calm realism both in criticism and in public debate. The 'critical attitude', then, was deeply implicated in Edwardian political tensions, and *The English Review* was as responsive to public life and major issues as Dr Leavis' *Scrutiny* (1932–1953) or T. S. Eliot's *Criterion* (1922–1939).

And so, as we read Ford's work of this decade we don't sense that we are in the company of a man uninterested in the world, though we may well be surprised by what appear from this distance to be paradoxes or instances of short-sightedness. In this respect, however, Ford was only conforming to the larger inconsistencies of Edwardian literature. Many of his dilemmas were not personal, but were rather the common property of the intelligentsia of his class and time. Ford was indeed 'an interesting case of an Edwardian Man of Letters', struggling to make sense of rapid social upheaval.[36] Thus, despite his awareness of the various forces making for change – the Boer War; the collectivist movements; urban poverty; the excitement of provincial working-class culture which Lawrence enabled him to glimpse and which brought home to him the disabling philistinism of the metropolitan bourgeoisie – despite all these insights, perceptive but local, Ford remained wedded to the ideals of conservatism and preservation.[37]

Fascinating in this respect and wonderfully revealing of the period is Ford's retrospective account in *Mightier than the Sword* (1938) of his first meeting with the young Lawrence, whom, he claims, he mistook at first for a fox. (Noting, or inventing, his first impressions of those he met was a device commonly used by Ford in his memoirs to 'draw' a character speedily and memorably.) Ford was very clear about the strengths of Lawrence's story, 'Odour of Chrysanthemums', and about its author's innovation in opening up a quite new territory for literary exploration, the world of the industrial working classes, seen from the inside. Ford aptly remarked that the English middle class of 1909 knew less about this world than about 'Central Africa and its tribes'. Nevertheless, Ford's receptivity to Lawrence is accompanied

by a confession that he found this first meeting acutely disturbing, since, though priding himself on his theoretical
egalitarianism, he still felt himself one of the governing class.
Consequently he didn't quite know how to deal with a
proletarian artist. This encounter brings to the surface the
main tensions in the Edwardian Ford: the coexistence of a
modern literary sensibility, acutely responsive to the significance of new work, with a social code that was regressive and
blinkered.

2

THE 'FIFTH QUEEN' TRILOGY: THE POLITICS OF NOSTALGIA

I

More than seven years seem to intrude between Ford's completion in 1908 of the Tudor trilogy, *The Fifth Queen*, *Privy Seal* and *The Fifth Queen Crowned*, and the publication in 1915 of *The Good Soldier*, that modernist and unrelentingly demanding novel. The two works are products of entirely different fictional poetics. The trilogy is ample, leisurely, spacious and so completely coherent at a first reading that our return to the text only serves to confirm its virtues. There is no 'instability' or 'turbulence' in the pages of the Tudor novels; no gap between page and reader which must be filled 'productively'. The trilogy establishes 'a single standard of veracity', as Frank Kermode has put it, excluding any elements which might be uncertain or problematic. It continues to maintain that 'illusion of the single right reading' which *The Good Soldier* will shatter. The Tudor novels, like *A Man of Property* or *Clayhanger*, are to be read once and 'consumed'. They invite a reading that is passive and 'consumptive', whereas *The Good Soldier* forces us to read in a fashion that is active and productive, based on 'the evidence of conflicting and ambiguous clues'. The latter is so compressed and frugal that it can only be read recursively, when we return to the text and

[code] it in accordance with later discoveries. . .The more self-reflexive [the] text, the more recursion is necessary, and the harder it is to code information unequivocally.[1]

Any search for 'clues' or 'codes' in the trilogy, though, would be futile.

In the opening sentences the reader is invited to believe in the solidity of character and setting:

Magister Nicholas Udal, the Lady Mary's pedagogue, was very hungry and very cold. He stood undecided in the mud of a lane in the Austin Friars. The quickset hedges on either side were only waist high and did not shelter him. The little houses all round him of white daub with grey corner beams had been part of the old friars' stables and offices. (*FQ*, 11)

Udal may be hesitant here, but the reader knows immediately, from the self-assurance of these first few words, that no indecision is expected of him. (We may contrast this opening with the first paragraph of *The Good Soldier*, in which the six appearances of the verb 'know' and the repeated switching from 'I' to 'we' order us to read with caution and suspicion.) In the trilogy, however, we don't have to 'worry' over the text, for all is above-board and attractively innocent. These, then, are 'pre-modernist' novels, affirming the vitality of a tradition of realistic fiction that runs back through what Ford called the Victorian 'nuvvle' to Defoe.

In the Preface to the 1913 edition of his poems Ford was to remark that the main business of the poet is to give a 'faithful rendering of the received impression', and he praised Flint, Lawrence and Pound for their success in reflecting the present as it appeared to them, in words that were neither imitative nor derivative. (*COLLP*, 28, 24) In his collaboration with Conrad, Ford had proposed similar aims for the impressionist novelist, and in his final commentary on impressionism in fiction, in the late thirties, Ford was still emphasising the importance of a style that was 'unnoticeable', self-effacing, 'low-keyed' and 'vernacular'. (*MOL*, 767–71) Impressionism, in both poetry and prose, was concerned with finding ways of escaping from a language that was formal and 'literary'.

Within the context of these theories, which he had attempted to practise in *The Benefactor* and was to return to in *A Call* (1910), the 'Fifth Queen' novels seem markedly regressive. It was as if Ford had simply decided to by-pass the discoveries about fiction he had made with Conrad ten years before and to take up earlier models – Dickens, Thackeray and, above all, Scott – or the conventional historical novel of his own time, Maurice Hewlett's *The Queen's Quair* (1903–4). The Tudor novels don't present 'received impression[s]' with all their incoherencies and contradictions. Instead they are novels of scenes, panoramas and tableaux, presented by an authoritative, omniscient novelist. Their style, too, is far from the self-effacement advocated by Ford and Conrad earlier. It is indeed always consciously 'literary' and 'written':

[Katharine's] knees felt suddenly limp and she clung to the latch for support; she believed that Mary had turned the heart of this villain. He repeated that he smelt treason working in the mind of an evil man, and that he would have her tell the Bishop of Winchester. (*FQ*, 147)

The heroine's emotional crisis is presented to us externally, as if we were spectators watching Katharine Howard. We aren't given, from the inside, the uncontrolled, unformed, raw impressions that passed quickly through her mind. The language too – the limp knees, the clinging to the latch, the villain's heart and the smell of treason – is conventionally 'literary'. We may set against Ford's notation of Katharine's crisis the passage in *The Good Soldier* in which he attempts to make the reader share, from the inside, Dowell's reactions immediately after he has learnt that his wife has in fact killed herself:

And I thought nothing; absolutely nothing. I had no ideas; I had no strength. I felt no sorrow, no desire for action, no inclination to go upstairs and fall upon the body of my wife. I just saw the pink effulgence, the cane tables, the palms, the globular match-holders, the indented ashtrays. (*GS*, iii, i, 101)

Here Ford captures the blankness of the mind in upheaval; how, at a moment of acute mental anguish, the mind becomes merely the passive recorder of trivial random external impressions, of furniture and pastel lighting. This extract from *The*

Good Soldier exemplifies fictional impressionism, but nowhere in the 'Fifth Queen' novels did Ford attempt this kind
of inwardness. To use his own critical terminology: the Tudor
trilogy was 'narrated', *The Good Soldier* 'presented'. The
formal demands of the historical novels are untaxing.

Ford and Conrad had intended that the impressionist novel
should reflect in its style and language what they perceived
as the formlessness of their world, England of the Boer War
and its immediate aftermath. Ford's fictional theory committed him

to rendering life dispassionately, to giving the effect of the formless and fragmentary nature of life as it meets the individual
consciousness, and to directing the story to its inevitable conclusion. His concern with language [was] designed to achieve these
aims – the point of view, the time-shift, the *progression d'effet*,
the selection and juxtaposition of events and impressions, and an
objective, non-literary language. (*Cassell*, 72)

The impressionist novel would record disorder in a form that
was actually highly ordered, disciplined and self-aware. Ford
evidently felt that the decision to set these three novels in the
past freed him from the obligations that had to be met by the
honest recorder of the contemporary world. He would
describe the past in a way that would suggest that, in being
comprehensible and lucid, it was fundamentally different
from the inchoate present. The Tudor trilogy implies, then,
the pastness of the past, whereas *Nostromo*, for instance,
underlines its presentness. Ford never once invites us to
believe that Henry VIII or Cromwell saw their world through
the same unfocussed eyes as Dowell or Granger. His view of
the past is radically different from his apprehension of the
present. Motivation and action are often complex in the
Tudor novels, but they are *presented* as if they are comprehensible to the novelist. Ford's formal regression, the temporary abandonment of impressionism, is thus closely connected
with his thematic regression, the decision to place his novels
in the sixteenth century.

Yet although the 'Fifth Queen' trilogy is, in both setting

and technique, undoubtedly 'dated', it is far from being naive. On the contrary, it's the work of an intelligent, coherent novelist, ably controlling the large forces he has set in motion amidst the vast spaces of his Renaissance world. Ford makes full use of his commitment to the third-person narrative and to the actuality of time and space. The trilogy is full of passages of great descriptive power, which led Goldring to suggest the influence on Ford of his grandfather's large medieval canvasses.[2] Graham Greene remarked that the three novels were 'lit as carefully as a stage production'.[3] Always, though, such realistic descriptions, of buildings and clothes, are controlled by the whole design of the trilogy in which the places occupied by Ford's characters are meticulously 'blocked'. Indeed Ford wrote a play based on *The Fifth Queen Crowned*, and all the characters of the novels are presented as if they were on stage, their interrelationships delineated through dialogue and 'business'. The essentially visual, scenic appeal of the trilogy is also suggested by the novelist's reference to Holbein, on whom he had earlier published a critical study. (*FQ*, 157) The realism of the German painter served as Ford's model in the trilogy, rather than the Impressionism of Manet or Monet, but historical realism of any period isn't achieved simply by ornate descriptions. Ford's lengthy, detailed rendering of the royal stables in *The Fifth Queen* could be superficially paralleled in the later *Ladies Whose Bright Eyes*, yet the latter's medieval scenes fail to convince us because they lack any controlling intellectual framework. Colour and brightness must be substantiated by the author's understanding of the social forces prevailing at the time, and the effect of these pressures on his characters' lives. It was to just this understanding that Ford was referring when he praised Holbein for his 'realism'. (*HH*, 56)

Ford's extensive reading had taught him that Henry's stable-lads wore a livery decorated with the roses of both York and Lancaster, and that the rushes for the thatch at Greenwich were cut from the banks of the nearby Thames.

The real distinction, though, of the trilogy lies more deeply, in its successful rendering of the fundamental pressures in mid-sixteenth-century England. At that time the old feudal landowners were in conflict with a rising bourgeoisie, and this is the clash that underlies the whole of the trilogy. It was an age of transition between feudalism and early capitalism, and the 'Fifth Queen' novels both reflect and, in their juxtaposition of contrasting scenes, are even moulded by this tension. In terms of England's foreign policy, a key theme in the novels, the battle between dying feudalism and nascent capitalism was expressed in a permanent oscillation between pro- and anti-Spanish strategies.

All the characters of the trilogy, even minor figures such as Udal, the lecherous classicist, are seen to be circumscribed by these forces. Ford had remarked upon 'the amount of subsidiary addition to the dramatic centre' of his grandfather's paintings, and it's similarly true of the trilogy that the central conflict ripples out to the circumference. (*FMB*, 372–3) At the opening of *The Fifth Queen* the Protestant faction is in the ascendancy, because the King has committed himself to Anne of Cleves, and Cromwell's life depends on the success of this alliance. Accordingly, the kiss that Henry bestows on Katharine in Part One is imbued with great political significance, for the abandonment of Cleves in favour of the Catholic Katharine would mean the defeat of the Protestant wing. The characters in these novels are alert to every whim and nuance of the ruling class. His achievement in the trilogy lies in showing how the freedom of action of each of these people is vitally affected by the central collision between the old nobility and the rising bourgeoisie. Even the monarch must continually be playing off one group against the other. At the end he has as little control over his own life as *Nostromo*'s Gould, for, as Katharine acutely observes, Henry is but a 'weathercock' and nobody in his court can escape the intrigue and plots hatched in a 'world of men who did one thing in order that something very different might happen a long time afterwards'. (*FQ*, 186) Ford's chosen technique may emphasise the pastness of this world, yet it's well able to unravel its internal complexities.

Action in the trilogy, then, is always rooted in social and economic foundations that Ford articulated with great lucidity. He made his Tudor characters 'live', because they are rendered with the same complexity as those of a novel set in the present, such as *Parade's End*. The externality of Ford's approach to character in the historical novels is a very different method from the internality through which Dowell and Tietjens are rendered, yet both approaches are capable of making the reader 'see'. Ford, using a 'pre-modern' method, has created credible people and has re-created the world of Tudor England, within whose tensions their lives are spent. Reliance upon earlier models, Scott especially, doesn't lessen the trilogy's intellectual and aesthetic distinction. The trilogy demonstrates Ford's ability to root character 'in milieu, and particularly in politics', and for the first time in his career he shows that he can marshall and analyse political forces, reveal the relationship between conflicting ideas and show how these are embodied in completely credible characters.[4] It is a success he was to repeat – with less tractable, modern materials and with a modernist method – in *Parade's End*.

II

The Inheritors had been designed to support Balfour in the Conservative Party, and the Tudor novels have similar sympathies. Ford's fear of the collectivist forces in English politics is once again the dominant pressure behind the Tudor novels. Moreover, now that he was engaged on a series of historical novels, his own particular – or peculiar – view of English history came into play. These two factors – his attitude to contemporary politics and the larger scenario of historical development – played a considerable part in the construction of the 'Fifth Queen' series.

In the last years of his life Ford began his Wellsian *March of Literature* at a point two thousand years before Christianity; elsewhere he described himself as a 'Tory mad about historic continuity'. (*HJ*, 103) This obsession with tradition and continuity lies at the heart of the Tudor novels. It was indeed Ford's preoccupation with the idea that the England of his day had lost touch with its roots that led him to design a fictional history from the fourteenth century (*Ladies Whose Bright Eyes*), through the Tudor trilogy, the Stuart '*Half-Moon*', the eighteenth-century *Portrait*, the Napoleonic *A Little Less Than Gods*, and into the twentieth century with *Parade's End*. Thus the 'Fifth Queen' trilogy is only one section of a large tapestry that, with varying degrees of success, attempts to express the novelist's sense of the importance of the past. His aim, as he noted in 1900, was to instil 'a just appreciation for the lessons of tradition – a possibility of being able to mould the future with some eye to the institutions of the old times'. (*CP*, 270) Ford was never to lose a sense of the weight of the past and when he died he was at work, characteristically, on an unpublished 'History of our own Times'. The past was truly 'the lodestar of his career from its beginnings'.[5]

The lineaments of Ford's theory of English history are exemplified by his comment that western civilisation had failed to improve upon the Roman Empire, and that our banking system was indeed much inferior. (*GTR*, 432) Ford was a pessimist, who saw history as a decline from a distant glory and argued that there had been a progressive decline from feudalism down to the present. Though riddled with contradictions, Ford's theory divided English history into four distinct 'ages', which themselves grew and decayed within the larger overall pattern of general decline. The ingredients of this theory, as of other views of history current at the turn of the century, were a regressive Darwinism, elements of Taine and Hegel, and traces of a *fin-de-siècle* gloom. Rigidly deterministic, it was sceptical of any prospect of ameliorating the human condition. When applied to the world of Chamberlain and Balfour, Ford's theory aligned him with that section of the Conservative Party most hostile to reform.

These theories of Conservative pessimism affected Ford's rendering of Renaissance history. He was fond of dividing mankind into two groups: the idealistic and sentimental 'Platonists', and the 'Aristotelians', empirical, cynical and realistic. (*IWN*, 49; *MOL*, 119, 142, 150) Ford always prided himself on being an 'Aristotelian', but the pattern of his thinking about both the past and the present actually incorporated a highly romantic 'Platonic' assumption. This was, in historical terms, that feudalism was a near-perfect system; in modern terms, that the English upper class had found the elixir of social life. Both were questionable propositions and, as *The Spirit of the People* (1907) and *The Good Soldier* suggest, Ford had some difficulty in reconciling the actual data of English upper-class life with his idealised version of that world. Similarly, his veneration of feudalism, the keystone of his view of history, often runs counter to his deeper insights into the reality of the past. The Tudor trilogy is Ford's fullest portrait of the feudal world, with Katharine a personification of his vision of feudalism, so we cannot ignore the effects of his theory of history on these novels.

His view of the feudal world was akin to T. S. Eliot's 'nostalgia for closed, immobile, hierarchical societies' and to T. E. Hulme's affection for Byzantine civilisation.[6] These poetic 'worlds', and the analogous worlds of Pound, Yeats and Lewis – authoritarian, rigid, highly formal – were built as bulwarks against the anarchistic forces they discerned around them. Similarly Ford, like many writers of the previous century, turned back to feudal England as a repository of idealism and communalism. Idealisation of the Middle Ages ran through much social criticism of the nineteenth century and Ford drew on these Victorian sources in arguing that 'the old feudalism and the old union of Christendom beneath a spiritual headship' was an ideal social framework. (*HJ*, 47; *RTY*, 82) This version of feudalism had only tenuous connections with the historical reality of the same name. Its value

for Ford resided less in its accuracy than in the private need
it fulfilled by recreating a society in which order and ritual
were central. In an England in transition, Ford, like Chesterton and Belloc, required the assurance derived from a set of
private myths. His account of the world of Henry VIII and
Cromwell was certainly shaped by his mythology of history.

However, besides being an expression of his own individual reading of English history, Ford's Tudor trilogy was
also intended to reflect upon the politics of Edwardian
England. Thinking about the parallels between the two ages,
Ford commented that his Henry VIII

represents the modern world being born out of the medieval. As
a ruler at home he had to face almost exactly the social problems
we are still facing, even to the relations of capital & labour & the
question of agricultural depopulation. As a foreign politician he is
one of the first & certainly one of the most portentous of the type
of Bismarck. (*Mizener*, 470)

The Tudor trilogy, like *The Inheritors*, was planned as a
commentary on Edwardian politics. Ford felt that a man
should retain his idealism by retreating from public life, as
Granger had done at the end of *The Inheritors*. He believed
that freedom lay in the retention of a set of ideals, irrespective of their validity. Ford was preoccupied with the austere
glory of martyrdom, renunciation and resignation, for these
were his response to the increasing dominance of the collectivists within English politics.

But Ford sometimes failed to detect the arrogance and
blindness of his victims' inability to respond actively to
change. There is an element of this, of martyrdom's conceit,
in the 'Fifth Queen' trilogy, in which Katharine is not only a
martyr, like Granger or Moffat in *The Benefactor*, but a
feudal martyr as well. Ford certainly tried to depoliticise
Tudor religion, to make it appear as if the Queen's ambition
to re-establish Catholicism in England could really be
divorced from the political and economic realities of that age.
She herself is blind to the political implications of her aspiration, and Ford seemed to condone such myopia, in order,

once more, to try to make failure admirable, more estimable even than success. He omitted to criticise Katharine's egoism out of a desire to highlight the conflict between idealism and reality, ennobling the former's inevitable defeats. The pattern of *The Inheritors* is being repeated in the Tudor novels. But Katharine cannot reinstate Catholicism by pretending that her enemies don't exist. Indeed it's arguable that the real heroes of the trilogy are in fact Cromwell and Throckmorton, because of their awareness that freedom only lay in 'the recognition of necessity'. The latter, however, was too close to the Fabian policy of 'permeation' to hold much attraction for Ford. On the contrary, he admired Katharine's obsession with the purity of her feelings, the beauty of her own motives and the stubbornness of her refusal to manoeuvre and lobby, for these constituted another illustration of the nobility of remoteness from public life.

These, then, were the twin pressures at work behind the Tudor novels – Ford's Edwardian conservatism plus his pessimistic view of history in general. He had temporarily abandoned the tenets of impressionism in order to take up the traditional realism of Scott. Yet this kind of 'scenic', omniscient presentation was by no means devoid of political implications. Holbein, Ford's acknowledged model, hadn't been a neutral, dispassionate observer of Renaissance England, and Ford's novels of the same period were no less affected by their creator's presumptions and prejudices. Under these pressures Ford made a number of modifications to the historical reality of the period. In particular, he was forced to alter the characters of Katharine, his heroine, and of her major enemy, Thomas Cromwell.

III

Outside the trilogy Ford recognised in full Cromwell's historical importance. In *The Spirit of the People* he noted that Thomas was the great man of the age, who 'welded England into one formidable whole' (*SP*, 71) and a few years later, in

When Blood is their Argument (1915), that he was 'the founder of modern England' and a 'genius'. (*WBITA*, 11) Yet in the Tudor novels the same man is portrayed as a sinister Machiavellian villain, first introduced in the cold and darkness of his barge:

The Lord Privy Seal was beneath a tall cresset in the stern of his barge, looking across the night and the winter river. They were rowing from Rochester to the palace at Greenwich, where the Court was awaiting Anne of Cleves. The flare of the King's barge a quarter of a mile ahead moved in a glowing patch of lights and their reflections, as though it were some portent creeping in a blaze across the sky. There was nothing else visible in the world but the darkness and a dusky tinge of red where a wave caught the flare of light further out.

He stood invisible behind the lights of his cabin; and the thud of oars, the voluble noises of the water, and the crackling of the cresset overhead had, too, the quality of impersonal and supernatural phenomena. His voice said harshly:

'It is very cold; bring me my greatest cloak.' (*FQ*, 24–5)

Cromwell's association here with the crackling torches and the 'dusky tinge of red', an 'impersonal and supernatural' occurrence, is slightly satanic, for, in this kind of novel, darkness and cold are always loaded with ethical assumptions. A man of arctic blood and of few words, described but 'invisible', Cromwell is portrayed in Ford's fiction with near-total disfavour. On no occasion in the trilogy does Ford attempt to evoke the reader's sympathy for the Privy Seal, and even his death, which might have drawn our sympathy, is not described. It's significant that in a work not notably squeamish about physical violence Ford allowed Cromwell to disappear from view after Throckmorton's accusations at the end of *Privy Seal*. Ford's antipathy to Cromwell accorded with his need to idealise Katharine and medievalism, but it hardly squared with what the novelist knew about the innovative features of Cromwell's rule.

Superficially at least, Ford appears to have succeeded in this attempt to vilify Cromwell, though there is one scene in *Privy Seal* – the interview between Cromwell and Wriothesley

– where the author permits us to see what we may have suspected: that Cromwell was in fact no less disinterested or idealistic than Katharine herself. Cromwell, Ford there wrote, paused and then, surprisingly, spoke 'gently':

'And assuredly ye do me more wrong than ill,' he said. 'For this I swear to you, ye have heard evil enow of me to have believed some. But there is no man dare call me traitor in his heart of them that do know me. And this I tell you: I had rather die a thousand deaths than that ye should prop me up against the majesty and awe of government. By so doing ye might, at a hazard, save my life, but for certain ye would imperil that for which I have given my life.' (*PS*, 375–6)

And Cromwell concludes with words that, only slightly altered, we might be tempted to attribute to Katharine:

'that before all creeds, and before all desires, and before all women, and before all men, standeth the good of this common-wealth, and state, and King, whose servant I be. Get you gone and report my words ere I come terribly among ye.' (*PS*, 376)

In its subordination of self to a larger ideal this speech anticipates some of Katharine's words before her death in *The Fifth Queen Crowned*. The stylistic affinities serve to remind us of the psychological kinship of the trilogy's two protagonists. Their ideals were indeed very different – Cromwell's fidelity being to the State, Katharine's to the Catholic Church – yet each held to these ideals with a similar fortitude and consistency. Both, also, though fundamentally loyal to Henry, died as traitors. In this isolated scene, then, Ford presents Cromwell with some of the generosity accorded him in his non-fiction, but the rhythms of Cromwell's speech to Wriothesley, and its passionate affirmation of selflessness, are quite untypical of the presentation of the Privy Seal else-where in the trilogy. Despite the fact that Cromwell was as dedicated a visionary as Katharine, and despite the novelist's understanding of his political modernity, Ford does his best to devalue Cromwell, consistently associating him only with the most brutal aspects of Tudor life.

Alongside, and closely related to Ford's denigration of the

real Cromwell, lay Ford's idealisation of the real Katharine
Howard. There is, it is true, nothing sacrosanct for the artist
about the biographies of historical characters. The novelist's
duty lies not in fidelity to minutiae – this is the 'pseudo-
historicism of the mere authenticity of individual facts' – but
rather in preserving the broad outlines of the social forces
obtaining in his chosen period.[7] We cannot, therefore, criticise
Ford simply for having transformed a rather ordinary Tudor
aristocrat into a Catholic martyr. Nor is there any basic
improbability in Katharine's character in the novels, though
the ending of *The Fifth Queen Crowned*, like the conclusions
of his other Edwardian fictions, does leave the impression of
being too hurried. Ford seems to take insufficient time to
prepare us for the change in Katharine from a tough, resilient
fighter to a resigned martyr; though this development itself
isn't fundamentally improbable. The real criticism to be made
is that Ford has idealised Katharine's own idealism, failing to
provide sufficient distance between himself and his heroine.
(This weakness can be located in all Ford's fiction of this
period and is surely present too in Galsworthy's Irene and
Forster's Schlegel sisters.) In the case of Cromwell – as with
the Wilcoxes and the young Soames – we are distanced from
the character's aspirations by the novelist's creation of a large
gap between his ends and his means. With Katharine, however, her creator failed to be sufficiently critical of her aspirations.

   In summary, then, the changes Ford made to his real-life
models differ, yet each is closely related to his overall historical purpose. With Cromwell, Ford gave us a partial view
in order to minimise the actual historical importance of those
forces he stood for. Cromwell was a remote ancestor of the
reformists and collectivists who were working towards the
intensification of State power in Edwardian England. With
Katharine, he chose to magnify her idealism in order to
glorify the regressive forces she personified. In both cases,
Ford, exploiting the novelist's proper freedom, altered historical fact. More dangerously, he attempted to tilt the

balance in the actual *forces* at work in Tudor England so as to manufacture material supporting his own belief in 'feudalism' and in renunciation, 'the seductive appeal of pretending that ideal virtue is humanly possible'. (*Mizener*, 476)

IV

A continuous tension exists in the trilogy between a centripetal system that the intellectual desires to impose on his world and the centrifugal energies of the created world. Irving Howe has identified such forces as the pressures of 'ideology' and of 'emotion', arguing that in their inevitable clash

Abstraction. . .is confronted with the flux of experience, the monolith of program with the richness and diversity of motive, the purity of ideal with the contaminations of action.[8]

This was what occurred in the trilogy, where the monolithic structure of Ford's view of history pressured him to distort Katharine and Cromwell. He certainly sympathised with the former's vision of the chaste rectitude of escapism. To this extent Fleishman is right in detecting evidence that Ford intended to use the trilogy as a vehicle for his own escapism:

Ford's imagination is poised upon the dichotomy of historical corruption and civilized retirement, and his escapism avoids a personal tone by being expressed in the language and myths of the men of the past. By identifying his own escapism with that of the Renaissance, Ford achieves genuine historical sympathy with another world-weary age.[9]

But the essential point is that the mid-sixteenth century was *not* decadent, bored or enervated. Indeed Ford's actual achievement in the trilogy lay precisely here: in his re-creation of the basic energy and vitality of the period, despite his own private, 'ideological' leaning towards hypostasis and retirement.

Ford's 'ideology' thus fell victim to his 'emotion', to his deeper insights as an artist in tune with the period's conflicts.

The Tudor trilogy depends for its strength upon the framework of *actual* history, not on the mythical pattern Ford sought to impose. History was an invaluable discipline, which finally prevented the trilogy from being a fictional enactment of Ford's own leanings. His accomplishment is to show, through the lives of a few individuals, a particular society in change, evolving inexorably from late feudalism towards modern capitalism. He has presented us with a vision of 'time as change', despite the attraction of the closed, hierarchical, static world of his 'feudalism'. In the most concrete and realistic way the trilogy demonstrates that Katharine's aspirations are determined by 'the form of organization of society, by the relation of forces within it',[10] despite Ford's interest in proving that such forces were most nobly ignored. Although Ford himself may have disliked 'the relation of forces' within both Tudor and Edwardian England, he still created three novels whose every episode and character bore witness to the potency of what Katharine abhorred, the ambitious Protestant bourgeoisie, determined, in Marx' celebrated phrase, to 'put an end to all feudal, patriarchal, idyllic relations'.[11] Superficially the trilogy is pessimistic, ending with the bare record of Katharine's death. More fundamental, however, is the vitality with which it renders the claims of historical progress and its truthfulness in portraying human behaviour, what Lukács called the complex 'intertwinement of the individual and the social. . .of private interest and public affairs'.[12]

v

The Tudor trilogy is a highly sensuous work, communicating through an appeal to sight, smell, hearing, taste and touch:

A man with a conch-shaped horn upturned was suddenly blowing beneath the archway seven hollow and reverberating grunts of sound that drowned his voice. A clear answering whistle came from the water-gate. Cromwell stayed, listening attentively; another stood forward to blow four blasts, another six, another three. Each time the whistle answered. They were the great officers' signals for their barges that the men blew, and the whistle signified that these lay at readiness in the tideway. A bustle of men running, calling, and making pennons ready, began beyond the archway in the quadrangle. (*FQ*, 57)

Ford tells his tale through the management of texture, tone and colour, with the implicit assumption, so deep that it is not verbalised, of a harmony between man and nature. This is 'romantic' art – in the sense that T. E. Hulme was shortly to employ – the product of an optimistic humanism that upheld the possibility of human communication. As such it provided the perfect vehicle for Ford's commitment to tradition and continuity. The sanctity of the individual consciousness, which he feared was being threatened by the new movements in English politics, was here given its fullest expression.

Nevertheless, Ford knew that his own world, the London of the 1900s, couldn't be rendered in the same leisurely humanist way. The theories of the impressionist novel developed with Conrad a decade earlier had indeed been posited upon the existence of a world that was stressful, hurried and uncertain: a world, in short, recognisably 'modern'. Ford's future lay here, in the refinement of a modernist medium capable of rendering his own world with the expressiveness of the traditional trilogy. Though brash and intolerant, Hulme's prognosis that the kind of art exemplified by *The Fifth Queen* was moribund certainly corresponded to the development of Ford's career. Through *A Call* (1910), *The New Humpty-Dumpty* (1912) and *Mr Fleight* (1913) he was to approach *The Good Soldier* (1915), a novel that, in its pervasive nihilism, questions all the romantic assumptions of the Tudor tapestry, especially its 'texture of actuality'.[13]

When Conrad – like James, a skilled exponent of the backhanded compliment – commented, in a letter to Galsworthy, that

Ford's last *Fifth Queen* novel is amazing. The whole cycle is a noble conception – the swan song of Historical Romance – and frankly I am glad to have heard it[14]

he was putting his finger on an important feature of the trilogy. Whether or not it marked the demise of a genre, and Conrad plainly hoped it did, the Tudor trilogy assuredly constituted Ford's last bow as an historical novelist. Never again was he to invest any serious energy in this genre: *The 'Half-Moon'* (1909), originally part of another trilogy, was never completed. In the future the main direction for Ford lay elsewhere, in the articulation, through *The Good Soldier* and *Parade's End*, of his own age. Still, although the Tudor novels can easily be dismissed as a diversion in his career, a playful intermission in the stern business of impressionism and the search for formal exactitude, they did have some lasting value for Ford, which Conrad was in no position to anticipate.

There is no evidence that they presented Ford any great technical problems – there are no records of the agonised rewritings that punctuated *Romance* or *The Inheritors* – yet they did give him the opportunity to practise working on an extended canvas. The experience of manipulating large numbers of characters with complex political and personal motives must have stood him in good stead when he came to write *Parade's End*. The latter involved difficult formal problems but at least Ford was now aware of some of the demands that would have to be met in writing about modern politics. His apprenticeship, then, was now complete. He had experimented in both the small-scale, concentrated impressionist novel as well as in the larger chronicle. He was now equipped to move towards his major fictions, *The Good Soldier* and *Parade's End*. Collaboration with Conrad and his own historical experiments provided the twin foundations for his later career.

PART TWO

1910–1915

1910–1915

Date	Novels	Prose	Poetry
1910	*The Portrait* *A Call*	*English Review*	*Songs from London*
1911	*The Simple Life* *Limited* *Ladies Whose Bright* *Eyes*	*Ancient Lights* *The Critical* *Attitude*	
1912	*The Panel* *The New Humpty-* *Dumpty*		*High Germany*
1913	*Mr Fleight* *Young Lovell*	*This Monstrous* *Regiment* *Desirable Alien*	*Collected Poems*
1914		*Henry James*	
1915	*The Good Soldier*	*When Blood is their* *Argument* *Between St Dennis* *and St George* *Zeppelin Nights*	*Antwerp*

3

GEORGIAN PESSIMISM: SKETCHES
FOR *THE GOOD SOLDIER*

'The place is vulgar, the time is vulgar. The language we speak is vulgar. So are the thoughts we think. Everything is vulgar. Even the air!'

(Ladies Whose Bright Eyes)

'There be summer queens and dukes of a day,
But the heart of another is a dark forest.'

(The New Humpty-Dumpty)

I

One fine summer day shortly before 1914, Blood, an aristocratic landowner, is sitting in his club staring out on the Embankment and calculating the relative numbers of motor cars and horse-drawn carriages. The rest of his class, London's smart 'society', has decamped to Epsom, there to participate in one of its annual rituals, the 'Derby', but Blood cannot even muster the energy for trivial social intercourse. At one time he had espoused radical causes, but is now totally disillusioned with politics, as with everything else, believing that the structures of parliamentary democracy will soon be swept away by 'corruption and boredom and dilettantism'. (*MF*, 275) He is rich and intelligent, but won't bestir himself to intervene. An anachronism, he is totally withdrawn from the present, living as if he were in the early nineteenth century. Life, he believes, is only a 'dirty comedy', at which he is content to be a cynical spectator, and he adopts Fleight, an ambitious Jew, because he is amused by the opportunity to demonstrate that the possession of wealth will now open every door, to the boardroom and the boudoir. (*Mr Fleight* is set in London in 1913, the year of the notorious Marconi Scandal.) At the conclusion of Ford's novel, Blood is successful, for his puppet has bought himself a parliamentary seat and a blonde, gentile wife. But the sponsor is, a year later, still seated in his club chair, counting London's traffic. The only change is that motor cars are now fast replacing carriages.

Mr Fleight is a mediocre novel, unredeemed by some crude political and literary satire. Nevertheless the portrait of Blood, 'lazier than a buffalo and prouder than a hog', illuminates Ford's own problems at the beginning of this decade, his personal difficulties and, more important, the obstacles he faced as a novelist. (*MF*, 7) It is the latter with which the critic is properly concerned and the crux of the problem is the self-indulgence in all Ford's fiction before *The Good Soldier*. Blood 'feeds on the very object of his contempt, creating a cult of his own nausea', and Ford's conduct as a novelist is similar. (*Huntley*, 6) Blood can find no mode of action in the present that won't involve him in a repetition of the violence he had committed earlier. (He had murdered his groom in America for having pocketed a thousand-dollar bribe to dope his horses.) By way of compensation for his impotence Blood stage-manages the violent improbable comedy of *Mr Fleight*. (The plot is as unlikely as some of its author's autobiographical fantasies.) Ford, too, is baffled by the world around him and assiduously cultivates his own bewilderment.

The stock character of Ford's fiction between 1910 and 1915 is the honourable man beset by rogues; the saint suffers before he is saved through love. Thus in *The Portrait* (1910), Bettesworth emerges from all his tribulations, his high principles vindicated by the hand of the woman he loves and the winning of a £20,000 wager. Similarly, Sorrell in *Ladies Whose Bright Eyes* is anguished by the contrasts between the chivalric idealism of Wiltshire in the fourteenth century and the urgent materialistic pressures of pre-war London. Only the love of his wife, in the novel's artificial conclusion, restores his equilibrium. The pattern recurs in *The Panel*

(1912), where Ford's man-of-honour, Major Edward Foster, is finally united with his beloved after a series of disasters, the price he pays for his upright principles. Finally, *The New Humpty-Dumpty* shows us the Fordian idealist, Count Macdonald, leading a counter-revolution in Galizia as a first step to the regeneration of the world. Ford commented about this character that

It is impossible to represent [Macdonald] as being in any way rational or coherent in his idealism. All that can be said is that he was consistently an idealist. (*NHD*, 366)

The reader of *The New Humpty-Dumpty* might well reply that Ford did not say 'all that can be said', that he was insufficiently critical of his idealistic hero. In an attempt to glorify Macdonald's heroic recklessness Ford likens him successively to the otter who hides his nose in hay to escape the hounds, to Thomas à Becket, and even to Christ. (*NHD*, 330–1, 340) But whereas in the Tudor trilogy Ford had given considerable attention to the 'hounds' who hunted Katharine, in his Georgian fiction before *The Good Soldier* he has become myopically concerned with his martyrs to the exclusion of all else – credible characterisation and the creation of a realistic world.

Like his hero in *Mr Fleight* Ford appears to be neurotically fascinated by the despair he projects onto his creations. The politician's rejection of politics may itself be a positive, affirmative action, but in literature there will always be a gap between the writer's sense of despair and the publication of a novel which transmutes that emotion. In these novels Ford was attempting to create art out of his own despair and his failure may be further evidence that a literature of despair – though not the politics of despair – is a contradiction in terms. In his search for a novel that would communicate the experience of life at the edge of an abyss Ford experimented in a variety of forms: a parody of Restoration comedy in *The Portrait*; the historical romance in *Ladies Whose Bright Eyes*; Feydeau farces, the stock of pulp-fiction, in *The Panel*; and a

Ruritanian melodrama in *The New Humpty-Dumpty*. He produced no fewer than seven novels in these five years, the range of forms attempted being wider than at any other period of his career. It's also true, though, that he was never to write as many undistinguished novels so quickly. Of the work of these years only *A Call* and *The Good Soldier* can now be read with any pleasure.

Part of the weakness of these novels is the lack in them of any 'felt life', of any social or historical verisimilitude; we simply can't *believe* in them. Deeper, though closely related, is the difficulty Ford evidently had from 1910 to 1915 in creating a sense of time in his fiction. In *Mr Fleight*, for instance, a year has passed but Blood still occupies the same chair, thinking the same thoughts at the end as at the beginning. None of the intervening events seems to have affected him in any way. Nothing seems to have changed. Nothing seems to have happened, despite the many violent episodes in the novel. Indeed the numbness of his characters' withdrawal from an active engagement with life seems, in its turn, to have paralysed Ford, their creator.

This inability to communicate a sense of the passing of time wasn't simply a formal, technical problem, for the 'Fifth Queen' novels are evidence of Ford's ability to tell a story coherently and credibly, and it's unlikely that these skills suddenly deserted him. Rather, as Ford lost his belief in the efficacy of either of the two political parties in opposing the State's growing power and as he became increasingly sceptical of parliamentary democracy in general, so he was faced with the need to develop his own medium to express this new pessimism. Ford deplored what he saw as England's slide towards a Bismarckian state, but could discern no forces which would avert such a catastrophe. His novels between 1910 and 1915 were a search for a form through which to mediate his feeling of helplessness. There were several failures during this search and it wasn't until *The Good Soldier* that he found a way of objectifying despair. Only here did he light upon a means of communicating the numb monotony of a world in which time is not *felt* to pass, in which clocks *seem* to have stopped – that medium was Dowell, the narrator of memory, illusion and retrospection.

Closely connected to the frenetic experimentation of these years is the widespread violence of the *content* of his Georgian novels. Husbands and wives are estranged, suicides seem almost commonplace, and class is divided against class. His earlier novels had contained scenes of physical and mental torment, but what is new in the pre-war novels is the arbitrariness of the violence; the sense that cruelty is both fortuitous and, at the same time, quite typical of the period. Perhaps it's only in periods of deep social convulsion that violence can be viewed as both contingent and unremarkable. In E. M. Forster's fiction of this period, too, violent and unexpected deaths frequently disturb the placid gentilities. Ford and Forster both foretold the macabre democratisation of death, its unspeakable ordinariness, in Europe between 1914 and 1918.

At first glance, then, the violent Georgian fiction of middle-class novelists such as Ford, Forster and 'Saki' only seems to be a further manifestation of the widespread tensions of these years. More and more strikes; the conflict between the Commons and the Lords; agitation by the Suffragettes and the Irish independence movements; the European political crises – everywhere they cared to look the propertied classes felt their security jeopardised, since all these movements of revolt seemed to presage 'the moral and economic destruction of Victorian capitalism'.[1] Blood in Ford's *Mr Fleight* wasn't alone in fearing that the whole fabric of democracy might be in imminent danger, for there was, as Thomson has observed, 'a universal note of desperation, of hysteria, of pent-up passion, in all these events of the decade before 1914'.[2] Nevertheless, although these qualities were common in literature as in life before 1914, we must distinguish between the actions of, say, the Suffragettes, aimed at righting a social injustice, and the extreme deeds portrayed in *Mr Fleight* and *The Good Soldier*, the results of ignorance and of a frustrated lassitude. Whatever else they were, Georgian feminists were not bored.

In Ford's fiction pain is the product of boredom, rather than the consequence of political frustration. Injury seems the result of his characters' inability to understand themselves and their intimates, but is never employed as a tool of political action. It's true that in his best work, in *A Call* and *The Good Soldier*, Ford demonstrated that his most percipient characters were aware of the existence of rapid social change, and that their inability to govern their lives was connected with the bewilderment they felt in the face of such upheavals. But their first reaction was not to unite as a class to defend their interests. Instead, they fractured and quarrelled among themselves. The suicides and sadism of these novels were, then, the actions of frightened, frustrated people, unable to understand their own circle or the changes around them. In such circumstances the aloof, aristocratic detachment of Blood and the cruel machinations of Florence Dowell were two sides of the same coin, two consequences of frustration. Similarly, the 'heroism' with which Ford so generously endowed the men of these novels was escapist and fugitive. It involved abdication and renunciation rather than confrontation, and was a further strain of Georgian pastoralism. For these reasons, it too often seems unreal, almost dilettante, an epicene delight in its own impotence.

Impotence, sexual, linguistic and social, is indeed the central theme of *A Call*, as the novel's epigraph hints:

> 'We have a flower in our garden,
>   We call it Marygold:
> And if you will not when you may,
>   You shall not when you wold.'

Robert Grimshaw, in appearance like a seal or his own pet dachshund, 'wills not when he may', by donating the woman he loves to his best friend, Dudley Leicester, an 'obtuse hypochondriac'. (*CALL*, 14) The latter, a wealthy young landowner, is reduced to a state of senile aphasia by an anonymous telephone call, and spends most of the novel looking like 'clothes carelessly thrown down'. (*CALL*, 140) Before the end of the novel, however, he has been cured and become Foreign Secretary. The country's male rulers are portrayed as too weak to control even their own lives, but they are supported by some very determined women. *A Call* indeed 'offers a depressing view of the cultural decadence and neurotic indecision that beset Europe in the years just before the First World War'.[3]

The shrewdest comment on the sexual and political paralysis of this class is provided by Leicester's servant when he remarks that 'It's only gentlemen of leisure who can think of their hats at all times.' (*CALL*, 132) Dress and deportment are the sole preoccupations of a man like Leicester, who had 'never in his life done anything', and the novel renders with some success the hot-house atmosphere of a parasitic class. (*CALL*, 46) It demonstrates that the *mores* of the ruling class, which Ford had analysed in *England and the English*, are dependent on emotional calm, and that this 'honour' is help-less when faced with any strong feeling, such as jealousy, love or anger. This 'facile sense of honour' is 'adapted only to the life of no strain, of no passions'. (*CALL*, 281) The regimen of the invalid has been erected into a code of conduct govern-ing the lives of healthy adults. Ford, then, had detected the dangerous naivety of this value, 'honour', and *A Call* success-fully renders the dislocations that result when genuine emotions intrude into a society whose existence depends on their being repressed or ignored. As one of the characters remarks, 'we haven't learned wisdom: we've only learned how to behave. We cannot avoid tragedies'. (*CALL*, 274)

And yet, for all the novel's insights into the relationship between sex, class and political incapacity, D. H. Lawrence and Arnold Bennett were surely right when they pointed out the novel's damaging lack of reality. Ford had seen so much, but the final effect of *A Call* is slight.[4] The episode in which Leicester's ex-fiancée flirted with a farrier's son and caused him to break off their engagement is, in isolation, a Lawren-tian intuition, reminiscent of *The White Peacock*, but the novel as a whole is considerably less than the sum of its excellent parts. It possesses the intensity of a successful novel and is much superior to anything else Ford wrote between *The Fifth Queen Crowned* and *The Good Soldier*, yet finally its achievement is much slighter than its potential.

In an 'Epistolary Epilogue' to *A Call* Ford remarked that he found Grimshaw 'an amiable but meddlesome and inwardly conceited fool', and the events of the novel, in which Grimshaw's clumsiness causes him to lose the woman he loves and be yoked to one he doesn't, confirm Ford's criticisms. (*CALL*, 301) Ford went on to claim that his ambitions for the novel were Jamesian; that he 'sought to point no moral', merely to tell a 'plain tale':

[My] sole ambition was to render a little episode – a small 'affair' affecting a little circle of people – exactly as it would have happened. [I] desired neither to comment nor to explain. (*CALL*, 303–4)

Ford's comments here are of interest, because they highlight the failure of *A Call* and indeed of all the novels of this period before *A Good Soldier*. The crucial point is that Grimshaw is not treated like an interfering fool, nor is the 'affair' presented with the objectivity the novelist claimed. Rather, the cruel futility of the lives of Grimshaw and his set seems to have attracted Ford's admiring sympathy. In a fashion that runs counter to the novel's deepest perceptions, Ford condones, even praises, Grimshaw's renunciation of his woman because such abnegation is, the hero feels, the duty of 'our class'. (*CALL*, 34) At one point, it is true, Grimshaw muses that 'we're an idle, useless crowd', but he himself is too deeply implicated in the novel's arabesques to act as a critical voice, while Ford, for his part, is too close to his hero. (*CALL*, 153)

The strangely lifeless quality of *A Call*, which Bennett and Lawrence diagnosed as the novel's failing, wasn't the result of anything incredible in the behaviour of Ford's characters. (After all, Nigel Nicolson's *Portrait of a Marriage* records, as documented fact, events among this class more bizarre than any Ford invented.) No, the real mystery is that a writer as perceptive and sensitive as Ford should have been 'conned' into mistaking the theatricalities of his creations for honesty and sincerity. We can see – as can Ford, from the safe refuge of the 'epilogue' – that Grimshaw is a dangerous psychopath, but as soon as he starts to talk of sacrifice for the sake of 'civilisation' we can sense Ford being swept away by his hero's shabby idealism and tawdry rhetoric. At a period of great social instability Ford was desperately searching for any form of idealism – even, in *The New Humpty-Dumpty*, that of the opportunistic adventurer, the mercenary – and his fiction before *The Good Soldier* is a saddening record of his inability to distinguish the hero from the 'ham', magnanimity from mulishness. Of these failures and their relations with the troubled history of the period, *A Call* is paradigmatic. The novel is weakened by the lack of any probing, sceptical irony with which to flail the self-deception and pomposity of a Robert Grimshaw, and to throw a harsher critical light on the 'civilised' values his class claimed to be treasuring.

Ford's inability in the majority of his seven Georgian novels to combine objectivity and despair, to fictionalise the meaninglessness he saw around him without trivialising or brutalising it, can't simply be reduced to the failure of a 'technique'. Instead it resulted from his inability to comprehend, let alone sympathise with the world about him. The gentility and fastidiousness of his earlier conservatism could make little of the events of, say, the summer of 1911, when the threatened General Strike coincided with the Agadir Crisis in the Mediterranean. It's useful to be reminded that the Irish Crisis and the labour unrest were both remarkable for their order and discipline, and that the really dangerous manifestations of violence were international, not domestic.[5] It's undoubtedly true that English politics were less violent just before the war than in the 1880s, and these are useful correctives to the earlier view that the years preceding the war were marked by a general 'pattern of extremism amounting to a pathological social morbidity'.[6] Nevertheless, Ford's fiction of these years suggests that he, at least, was profoundly

sceptical of the future of democratic institutions. From the
perspective of the present, his Georgian novels, like the common belief that England was becoming ungovernable, may
now seem hysterical and excessive. The fear of anarchy,
justified or not, was evidently real enough at the time. The
political history of England between 1910 and 1916 is characterised by the search for a new form of government, that bore
fruit in the establishment of the Lloyd George Coalition of
1916. Ford's novels in these years were similarly unstable,
yet an undue emphasis on his working life as the search for a
perfect fictional form has implied that he always knew what
he wanted to say and merely lacked the means of expression.
However, the evidence of Ford's non-fiction of this period –
Ancient Lights (1911), *Henry James* (1913), *The Critical
Attitude* (1911), his journalism and his two propaganda books,
When Blood is their Argument and *Between St Dennis and
St George* (1915) – suggests that he himself saw the problem
in different, rather more complex terms, terms indeed which
give a more influential role to public stresses as conditioning
factors in an artist's work. All these volumes, in different
ways, attest to Ford's sense of derangement and helplessness
that is manifested by his uneven work as a novelist before the
war. The urbanity and detachment of *Romance* and *The
Inheritors* were clearly unsuitable as ways of recording Ford's
view of Georgian England, and he had to find another form,
one that could articulate breakdown and bafflement. In
Europe at this time the early work of Proust, Mann and Gide
was 'suffused with the sense of things not being what they
appear to be, of contradictory versions of the same reality,
of a deeper truth that cannot be explained but can only be
glimpsed in moments of heightened awareness'.[7] With *The
Good Soldier* Ford discovered the means of expressing the
new problematical reality for which he had been groping in
the earlier novels. His non-fiction is worth looking at if only
because it serves to place *A Call* and *The Good Soldier* in the
context of the history of pre-war England and of Ford's
response to public life.

One of the most interesting of these documents is *Ancient Lights*. Ford's ostensible subject here is the decay he found in politics and literature following the Boer War, which he took to be the watershed between the two centuries or, in his metaphor, the 'iron door between the past and the present'. (*AL*, 175) Ford's method is to evoke the great figures of his childhood in the seventies and eighties – Rossetti, Morris, his grandfather Ford Madox Brown – and to contrast them with what he saw as the pigmy literary world of 1911. *Ancient Lights* can scarcely be taken seriously as 'literary history'. Victorianism as a cultural concept had expired before the South African War, and 'decay' and 'decline' are strange descriptions of a culture that was in the process of renewal and innovation. Later historians would claim that 1911 was one of the key years in this development, and Leonard Woolf's portrait of that year in *Beginning Again* (1964) evoked the excitement and atmosphere of glorious change. To Woolf the period was far from being defunct or moribund. *Ancient Lights*, too, is scarcely consonant with the receptivity to experiment and renewal that Ford himself demonstrated as editor of *The English Review*. Ford's main aim here, though, as it had been in *The Cinque Ports*, was not to produce an account of the past that would satisfy the historian. Instead he wished to create an adorned, impressionist view of the past in order to contrast it the more clearly with what he saw as the decadent present. *Ancient Lights*, then, should be read as if it were fiction. The excitement Ford had experienced on first reading a short story by the young Lawrence finds no place in *Ancient Lights*, not because that experience has been disowned but because his purpose now is to suggest the collapse of tradition rather than the process by which traditions were being reshaped and reinvigorated. The book is another elegy on the now-defunct conservatism of Balfour and Salisbury.

Ford grants that there was less social justice in 1873, when

he was born, than now, in 1911. (This was the year of Lloyd
George's monumental Insurance Bill, the first example of
what the Social Imperialists, the hated 'Inheritors', had been
working for since the Rosebery Revolt – a great measure of
national reconstruction achieved above party divisions.)
Ford, however, complains that social amelioration has been
purchased at the cost of 'individuality'. He is repeating,
though now more emphatically, the keynote of his Edwardian
trilogy, *England and the English*, the fight for individualism
against the claims of the State. The incredible antics that
punctuate Ford's Georgian fiction, the social and political
recklessness of his characters, is an attempt, often ridiculous
and always futile, to recapture the lost 'individuality' of
Ancient Lights. In many cases, the latter argues, life is more
agreeable, yet it is greyer, less adventurous, than in Ford's
childhood. The great artists and writers of those years are
used as a stick to beat the Social Imperialists of 1911. Characters are employed to denigrate collectivists. 'We are making
a great many little people more cheerful and more comfortable in their material circumstances', Ford admits, but this is
less important than the fact that 'we are knocking for the
select few the flavour of the finer things out of life'. (*AL*, 270)
Faced by the choice between widening social justice or
preserving the privileges of the minority, Ford is unambigu-
ously clear. The doubts and hesitancies recorded in the three
essays about England written between 1905 and 1907 have
been resolved; Ford now stands for the preservation of in-
equality. In adopting this position in 1911 Ford was, of
course, effectively cutting loose both from the Liberals and
the Conservatives, since both parties had by now committed
themselves to reform. While still maintaining that he didn't
yet know his political opinions, Ford offers a good deal of
evidence in his concluding chapter, entitled firmly 'Where
we stand', of the development of his views since leaving the
Liberal Club in 1908. He is surprised, he claims, that *Ancient
Lights* has turned out to be a jeremiad, because really he only
wants life to be a constant succession of little pleasures, and

he even confesses to enjoying the present's greater politeness and civilisation. Actually, however, this materialism has soured him and Ford loathes the modern obsession with such practicalities of life as workers' insurance. 'In a mild way', Ford writes, 'I should call myself a sentimental Tory and a Roman Catholic', but the prevailing tone of *Ancient Lights*, as of his fiction in these years, is some distance from either mildness or sentimentality. Indeed, very close to the surface of the book is a frustrated desire for a violent confrontation, a passionate resolution of social contradictions, that was to find release in the splenetic *New Humpty-Dumpty* and *Mr Fleight*.

H. G. Wells' novel of the same year, *The New Machiavelli*, also reveals a profound disillusionment with English public life, and it's interesting to compare the two works because Wells at this stage was enunciating the very collectivist doctrines Ford had for years been opposing. And yet, although their attitudes and proposed solutions were so totally at variance, the two books have in common a distaste for the present. For Ford the homogeneity of Victorianism provided an escape from the present: his history was fugitive and escapist. Wells, on the other hand, saw the nineteenth century as the cause of the present impasse, 'a hasty, trial experiment, a gigantic experiment of the most slovenly and wasteful kind'.[8] Ford regretted the disappearance of the Victorian cultural order: to Wells the past was still regrettably alive, blighting the present. Ford looked back to an age of greater 'individualism', Wells to the future, to the State's creation of an era of 'construction, order, education, discipline'.[9] By the end of the novel, though, Wells' hero, Remington, has become totally frustrated with English politics, with 'all this dingy, furtive, canting, humbugging English world', and he and his mistress escape to exile on the continent.[10] Wells' tone and vocabulary here, bitter and soured, are close to the texture of much of Ford's Georgian work. Underlying both *Ancient Lights* and *The New Machiavelli* is a sense that the present can only be changed through violent means. Reming-

ton at one point prays 'for a chastening war', imagining
that the outbreak of hostilities would be 'a dramatic episode
in the reconstruction' of the nation.[11] The cynicism and
amorality characterised in both these visions of English
politics and culture in 1911 can only be purged violently.
Both are symptoms of Europe's need for a deep cleansing,
evidence that the coming of war was to be, in Bergonzi's
words, 'an act both of fulfilment and of deliverance'.[12] In
Ford's case, *Ancient Lights* suggests that he found it easier
to objectify and distance his frustrations through the literary
memoir than through fiction. His fictions before *The Good
Soldier* were a search for the novel that would give him the
same control over his material that he found in non-fictional
forms.

Also published in 1911, *The Critical Attitude* is largely
the garnering in a more permanent format of essays that had
previously appeared in *The English Review* and in two other
journals in 1909 and 1910. In its general attack on art and
criticism that was 'Romantic' – a term of central importance
in T. E. Hulme's aesthetic – and occasionally also in its verbal
details *The Critical Attitude* was a markedly 'neo-classical',
Hulmian document. It was related to *Ancient Lights* in that
Ford's yardstick was once more the great Victorian figures
who had, in his view, helped propagate a single social and
philosophical attitude, generally accepted in the previous
century. This was what Ford calls 'sentimental altruism'
and was the foundation of, say, Tennyson's verse and Eliot's
fiction. Victorian art was 'Romantic' in Hulme's sense, because it concerned itself with making 'humanist' generalisations about life and erecting a moral system by means of
intellectual synthesis. Ford argues, though, that this unified
code has now fractured and that his society is in a period of
transition between the past and an unknown future. 'The old
order. . .is changing; the new has hardly visibly arrived.' (*CA*,
128–9) As a result, all social and political questions are now
immensely complex for Ford. He can't discover one single
belief upon which he can draw, confident of its general

acceptance, but instead perceives myriads of conflicting
ideologies, all claiming man's approbation. This condition,
which Shannon calls a 'sense of psychological bereavement,
of morally isolated individualism' was the consequence of the
age's loss of religious and melioristic faiths.[13] The cultural
programme of Liberalism before 1914 was founded on the
refurbishment of the Victorian ideal of a 'collaborative relationship between society and art', and Liberals believed
that their political ascendancy before 1906 'would result in a
new wholesome integration of art and the march of the
mind'.[14] This indeed was Masterman's design in *The Condition
of England* (1909). But the modernism that Ford was voicing
in *The Critical Attitude* was sceptical of any such melioristic
theory of politics and history. His age being 'a dance of
midges', Ford believed that the modern writer shouldn't aim
at making moral statements, at generalisations and syntheses
of the kind exemplified in the neo-Arnoldian *Condition*.
Ford's writer should simply concentrate on throwing 'light
upon the human heart', because in a time of isolation and
alienation the public was in danger 'of losing alike human
knowledge and human sympathy'. (*CA*, 183, 67) *The Critical
Attitude* was an early articulation of the split between the
melioristic realists and the sceptical modernists.

At a time when the vitality of liberal democracy was felt
to be problematical and there were calls for the abolition of
'party' government, it's no surprise to find Ford describing
his age as fragile and evanescent. Nevertheless, *The Critical
Attitude* was a more responsible, active book than *Ancient
Lights*, since Ford was seeking a remedy, some aesthetic
code that would fill the vacuum left by the collapse of
'Victorianism'. He holds that literature and the arts, together
with their attendant criticism, now have a more vital function
in the republic torn with dissension than in the age of the
'ancient lights', the Victorian seers, those 'schoolmaster[s]
endowed with great moral prestige'. (*CA*, 124) Now, in these
changed conditions, the artist has the opportunity to guide
and educate his readers without browbeating them; to show

them, in Ford's Jamesian metaphor, the pattern in the con-
fusing, multi-coloured carpet that is modern life, without
establishing another set of 'spiritual dictatorships'. This can
no longer be effected through the synthesising intellect, in
the fashion of Galsworthy and Wells, but only through an
aloof detached and remorseless 'registering of life as it really
is'. Realism, as represented by the fiction of Wells, Galsworthy and Bennett, was ineffectual, because its melioristic
rationalist attitudes linked it with the discredited Victorian
sensibility.

Thus *The Critical Attitude* associated itself with the movements of renovation and re-creation then current. For
example, Virginia Woolf's analysis of the function of the
modern novelist in her celebrated essay on Arnold Bennett
was remarkably similar to Ford's, even though they differed
in their practice as novelists. Like the divine manicurist, the
artist for Flaubert, for James Joyce, who was also formulating
a new poetics of fiction at this time, Ford's imaginative artist,
and the critic, 'must, as far as possible, put aside sympathy
with human weaknesses', and be content to 'register', *con-
stater*, his age in a 'splendid aloofness', for only in this
fashion can he show us life 'whole'. (*CA*, 21, 34) E. M. Forster,
too, was searching for a 'wholeness' in his pre-war fiction. It
is striking how the same terms and attitudes are clustered
together in these years. 'Essentially the function of the novel',
Ford continues, is 'to render life, even though its ultimate
aim should be to make life a better thing', and he criticises
the fiction of his contemporaries because of its failure to
'render', its preference for the attractions of the social 'cause'
or the escapist creation of unreal, 'heroic' figures. (*CA*, 15)
Joyce, too, in *A Portrait of the Artist*, had shown his artist
moving towards a similar position, rejecting the temptation
to use his writing in the service of Irish nationalism. Such
temptations are among the vices of 'Romantic' art, of 'dilettantism', and spring, Ford argues, from the artist's refusal to
confront the unheroic muddled present. 'We live', he sternly
concludes,

in our day, we live in our time, and he is not a proper man who will not look in the face his day and his time. (*CA*, 187)

The Critical Attitude was, then, very plainly a manifesto, a call for action, a programme which was to be executed with great success in *The Good Soldier*, the most aloof, detached and remorseless of Ford's novels. Nevertheless, from 1910 to 1915 the relationship between theory and practice in Ford was problematic, and the road to the world of Ashburnham and Dowell was littered with Ford's failures to translate perplexity into adequate 'classical' terms.

What needs stressing about Ford's programme in *The Critical Attitude*, and the various attempts to implement it in the fiction between *A Call* and *The Good Soldier*, is that criticism and fiction alike were both founded on a set of social assumptions far removed from the melioristic liberalism of Masterman, Galsworthy and Bennett, and equally distant from the social reformism to which both parties had by now come to subscribe. In *The Critical Attitude* and the accompanying novels a writer's concern for material improvements is at best irrelevant; at worst, as Ford argued in the case of Galsworthy, corrosive. Indeed the implicit basis of *The Critical Attitude* is the astringent neo-classicism of T. E. Hulme, whose political sympathies were far to the right of Bonar Law's conservatism or of liberalism, which he regarded as a dying, 'humanist' aberration. In its abhorrence of all sentiments – an aversion that, transformed into fiction, may topple over into a self-indulgence that is, paradoxically, full of sentimentality – *The Critical Attitude* anticipates some of Ford's least savoury comments about the benefits of war in 1914 and 1915. While not an explicitly political book, *The Critical Attitude* nevertheless developed a set of attitudes that had a distinctly political dimension. Ford's aversion to both parties and his disillusionment with the Conservatives was stated most fully in the 'Declaration of Faith' in the February 1910 number of *The English Review*. This was paralleled by his belief that the artist was incapable of making order out of chaos and should not be tempted to employ his art in the service of a particular 'cause' or party. Such an exercise, Ford suggested, was doomed to failure, because in 1911 the material upon which the artist must work was too recalcitrant and no simple rational structure could then be expected to embrace all the paradoxes and mysteries of the contemporary world. Instead, Ford stated, the novelist should concentrate on catching a few glimpses of the individual heart, abandoning the search for an illusory coherence.

The assumptions underlying Ford's Edwardian *roman à clef*, *The Inheritors*, and his Tudor trilogy had been centripetal, in that he had posited the novelist's sensibility at the centre of the world, a sensibility capable of pulling together and reconciling contradictions. The trilogy and *The Inheritors* had both been versions of allegory, allusive commentaries upon political life which assumed that the latter was amenable to synthesis and comprehension. For all their differences these novels shared a common foundation in confidence and stability: the external world could be grasped as a whole and articulated. Neither kind of novel could easily be created out of a world that seemed absurd or unknowable. By 1910, however, Ford's thinking about the relations between the novelist and his material is altogether less assured. The relation has become centrifugal. Social beliefs and institutions are conceived of as whirling outward to a distant circumference that the artist is unable to discern. A neat Newtonian world has given way to the astronomy of 'black holes' and incalculable distances. Ford, like Hulme, believed that the intellect was impotent to control the 'flux', the 'dance of midges'. What replaced the synthesising capacity of the artist was his ability to 'register' his environment in a manner analogous to the procedures of the Bergsonian 'intuition'.

These beliefs, so central to an informed reading of *The Good Soldier*, were also elaborated in *Henry James*, the first full-length study of the novelist. As a scholarly, academic critique of James, Ford's book is of slight value, yet it does indicate with some precision its author's preoccupations as war approached. Aside from its intrinsic interest as a highly readable response to James' canon from a fellow-novelist and acquaintance, Ford's essay suggests some of the socio-aesthetic attitudes that underpin *The Good Soldier*, the novel on which he began work in that same year.

The main point about *Henry James* is that Ford used James' fiction as an illustration of the theories set forth in *The Critical Attitude*. He demonstrates that James' methods, the felicitous ambiguities and elusive parentheses of his style, were perfectly attuned to the society in which he was writing. For Ford in 1913, James' value is that 'he is the only unbiased, voluminous and truthful historian of our day', a writer who can render Edwardian and Georgian high society without being overbearingly dogmatic or moralistic. (*HJ*, 66) Through his meticulous portrayal of the 'affairs' of the leisured classes, James could hint at the existence, or absence, of basic human values without resort to the explicit moral statements of the Victorian 'nuvvlists'. The case Ford here makes out for James is based upon a recognition of the parti-cular specific difficulties created for the artist by contempor-ary conditions; the whole argument is grounded upon his appreciation of the skill with which James surmounted these obstacles. Ford contended that 'you cannot write about Euripides and ignore Athens', and so he delineated the social context within which James had to operate as a factor which neither James himself nor his critic could afford to overlook. (*HJ*, 16) Three-quarters of the book examines the novelist's umbilical relationship to his subject-matter, the Anglo-American bourgeoisie, Ford's conclusion being that the refine-ments of James' style are a vivid embodiment of his subjects' devotion to the indefinite statement, the imprecise velleity. At a period when, Ford argued, no one particular theory was dominant and the Victorian homogeneity had splintered, what was needed from the novelist was not another set of dogmas but rather 'a ray of light [cast] into the profound gloom, into the whirl of shadows, of our social agnosticism'. (*HJ*, 66) At a time of bewildering transition only the novelist, Ford held, can rescue us from the whirlpool of conflicting ideologies, only he can 'give us the very matter upon which we shall build the theories of the new body politic'. (*HJ*, 48) The novelist's vocation is not to publish theories, only to provide the facts of human motivation and ambition upon which theories can be constructed. Hence in an illuminating way Ford associates the perplexities of contemporary life, evanescent and transient, with the very methods James chose to render that world.

III

For all their distinct local differences these three books, *Ancient Lights*, *The Critical Attitude* and *Henry James*, are linked by the common preoccupation with the literary and artistic world at the turn of the century. Ford's other non-fictional prose of those years, his journalism and two propaganda essays, does not have this same aesthetic concern. Nevertheless this material shouldn't be overlooked, for it casts a revealing light on the contemporary fiction.

The essays Ford published in the journal *Outlook* are indeed remarkable for the frankness with which they record the novelist's reactions between the beginning of 1914 and January 1915. In January 1914 Ford sounded supremely confident in his adherence to the 'feudal' ideals of the ruling class he had adopted, and was contemptuous of anyone who reneged on those ideals. His tone is aristocratic as he enquires of his *Outlook* readers:

How can a man, an educated man, a man ex-officio a member of the ruling classes – or any man who can read at all – hold the vast number of contradictory opinions that are necessary to a 'Progressive' of to-day?[15]

Even when we have offset the gameyness of this question with the fact that Ford, the son of a German music-critic with but slight material resources, was always tempted to affect the drawl of the upper middle classes, we are left with clear evidence that Ford is now disowning those progressives he had welcomed to the pages of his *English Review* only five years earlier – men as far from being illiterate as Hobson and Cunninghame Graham.

In another article in similar vein, published in May 1914, Ford lends his support to W. H. Mallock, a right-wing Conservative, arguing that now 'there are no poor in the sense that there were poor in the year 1801'.[16] Two months later, on the eve of war, he is registering his disgust with the Liberal government for having riled the Kaiser. Thus at the outbreak of war Ford's thinking was dominated by his

intense dislike of liberal democracy with – as he thought – its shady capitalists, venal politicians, and an electorate stuffed with fatuous ideas of its own wisdom by a shoddy system of universal education. (*Mizener*, 249)

Ironically Ford shared this distrust of parliamentary forms with some of the very men whose Social Imperialism he had long been attacking. The 'socialists of the Right' envisaged a solution through a 'national government', which indeed was to come to power under Lloyd George in December 1916. Their platform was modernisation, 'organisation and efficiency, social reform and national revival'.[17] Ford, from the opposite position of an aristocratic traditionalism, shared their disaffection with parliamentary democracy, but looked instead towards the 'feudalism' of his own invention, idealistic and chivalric, which he had fictionalised three years before in *Ladies Whose Bright Eyes*.

After the declaration of war in August Ford's first published comment was indeed to decry its lack of chivalric glamour. As the first soldiers were perishing in Flanders Ford claimed that he had no objection to men dying but that he was disturbed by the imbecility of the ideals for which they sacrificed their lives, the tawdriness of modern nationalism. In the first week of war the author of *The Good Soldier* is arguing that the hostilities will have been worthwhile if they prove to the survivors that they are feudal serfs, with duties but no rights. Three weeks later Ford invited his *Outlook* readers to consider Germany as the 'gallant enemy' rather than the loathed foe versified by the jingoist poets of the day. Though confessing that he disliked his father's nation for, among other reasons, its growing 'socialism', Ford urged those poets to extract poetry from the war instead of hatred.[18] The novelist who, a decade later, was to write one of the century's noblest anti-war novels, began the war, like Wilfred Owen, in a flush of frustrated idealism, defending militarism because it 'has, or implies, many high qualities'.[19] Indeed it was not Prussia's war-machine Ford hated so much as the way that the bureaucratic state, with its dangerous 'socialist' tendencies, had asphyxiated the idealisms of youth.

Ford's abhorrence of liberal democracy and his nostalgia for an altruistic, hierarchical, fictive 'feudalism' were stated at length in his two books of propaganda published in 1915, *When Blood is their Argument* and *Between St Denis and St George*. Though their ostensible subject is the materialism and chauvinism of Germany, and though both defend Britain's entry into the war, Ford's real concern is with British political institutions in peacetime. At the heart of these books lies his belief that Britain had become too much like Germany, too 'socialist', too 'materialist'. They contain the fullest, most explicit statements of Ford's hostility to collectivism and State power, the theme that had been preoccupying him since *The Inheritors*. Ford's attack here on his father's nation must be placed in the general context of English attitudes to Germany in the pre-war epoch. In particular it's necessary to remember that for the Social Imperialists Germany offered both a model and a threat. It was a threat militarily and economically, and English Social Imperialism was in many ways a response to the reality of Germany's superior economy.

However, Germany provided English thinkers and politicians with a paradigm for development as well as an indication of the urgency of modernisation. In several areas – in government, in the army, in industry, in higher education, but not, significantly, in culture, where France then offered the examples and stimuli – Germany was the country to

which English reformists looked for a lead. Many of the leading figures in the Social Imperialist movement – William
Cunningham the economist, Sir William Ashley, R. B.
Haldane – had deep intellectual affiliations with Germany.
To many English politicians the Germany created by
Bismarck indicated how the pressures for democratic reform
from the socialist and labour movements on the Left might
be safely drawn off. The English working-class electorate
might be saved from the Left by similar measures of social
reform.

To Ford, on the other hand, Germany was the living
embodiment of his nightmare of total State control, which he
had foretold as early as *The Inheritors*. His two propaganda
books of 1915, as well as reflecting much of that year's popular anti-German sentiment, may also be viewed in the context
of Ford's growing antipathy to Germany as the model for
English collectivists. His excoriation of Germany for its
'mania for organisation', its 'impersonalism', and for having
erected a system in which everything must tend towards the
glory of the State exceeded what was then required from
sponsored attacks on German militarism. (*WBITA*, xi) For
Ford these books were, rather, the climax of his consistent
and sustained criticism of *English* reformers. *When Blood*
argues for the return of 'altruism' to replace Bismarckian
'materialism', because Ford holds that 'no really satisfactory
art and no really great culture can arise except in an era of
noble political ideals and aspirations'. As well as trying to
inspire Germany's military defeat, these two essays warn
Britain that its own political parties had approached dangerously close to Prussian materialism. At the beginning of the
war Ford was obsessed with extremes. Like T. E. Hulme, his
vision was Manichean. He saw political and private life as a
straightforward choice between Prussian materialism and
Gallic altruism. Such are the alternatives posed for the State
in *When Blood* and *Between St Dennis and St George*. For
the individual a similar choice is presented, in the more
complex terms of imaginative art, in *The Good Soldier*.

In publishing a wide range of political opinion, Ford's *English Review* had been tolerant and pluralist. Now, in 1914 and 1915, Ford sounds much more 'hawkish', as he advocates a return to a rigid, hierarchical, quasi-feudal form of government, one in which men estimated their relationship to the State in terms not of rights but of duties. Ford's target here was the vision of the State's role held, for example, by the Webbs with their faith 'in a deliberately organised society. . .in the application of science to human relations with a view to betterment'.[20] Or the 'new spirit' perceived by Haldane in 1906, 'a spirit that was moving the democracy to go beyond the old-fashioned Liberal tradition, [which] would be content with nothing short of a demonstration that the democracy was for the future to have the last word'.[21] Ford's alternative to these developments was nothing if not 'old-fashioned'. *When Blood*'s sketch of his utopia, which Ford contrasts with the dystopias of Fabianism or the welfarism of Bismarck, indicates its nostalgic, unreal medievalism:

I should like to see revived a state of things in which port wine and long leisures over the table, and donnish, maybe rather selfish, manners and high gentlemanly traditions, possibly a little too heavy drinking, and classical topics for discussion – in which all these things were considered to be the really high standard of living. (*WBITA*, 300)

Such attitudes are, Ford concedes, anachronistic and regressive. They have to be 'revived' because they are dead, whereas in *The Inheritors* Ford's models of behaviour, though threatened, had been alive.

In another illuminating passage in *When Blood* Ford admits again that these are 'exploded traditions', and that his personal tragedy – and Ashburnham's, too – is that he continues to adhere to a set of principles formulated by a class (and a party) that has now discarded them. Ford's position, then, has become more embattled as a consequence of the Conservative Party's shift from its aristocratic and landed affiliations to a new fidelity to business interests. The relevant passage, though lengthy, merits full quotation because it clarifies the attitudes that underlie Ford's fiction between 1910 and 1915. 'I am', he confessed,

an unfortunate man – unfortunate in the sense that all men of forty and less, the world over, are unfortunate. For I came into, and took very seriously, English public-school life at a time when the English public-school spirit – in many ways the finest product of a civilisation – was already on the wane. I took its public traditions with extraordinary seriousness – the traditions of responsibilities, duties, privileges, and no rights.

And, in consequence, he continues,

I cannot now get away from the impression that I have the responsibilities and the duties of my station, and that if I perform them efficiently I shall possibly have certain privileges accorded to me. But as to a right – I have never known the feeling of having any right at all to anything. It is still ingrained in my bones – the idea that I must give unceasingly all that I have to the world, and that in return some day, with luck, some one will spoil me a little. . .

But, he concludes,

These are, in fact, *exploded traditions*, here or anywhere else. (*WBITA*, 301: emphasis added)

In all this aristocratic abnegation there is, of course, a sizeable theatrical element. Ford Madox Hueffer, with his paternal roots in the German petty bourgeoisie, is here claiming to bear the burdens of an alien class. The real aristocrats, whose miserable existence Ford is appropriating as his own, had acted more decisively and pragmatically. Few of them had waited to be spoiled a little. For reasons of his own, Ford is pre-empting the right, to which he was entitled by neither birth nor wealth, to have no *rights*. And, as a final irony, Ford is aware that the traditions to which he is laying claim, as an outsider, are now in fact dead and discredited. This was precisely the gap, between Ford's lofty assumptions and the banal realities of his life, which rendered his existence so frequently bathetic. Yet, to the novelist, these 'exploded traditions' were immensely fecund, giving birth to his two best works. *The Good Soldier* renders the tension between the world of an idealised, romanticised aristocracy and the

reality of debts, mortgages and marital dishonour. Ashburnham's courage is a sightless virtue.

An act of undeniable, sighted courage was Ford's decision
to enlist in the army, soon after the completion of the two
books of propaganda. The long-term effect of his war service
was undoubtedly to blur the certainties proclaimed in 1914
and 1915, although as early as January 1915 he was admitting
that he had 'nothing but questions left in the world' and was
'conscious of a profound moral change'.[22] Discussion of the
war's effect on Ford is best postponed, since the marks it left
– apart from his physical deterioration – only became visible
in his fiction of the twenties and thirties. (He published no
fiction during the war.) As regards the short-term effects of
the war and the nature of Ford's development between 1910
and 1919, there is no reason to doubt the testimony of his
friend Douglas Goldring that he left the army in 1919

very much advanced in his political thinking. His 'ivory tower'
period was definitely ended. All humanity was now his preoccupation. He was spiritually prepared for the advance from
being a good novelist to becoming a great one.[23]

Though Goldring is here pitching his claims for his friend a
trifle too high, the general drift of the comment is surely
just. After the war Ford's fiction does evince a new breadth
of sympathy and he becomes alive to international issues
that are wider – if not always more successfully rendered –
than the pre-war fiction's interest in the ethical minutiae of
one particular class, real or fantasised. The war was, then, a
truly educative and liberating experience for Ford in the way
that, as Trotsky saw, 'a catastrophe, whether it be personal
or social, is always a great touchstone, because it infallibly
reveals the true personal or social connections, not the showy
ones'.[24] For Ford, as for so many of his generation, the war
was a painful revelation, showing him through personal and
communal suffering the real nature of the world. As he noted
in a letter written shortly before his death, four years of conflict destroyed the 'Fine Illusions' he had cherished that faith,
loyalty and courage were the mainsprings of human action.[25]

Many of the uncomfortable questions he had become aware of by January 1915 were to be settled in the next four years. The decade between his editorship of *The English Review* and his demobilisation in 1919 was the most momentous of his life.

4

THE GOOD SOLDIER: THE POLITICS
OF AGNOSTICISM

When he wrote *The Good Soldier* Ford was still using the name of his German father, Hueffer, and nothing is so revealing of these German roots as the novelist's sustained fascination with the dynamics of illusion and reality among the English bourgeoisie at the turn of the century. As an alien, Ford could not command that innate familiarity with the minute tremors of upper-class behaviour ascribed to Tietjens or to Ashburnham. Yet, like Dowell, the American millionaire, Ford was uneasily attracted by a foreign code. Indeed the theatricality of the English upper class had been a source of wonder to Ford for some fifteen years: *The Benefactor, The Inheritors, A Call* and *The Spirit of the People* were all attempts to come to terms with what John Berger, in his novel *G*, calls the 'spectacle' or the 'theatre' of the English ruling class. Members of this class at the beginning of the century, Berger wrote, 'no longer claimed...justification by reference to a natural order: instead they performed a play upon a stage with its own laws and conventions'.[1] Ford's inability to grasp these rules stemmed partially from an outsider's failure to decode a complex rhetoric of speech and gesture, to demarcate the boundary between play and life; but the importance Ford assigned to the behaviour of his chosen minority must be linked to factors wider than the accident of his own Anglo-German pedigree. The anecdotal germ of *The Good Soldier* – Dowell's drive to a railway-station with a couple who chat calmly despite their inner turmoil – had made its first appearance in *England and the English* eight years earlier. Ford's return to, and the full fictional development of, this incident indicate that he was still fascinated with the questions it raised for him about the relationship between inner crisis and external calm among the English bourgeoisie. Ford was entranced by the power of the 'stiff upper lip' somehow to restrain and hide a man's acutest emotional conflicts. After germinating for a decade, an episode from an essay was transformed into a novel's Joycean 'epiphany'.

The Good Soldier was, then, a climactic novel in terms of Ford's own career, the most assured rendering of the theme which had absorbed him for so long. Yet it didn't offer any kind of exorcism, since the problems treated in the novel could only be resolved either by Ford's complete endorsement of a code from which he was alienated by birth and by class, or, alternatively, through his abandonment of the conventions of Edward Ashburnham, a decisive step for which he was still unprepared. The growing maturity of Ford's art was, rather, a result of the new clarity with which he was able to portray credibly the tensions between belief and social agnosticism. *The Good Soldier* doesn't present us with the agonies that result from conversion, the painful resolution of social tensions that we find in *Parade's End* in the twenties. Instead from its opening pages *The Good Soldier* records the pull and counter-pull within Dowell, as he tries to persuade himself that the 'long, tranquil life' he has enjoyed for nine years, the stately 'minuet' of his existence with Florence, Leonora and Edward – the 'good people' – is extant, has survived immortalised in some distant heaven. Working against this idealisation of the past is the narrator's certainty that in fact their foursome was 'a prison full of screaming hysterics'. (GS, i, i, 18) Which of these two incompatible views, Dowell vainly wonders, is the truth: the 'theatre', elegantly directed and costumed, of their public, visible lives; or the 'sub-text', barbarous and anarchic, of their private acts?

Even the terms in which Dowell formulates this question confirm the relevance of the theatrical imagery to the problem with which he's wrestling. He enquires

if for me we were four people with the same tastes, with the same
desires, *acting* – or, no, *not acting* – sitting here and there unanimously, isn't that the truth? (*GS*, i, i, 18; italics added)

'Acting – or. . .not acting' – the problematic and provisional
nature of 'sincerity' in Dowell's circle – is, of course, a crucial
question in a novel with such a high incidence of feigned
heart-conditions. Notoriously *The Good Soldier* provides no
answers to Dowell's constant self-interrogation. Indeed the
form of the novel, so totally unconcerned with the arousal of
any suspense in the reader – the suicide of Ashburnham at
the end must be one of English fiction's least surprising
deaths – militates against the novel's utility as a problem-
solving device. What it offers instead is a consummate portrayal of the nescience and frustration of the English
bourgeoisie just before the war, in which Ford now capital-
ises, positively and for the first time, on his own bewilderment. *Mr Fleight*, a pencil sketch for *The Good Soldier*, had
been marred by its hero's stunned disengagement from
human society. Dowell understands little more than Blood,
but, at least until the last two chapters, is prepared to question everything and to ruminate extensively. Ford's 'discovery' of Dowell allows him to treat in fictional terms what
he had previously only explored successfully in his non-
fiction, in *The Critical Attitude* and *Henry James*: the
evanescence and transience he found characteristic of his
age.

On its publication in 1915 *The Good Soldier* was widely
accused of undermining the values necessary in time of war.
Sixty years later we can now see that it did in fact imply an
allegiance to orthodox militarist beliefs, since out of the
pervasive chaos and scepticism of which Dowell was a focal-
point, Ford constructed a text that proclaimed the potential
of order and discipline. The *form* of *The Good Soldier*, so
engineered and modernist, indeed endorsed the promises
inherent in the title – of orderliness and self-control. The
crude reader in 1915 judged that a novel by Hueffer set, in
part, in Nauheim and Marburg and ending with the suicide

of a 'good soldier' was deeply subversive and pro-German. (Ian Hay's best-seller of the same year, *The First Hundred Thousand*, indicates what was required of a novel in 1915.) Yet, despite its superficial lack of tact, never Ford's strong point, *The Good Soldier* was fundamentally a 'soldierly' book, the work of a master fictional strategist.

Ford's creation of such a spare, pruned and efficient novel did not, however, indicate that he had finally cast in his lot with the social engineers, the 'Inheritors' of the earlier novel, the Social Imperialists. Ford's portrait of Leonora in *The Good Soldier*, that tough unromantic 'fixer', suggests that he maintained his hostility to the materialist ambitions of the political modernists. Now, though, on the eve of war, with the Conservative Party being led by a businessman, Bonar Law, and the Liberal government increasingly dominated by Lloyd George, Ford felt deeply unsure of the prospects for survival of the 'individualism' he cherished. H. G. Wells, an opponent of Fordian individualism, had chosen a markedly 'individualistic' form – the fictional memoir, subjective, reminiscential, private – to narrate the career of the collectivist Remington, the epitome of Ford's hated 'Inheritors', in *The New Machiavelli*. Equally striking was Ford's recourse to an authoritarian form as a means of transforming into fiction his own frustrated individualism.

The Good Soldier, then, provides another illustration from this period of the familiar conjunction, noted by Shannon, of political elitism with artistic impulses that were modernist, innovative but equally elitist:

The modern consciousness, concerned to insist on the lofty 'seriousness' of art's purposes and the need for formalistic structure and technical innovation, was fully attuned to an elitist social stance. The idea of resistance to the pressures of a mass or 'bourgeois' reading public became in itself one of the primary tenets of the new consciousness.

The Good Soldier belongs with the work of Hulme, Eliot and Pound as an index of the collapse of the Victorian faith in 'the homogeneity of society and intellect', the end of the 'synthesis of progressive politics and moral art'[2] that *The New Machiavelli*, say, still enshrined. Equally indicative of this collapse, though less often noted, is the absence from the pages of Webb's *Our Partnership* of any affiliation between her 'progressive politics' and a modernist culture. Her account of the year 1911, when she was busy publicising the Poor Law Commission's 'Minority Report', fails to recognise the cultural revolution then under her nose in London, the radical, scandalous developments in ballet, painting, sculpture, poetry and fiction. The modernity of the Webbs' dissenting 'Report', which anticipated the growth of Britain's Welfare State after 1945, and the innovations of *The Good Soldier*, which anticipated the later fictions of Joyce, Woolf and Richardson, were formally similar in that both valued discipline and centralisation, both opposed sentimentality. At the same time, however, they were politically and ideologically antagonistic, one harking back to the discredited conservatism of Salisbury, the other heralding the social democracy of Attlee and Beveridge.

The Good Soldier was as factitious as any complex Fabian or military stratagem, the most ordered of Ford's novels. He was aware, too, of the potential difficulties in such a structured, deliberate novel, writing in January 1914, while dictating *The Good Soldier*, 'that there is the danger of becoming too flawless, arid, soulless, and so on'.[3] He saw that 'the cold, clear flame' that was his high objective, an austere fashioning of perplexity, could become too arctic and rarefied in a genre as committed to contingency and the unforeseen as the novel. Ford's later comments on the novel seem designed to convince us that it was the first on which he had lavished any considerable attention, though it's clear that a great deal of research underpinned the achievement of the 'Tudor trilogy'. In these novels, however, Ford had tried to bring to life a vanished milieu and, despite his hard work on their 'locations' and costumes, the trilogy's relaxed and conventional form, inherited from Scott, scarcely exemplified the rigorous poetics of the novel formulated with Conrad at the turn of the century. In 1915 Ford crossed the line between conventional and innovative, between 'traditional' and 'modern'. In the terms recently adopted by David Lodge, he moved from the 'metonymy' of the historical trilogy to a text that was 'metaphorical', readerly and non-linear.[4] In *The Good Soldier*, that is to say, he concentrated powerfully upon the conceptual and the ahistorical, upon the deployment of his scenes to bring out clearly a patterned design that was neither chronological nor linear. Thus his nineteenth novel was the first – and arguably the last – sustained attempt to illustrate the demanding and monolithic theories Ford had long been advancing. Never again was he so driven by, above all, the search for a novel of perfect facticity.

Ford was frequently his own worst critic, yet the comments he recorded during the composition of *The Good Soldier* serve as a helpful guide to his intentions. What we now need, he wrote in a book-review in 1914, is

a novel uniform in key, in tone, in progression, as hard in texture as a mosaic, as flawless in surface as a polished steel helmet of the fifteenth century.[5]

Ford's demand here for a novel of neo-classical clarity is notable for its indifference to a large proportion of the novelist's customary concerns. There's no reference here to historical realism, dialogue, characterisation, narrative delight or moral fervour. Indeed its connection with any conventional 'metonymic' novel of the time – the fiction of Bennett, Wells or Galsworthy – is so remote that it's hardly surprising that Ford should borrow his similes from the non-verbal arts of music and sculpture. Ford's prescription – in effect a statement of his aims for the novel he was then writing – centres on the effect the novel should have on the reader, when it is recalled and recollected in tranquillity, as a whole autonomous construct, distilled from the experience of reading the work over a period of several hours. Ford aimed to produce an impression on his reader analogous to that of a sculpture whose shape can be perceived in a fraction of a second. The limiting factor here is that the experience of reading any novel must be spread and extended over a more or less substantial period. No verbal form longer than a haiku can be assimilated in a second. Ford's statement implies that in reading *The Good Soldier* we should deploy a strategy of distantiation or filtration, so that we can, as it were, suspend judgment of a character's moral health and concentrate instead on the place of an episode or chapter within an emerging design. This, at any rate, seems to have been Ford's modernist intention. The novel that met these exacting specifications, equally demanding on the reader's skills, would thus exist as autonomous and discrete, perceived spatially as a finite block of material, like a mosaic or burnished helmet, and enfranchised from fiction's usual linearity.

Dowell himself, Ford's narrator, addresses his attention to this point, the choice between time or space as the novel's axis, at the beginning of the second chapter, confessing uncertainty as to

how it is best to put this thing down – whether it would be better to try and tell the story from the beginning, as if it were a story; or whether to tell it from this distance of time, as it reached me from the lips of Leonora or from those of Edward himself. (*GS*, i, ii, 22)

He proceeds to reject the first, chronological, possibility, opting for a narrative method that will preserve the appearance of the casual and spontaneous. Indeed the chapter that follows his musing over the best presentation of his material ranges extensively and, it seems, extra-logically, over a wide terrain of reminiscence; yet all is controlled by the likely leaps of Dowell's consciousness: from Peire Vidal in medieval Provence to John Hurlbird's Waterbury factories, and from Dowell's first glimpse of Florence to his recent summons to Fordingbridge. These pages, then, provide us with the answer to Dowell's question. His rapid jumps are the means he will adopt for the whole of the novel.

The narrative method Dowell abandons, 'tell[ing] the story from the beginning, as if it were a story' – as if it were like, say, *The Old Wives' Tale*, which moves forward confidently from the sisters' childhood to their old age – implies the existence of a causative principle which was absent from the world of both Dowell and Ford. It was a framework which implicitly asserted an order in human affairs. The whole point of Dowell's choice of narrative method, under Ford's superintendence, is to bring out the arbitrariness of events, their lack of a sequential principle of cause and effect. In this sense *The Good Soldier* is not a 'story', but, as it were, an 'anti-story', proceeding from a recognition that 'unfractured prose' – in Dowell's phrase, 'the story from the beginning' – can only be utilised, in the words of Stuart Hampshire, as

the medium for representing citizens to themselves in a social and historical setting which they can recognise as their own and which they believe determines their existence and identity.[6]

Dowell didn't believe that the existence of himself and his three friends was determined by an extensive, public, temporal setting, the whole structure of implicit confidence that had held aloft *The Fifth Queen*. He rejected the nineteenth century's positivism, claiming instead that the reality of events lay only in his own perception of them – however fractured, subjective and uncertain this might be.

Ford's idea of the novel as a 'polished helmet' implies an abandonment of the chronological novel that is similar to Dowell's refusal to construct his narrative 'as if it were a story'. Dowell's choice, in its place, of a digressive mode, accumulating emotionally rather than historically, is given the appearance of the casual and unpremeditated as he determines that, in his words,

I shall just imagine myself for a fortnight or so at one side of the fireplace of a country cottage, with a sympathetic soul opposite me. (*GS*, i, ii, 22)

In truth, however, this unceremonious narrative posture is exceedingly demanding of both narrator and reader. Dowell's decision to converse 'in a very rambling way', as 'a sort of maze', because 'real stories', as opposed to fictions, 'are probably told best in the way a person telling a story would tell them', is an exacting choice, because, as he puts it,

It is so difficult to keep all these people going. I tell you about Leonora and bring her up to date; then about Edward, who has fallen behind. And then the girl gets hopelessly left behind. (*GS*, iv, i, 161; iv, iii, 192)

Dowell must therefore combine the most dizzying conjuring with the illusion of sitting at ease, and the strain of this procedure leads him at one point to wish that he could tell the story 'in diary form'. We know that Dowell is indeed a diarist, but a chronological narrative would be inappropriate for a story intended to communicate the absence of any nemesis or driving historical force. At the outset Dowell has likened himself to an historian, the witness to the 'sack of a city or the falling to pieces of a people' who desires to record what he has seen 'for the benefit of unknown heirs or of generations infinitely remote'. (*GS*, i, i, 17) Such Balzacian ambitions, however, are thwarted by Dowell's own scepticism: he is an annalist whose only reliable archives are his impressions. And so, in Schorer's phrase, 'from the very delimitation of form arises the exfoliation of theme'.[7] Historiography itself is called into question in *The Good Soldier*.

II

Ford's questioning of the very bases of western historiography, that sustained attempt since the Renaissance to schematise the past Hulme dismissed as 'humanist' and decadent, wasn't simply a quirk of his idiosyncratic historical fancy. It wasn't a cavalier exercise in private myth-making. On the contrary, Ford's work between 1913 and 1915 ran parallel with the main currents of literary and artistic modernism. In particular, *The Good Soldier*'s abandonment of linearity in favour of a spatial mode is another illustration of modernism's basic ahistoricism.

Joseph Frank, one of the early historians of this movement, has argued that the fundamental feature of the work of such writers as Eliot, Pound, Proust and Joyce was precisely this: that the reader is meant to apprehend 'spatially, in a moment of time, rather than as a sequence'.[8] Literature's 'spatial form' mirrored the non-naturalistic developments then afoot in the plastic arts. Spatiality was modernism's formal expression of its ahistoricism. Aspects of past and present are continually juxtaposed, as in Dowell's fractured narrative, so that they are fused in one comprehensive view that attempts to transcend historical limits and encompass all time. History, in Frank's words,

is no longer seen as an objective, causal progression in time, with distinctly marked out differences between each period, but is sensed as a continuum in which distinctions between past and present are obliterated.[9]

Modernism sought to transform the time-world of history into the timeless world of 'myth', whose appropriate expression is 'spatial form'. The actions and events of a particular time are no longer the constituents of a coherent historical design, but merely the embodiments of 'eternal prototypes'.[10]

Frank's observations about modernism's flight from history into myth and spatiality are certainly applicable to *The Good Soldier*, in which the narrator dissolves historical time and believes in a 'darkness' of the human heart that transcends anything as specific as, say, the changing economic and cultural relations between Britain and the United States at the turn of the century. Dowell's agnostic phrase, 'It is all a darkness' (*GS*, I, i, 22), reverberates throughout the novel and has a quasi-mythical status as his summary of the pointlessness and untidiness of experience. ('Two noble natures, drifting down life, like fireships afloat on a lagoon.' *GS*, III, v, 146) Dowell magnifies Edward and Nancy into creations of mythical scale, personifications of that passional force which 'society', any society, will always crush in favour of the more adaptable Leonora. We are actively discouraged from building any historical explication of the novel's discords and futility. Man's deepest passional energies are depleted and finally discharged, yet the novel suggests that no human

interference can reverse the process. The decelerating rhythm
of the novel – 'life peters out', Dowell remarks at the end
(*GS*, IV, vi, 218) – is placed outside of historical continuities
and within a timeless myth of human bewilderment and
frustration. The 'massive stasis' of *The Good Soldier* is the
atemporal quiescence of myth. (*Gordon*, 55)

And so we can place *The Good Soldier* within the modernist movement at the beginning of the century as another of
those works composed as

> aesthetic objects for contemplation, or [which] enact the leap out
> of time to the enduring artistic moment: the Joycean epiphany,
> the Imagist image, moments of stasis or aesthetic equipoise caught
> from the 'brutal chaos' of reality.[11]

Ford's prescriptive similes of the novel as a mosaic or helmet
have, too, a remarkable kinship with the 'strongly visualist'
language recognised by Bergonzi in the modernist masters.[12]
Indeed there's a good deal of evidence of Ford's intimacy
with the major radical developments in art and literature
before and during the composition of *The Good Soldier*.
(Aptly, the opening four chapters of the novel first appeared
in Wyndham Lewis' *Blast*.) Several of Ford's published comments on *avant-garde* art around 1914 suggest his familiarity
with Epstein, Lewis, Gaudier-Brzeska and Marinetti. More
important still, they imply that he felt some kinship with
these artists; that he was consciously struggling towards
some kind of insight into the non-naturalistic potential of his
own genre to express paralysis, both public and private; that
he was trying to compose a novel constructed like a Cubist
painting or like Epstein's sculpture 'Rock Drill', as an image
of his own bafflement. Ford commented, in the post-war
Thus to Revisit, that he had recognised in 1914 the attempt
of the Vorticists and Cubists to express themselves 'in abstract
Form or in abstract Sound'. (*TTR*, 174) Similarly, Ford
observed in May of that year that the Futurist painters

> were doing very much what novelists of the type of Flaubert or
> . . .Maupassant aimed at. They gave you not so much the reconsti-
> tution of a crystallised scene in which all the figures were arrested

– not so much that, as *fragments of impressions gathered during
a period of time, during a period of emotion, or. . .travel. . .*[13]

or during, indeed, the European and American trips that
punctuate, perhaps generate, Dowell's narrative. The plastic
technique of Futurist artists, in Ford's description, is similar
to Dowell's verbal procedures, his 'fragments of impressions'.
Again, to continue the possible analogues between art and
Ford's novel, the image of the 'vortex' printed in the same
issue of *Blast* and representing 'whirling concentrations of
energy' framed by the 'stable and self-contained' – the basic
Vorticist tenet of 'internal energy and external calm'[14] – is
suggestive of the novel's combination of phlegm and hysteria,
the presence in *The Good Soldier* of anarchy, fission and
incest within a rigid formal structure.

However, amongst all these various parallels the most productive may be the Cubist connection. (Frank Kermode
must have been alluding to this when he referred, glancingly
and without naming *The Good Soldier*, to Ford's 'Cubist
novel'.)[15] Wylie Sypher has been more specific, calling it a
novel 'about the unreliability of the modern self' and concluding that 'technically the novel is an exercise like Cubist
painting, which treated its subjects by seeing them from
contrary points of view simultaneously'.[16] Dowell writes in
similar terms about his principles of composition:

I have explained everything that went before [Maisie's death]. . .
from the several points of view that were necessary – from
Leonora's, from Edward's and, to some extent, from my own.
(*GS*, IV, i, 161)

He has told his story in a quasi-Cubist manner, dissolving a
space constructed from a fixed point of view and showing
instead that the events in Germany and Hampshire existed
in multiple relations with each other, changing appearance
according to the angle from which they were perceived. In
particular, those scenes which come to have the resonant
significance of an 'epiphany' – the first assemblage of the
quartet in the Nauheim restaurant, the 'Lutheran' episode

at Marburg – reverberate because they are told multi-
dimensionally, with a driving narrative concern for the
establishment of alternative modes of perception.

And yet Dowell too is a participant, however unwilling, in
these events, and his comments above indicate a recognition
that, like John Berger's Cubist, 'his awareness of nature was
part of nature'.[17] Similarly, post-Einstein physicists are
cognisant of their place in the environment they study. An
'uncertainty principle' operated in *The Good Soldier* no less
than in Cubism or the new physics. Just as Cubism was a
study in the techniques of representation, a new look at the
relationship between art and reality which gave us the
tableau-tableau, the painter's painting, so *The Good Soldier*
was a 'novelist's novel', a 'writerly' text, an investigation
both of 'the object and the means of painting this object'.[18]
The fact that most critical discussion of the novel since
Schorer has revolved around the moral worth of Dowell – as
if he were a Dickensian heroine – may perhaps be tangential
to Ford's intention. Conceivably he didn't intend us to evalu-
ate Dowell as we do Esther in *Bleak House*, Katharine in
The Fifth Queen, even Tietjens in *Parade's End*. Dowell
indeed may not be discussable in similar terms and earlier
readings of his character have failed to notice that ambivalence and unreliability are the very constituents of Ford's
particular design. As Kermode has noted, there is no 'single
standard of veracity' in *The Good Soldier* and 'the illusion of
the single right reading is possible no longer'.[19]

III

In his examination of the relations between modernist
literature and art Sypher took Gide as an example of the
'cubist novelist', that interesting oxymoron, and argued from
his work that

irresolution, an incapacity or unwillingness to endorse any one
perspective, was typical of the cubist temperament, the indecision
of the early twentieth-century intellectual who, having accepted

the notion of relativism, was aware of all the attitudes that could be held, but perhaps not acted upon: neutrality in art and life, and a clever investigation of alternative angles on every problem.[20]

Irresolution, intellectual and moral relativism, also dominate *The Good Soldier*, a novel whose form renders it impossible for us to elicit any clear-cut authorial ideology. In the earlier *Inheritors* Granger had stood for Ford's own identification with the values of individualism and tradition, and with the novelist's hostility to collectivist materialist forces. In *The Good Soldier*, though we are aware that these two modes are still in conflict, Ford's personification of such social movements through, respectively, Edward and Leonora, militates against a reader's identification with either. *The Good Soldier* discourages empathy. Our mixed and provisional reactions to Edward and Leonora make it impossible to believe that their creator was either wholly 'for' or 'against' the social alignments they represent. Although, as *What Maisie Knew, The Good Soldier* is patterned like a formal dance – perhaps the minuet to which Dowell refers – with Ford intending to imply 'a freedom from time, change and contingency' noted by Bergonzi as common in 'the iconography of modern art and literature', the novelist still remains faithful to the complexities established within each of the dance's several 'movements', rendering precarious any absolute moral judgment.[21] Ford doesn't oversimplify the crowded entanglements that constitute any individual's life. He puts no pressure upon us to believe that any single character in *The Good Soldier* offers a model of human behaviour. The novel wasn't conceived as a prescriptive document. Dowell's local condemnation of individuals in *The Good Soldier* must be read in the context of Ford's refusal to mount an outright and sustained assault on any character. The allusiveness and conditionality of the novel means that it cannot simply be read, as Wagner proposes, as an indictment of a leisured class, solely an attack on the excessive phlegm of the English bourgeoisie.[22]

Any narrow reading of the novel's historical dimension, focussed on only one of the novel's perceptions, will diminish its rich diversity. The paradox of *The Good Soldier*, as of *Wuthering Heights*, is that a mythopoeic fiction, despite its metaphysical, atemporal elements, can open up more historical perspectives than a 'documentary' fiction such as the contemporaneous *Ragged-Trousered Philanthropists* (1914). Thus we can make out a case for *The Good Soldier* as a 'war-novel', to be read alongside the post-war *Parade's End* and *The Marsden Case*. In such a reading, Gordon says, *The Good Soldier* is proleptic of the horror and madness of the imminent war. (*Gordon*, ch. III) We can, too, draw attention to the historical analogues, linking the private and public faces of the novel, the fictional microcosm and historical macrocosm. The collapse of domestic relations in the novel would, then, as Hoffmann suggests, be cognate with the breakdown in international affairs in 1914. (*Hoffmann*, 81) Equally plausible is a reading of *The Good Soldier* as an English domestic tragedy, as Ford's 'ultimate picture of the plight of contemporary upper-class society'; as an elegiac account of the defeat of traditional quasi-feudal virtues by 'a strident individualism governed by expediency rather than principle'; a bitter, nostalgic vision of a world in which a sense of responsibility has been whittled down to a mere façade of respectability, leaving only 'emotional and moral inertia and total meaninglessness'. (*Cassell*, 147, 161, 201) This last interpretation of the novel has the advantage of being in tune with Ford's central preoccupation since *The Inheritors*, his fear that England was being transformed into a Bismarckian bureaucracy. Yet even this reading is vulnerable to the charge of having made *The Good Soldier* a more conclusive, affirmative novel than it seems during our experience of reading it.

Some of the novel's willed inconclusiveness – the irresolution of a novelist who has lost hope in any political dispensation, even in his earlier nostalgic conservatism – can be suggested by placing it alongside Henry James' remark, in a letter written at the outbreak of war, that the conflagration effectively forced an individual to rewrite his own recent history, in a process that was as painful as it was unavoidable:

The plunge of civilization into this abyss of blood and darkness
. . .is a thing that so gives away the whole long age during which
we have supposed the world to be, with whatever abatement,
gradually bettering, that to have to take it all now for what the
treacherous years were all the while really making for and meaning is too tragic for any words.[23]

It was the widespread confidence that the 'treacherous years'
were the harbinger of a better world, the common optimism
towards the future, that made their being a prologue to the
war so darkly disturbing. James' comment reads almost like
the notation of some deep personal sense of betrayal. The
tragic contradiction exposed here is the product of retrospection. Dowell, too, is found meditating on a similar paradox, 'too tragic for any words', at the opening of *The Good
Soldier*:

The mob may sack Versailles; the Trianon may fall, but surely
the minuet – the minuet itself is dancing itself away into the
furthest stars, even as our minuet of the Hessian bathing places
must be stepping itself still. Isn't there any heaven where old
beautiful dances, old beautiful intimacies prolong themselves?
Isn't there any Nirvana pervaded by the faint thrilling of instruments that have fallen into the dust of wormwood but that yet
had frail, tremulous, and everlasting souls?
    No, by God, it is false! It wasn't a minuet that we stepped; it
was a prison – a prison full of screaming hysterics, tied down so
that they might not outsound the rolling of our carriage wheels
as we went along the shaded avenues of the Taunus Wald.
    And yet I swear by the sacred name of my creator that it was
true. It was true sunshine; the true music; the true splash of the
fountains from the mouth of stone dolphins. For, if for me we
were four people with the same tastes, with the same desires,
acting – or, no, not acting – sitting here and there unanimously,
isn't that the truth? If for nine years I have possessed a goodly
apple that is rotten at the core and discover its rottenness only in
nine years and six months less four days, isn't it true to say that
for nine years I possessed a goodly apple? So it may well be with
Edward Ashburnham, with Leonora his wife and with poor dear
Florence. And, if you come to think of it, isn't it a little odd that
the physical rottenness of at least two pillars of our four-square

house never presented itself to my mind as a menace to its
security? It doesn't so present itself now though the two of them
are actually dead. I don't know. . .
   I know nothing – nothing in the world – of the hearts of men.
I only know that I am alone – horribly alone. (*GS*, i, i, 17–18)

The wracked anguish of James' brief comment is here given
full fictional treatment in Dowell's lengthy rumination. The
painful strain implicit in James is marked in the novel by the
violence with which Dowell oscillates between the two available mental states ('No, by God, it *is false!*. . .And yet. . .it
was true') and the two verbal tenses, present and past. Just as
James looked back from the war-torn present to a past that
had been characterised by a widespread confidence – the
'goodly apple' in Dowell's phrase – so the latter, from the
vantage-point of 1914, when both Florence and Edward are
dead, is casting his mind back over the 'treacherous years'
that had begun in 1904. Burdened with their present knowledge, neither James nor Dowell can fully credit either the
malignity or the beauty of the decade before the holocaust.
For each, this pre-lapsarian period now has both a vivid
reality and a fabled gossamery thinness. This, precisely, is
the tension sustained throughout *The Good Soldier*, so that
Dowell's meditation in the opening chapter demands full
quotation as a theme which is to be repeated in different
keys all through the novel. A gentle idealising nostalgia is
counterpointed with a scatological rejection of illusion, both
moods ending in silence. James noted that the dialectic of
fidelity and scepticism was ultimately 'too tragic for any
words', could only be written in the 'language of silence'.
Similarly, the final point of rest in *The Good Soldier* is
Dowell's decision in the last paragraph not to reply to
Edward's valediction, because he 'didn't know what to say'.
   The rhythms and images of this passage stretch outwards
to the edges of the text, and beyond to that society which is
refracted in its pages. Dowell's rumination indicates that
what Spender, following Conrad, called 'the destructive
element' – modernist writers' 'experience of all-pervading

Present. . .a world without belief', a void from which artists either looked back or peered forwards – is the mingling of an enervated idealism with an abrasive demand that all human fallibilities be exposed to daylight.[24] (In much the same way, *Lord Jim*, the source of the seminal phrase, swings between an unavailing romanticism and suicidal cases of self-knowledge.) Dowell's delineation of his heaven, replete with its unceasing minuet, 'the faint thrilling of instruments that have fallen into the dust of wormwood' and the 'splash of the fountains from the mouth of stone dolphins', seems emblematic of the 'Georgian' voice, echoing much of that period's verse and the early fantasies of E. M. Forster. Into this idyll burst a rough, post-Freudian voice, assertive of the reality of the horrors suppressed, that violent, less urbane tone Hughes found characteristic of European social thought in the decade before the war.[25] Neither of these two 'voices' succeeds in establishing dominance in *The Good Soldier*. Ford maintains a precarious balance between his delight in the elegance of the old traditions, the theatre of good people, and an acknowledgment of the murky depths. The 'years' are rendered with their full treachery and their whole allure.

The novelist, then, will permit nothing more positive to emerge from this passage or from the whole of the work than the irreducible, ignorant solitariness of his narrator:

I know nothing – nothing in the world – of the hearts of men. I only know that I am alone – horribly alone.

Only doubt is irrefutable in *The Good Soldier*: a linguistic uncertainty as to the exact meaning of a 'rotten apple' long considered unbruised, which, radiating to the circumference of the text, even comes to inform the problematical nature of human character. Semantic, moral and political realities are all uncertain in the world of *The Good Soldier*, where only the narrator's agnosticism is beyond question. At its heart lies the only belief to which Ford had consistently adhered since his earlier disillusionment with Bonar Law's Conservative Party: the vanity of all human dogmas.

IV

In the concluding pages of *The Good Soldier* Dowell rumin-
ates on the 'ideological' implications of his story, wondering
what place his narrative will occupy in that wider debate
about the sexual and economic role of women to which the
final novels of Hardy and the life and art of Wells had contri-
buted. 'Modern Love' indeed might well have been chosen
as a sub-title for *The Good Soldier*, which offers a series of
cameos of triangular embroilments and erotic misadventures:
from the high comedy of the arranged marriage between
Edward and Leonora, through the former's affairs and the
worldly machinations of Florence with her *arriviste* black-
mailer, to, finally, the platonic volcano of Nancy and Ashburnham. All the central characters of *The Good Soldier* are
permitted to speculate about the nature of marriage, but
none is really revolutionary, and Dowell's summary of the
debate could hardly be expected to disturb any male com-
placencies:

Mind, I am not preaching anything contrary to accepted morality.
I am not advocating free love in this or any other case. Society
must go on, I suppose, and society can only exist if the normal, if
the virtuous, and the slightly deceitful flourish, and if the passionate, the headstrong, and the too-truthful are condemned to suicide
and to madness. . .

Yes, society must go on; it must breed, like rabbits. That is
what we are here for. But then, I don't like society – much.
(*GS*, IV, vi, 217–18)

The timid irony of this passage indicates why, for all the
many adulteries in its pages and the quasi-incestuous love of
Edward for Nancy, *The Good Soldier* ran little risk of being
burned by a Bishop, like Hardy's *Jude*, or indeed of inciting
that outraged hate which greeted *The Rainbow* or *Ann
Veronica*. Like so much English fiction before 1914 – Forster's
'Sawston' novels or his *Howards End*; the early tales and
novels of Lawrence – *The Good Soldier* mediates a conflict
between received conventions and urgent passional drives.
Authenticity was being privatised. And yet, despite its

criticism of certain bourgeois values, Ford's novel is far from being a revolutionary treatment of 'family life'. The dissenting, romantic assumption behind *The Good Soldier* – that a man, Ashburnham, can die of love – is fundamentally questioned by the casualness with which Dowell alludes, almost as an after-thought, to Edward's suicide, and, more widely, by the novel's 'Cubist' variety of perspectives, by its 'irresolvable pluralism of truths'.[26] Ford indeed brought the vortical conflict between public and private senses of reality into sharp focus, but he didn't attempt to resolve the dichotomy of individual conscience and social convention. The final climactic episode of the novel, with Leonora and Nancy 'like judges debating over the sentence upon a criminal...like ghouls with an immobile corpse in a tomb beside them' has been described as 'Gothic' in mood. Yet Ford so manipulates the text that, through Dowell, the pent-up power of this climax is succeeded by an atrophied, bewildered silence for which the Gothic tale provided no equivalent.

The difficulty in trying to put into words one's reaction to the conclusion of *The Good Soldier* is that almost every formulation seems too definite, too sharply-edged. Earlier attempts to encapsulate this mood – phrases such as 'the grim dignity of resignation' or the novel's 'stoicism' – appear slightly too severe in ascribing to the finale a saving power of endurance. Another attempt to pinpoint the novel's suffusing mood has likened *The Good Soldier* to the Absurd theatre of Beckett and Ionesco.[27] Though the comparison is plainly anachronistic, there is surely a sense in which Ford shared certain elements with later 'minimalist' writers:

I am [Dowell thought] that absurd figure, an American millionaire, who has bought one of the ancient haunts of English peace. I sit here, in Edward's gun-room, all day and all day in a house that is absolutely quiet. No one visits me, for I visit no one. No one is interested in me, for I have no interests. In twenty minutes or so I shall walk down to the village, beneath my own oaks, alongside my own clumps of gorse, to get the American mail. My tenants, the village boys and the tradesmen will touch their hats to me. So life peters out. I shall return to dine and Nancy will sit opposite me with the old nurse standing behind her. Enigmatic, silent, utterly well-behaved as far as her knife and fork go, Nancy will stare in front of her with the blue eyes that have over them strained, stretched brows. Once, or perhaps twice, during the meal her knife and fork will be suspended in mid-air as if she were trying to think of something that she had forgotten. Then she will say that she believes in an Omnipotent Deity or she will utter the one word 'shuttlecocks', perhaps. It is very extraordinary to see the perfect flush of health on her cheeks, to see the lustre of her coiled black hair, the poise of the head upon the neck, the grace of the white hands – and to think that it all means nothing – that it is a picture without a meaning. Yes, it is queer. (GS, IV, vi, 218)

Precisely: 'a picture without a meaning'. And a remarkable resonant paragraph inasmuch as all the articles of the Ashburnham code – the peace ascribed to the possession of a large isolated mansion; the sacred associations of landowning; the mysticism of a received social respect; the elegance of near-perfect etiquette; religious and sporting fidelities; the poise of a beautiful chastity – every single item of the creed of 'good people' is here evacuated of meaning, drained of vitality in the inertia of insanity. This 'interior' builds up a haunting permanence in the memory. Like the mad Duchemin breakfast in *Parade's End*, it stands as a monument to an exhausted social class, pathetic as the wrinkled sepia photograph of a dead beauty.

Dowell's tenancy of Branshaw with the vacuous Nancy is indeed a prophetic anticipation of a later *Endgame*, quite literally *Fin de Partie*, and the girl's belief in God bears some resemblance to the attendance of Vladimir and Estragon upon the ever-absent Godot. And yet, for all the superficial modernity of *The Good Soldier*'s over-arching sadness, Ford's novel cannot approach the universal reference of *Godot*. Didi and Gogo can be seen without strain as twin versions of a modern Everyman, ubiquitous and capable of infinite mutations. Ford's 'stage' too is desolate and empty, but, crucially, it has the specificity of fiction. Dowell and Nancy are individuals with a known history that would stubbornly resist translation into endless other locales. Branshaw has been located with some precision in southern England. We know with fair assurance the date of the happenings described. All in all, then, *The Good Soldier* is 'rich in precise if not actual details of life, organized into an imagined whole that has a remarkable inner consistency'. (*Mizener*, 257) Fiction's obstinate rootedness here works against a mythical universality.

Lassitude, rather than a metaphysical absurdity or an upright confrontation with suffering, is the keynote of the novel's final chapters, and Dowell's collapse into muteness allows Ford to side-step any resolution of the conflict built up between the individual and surrounding public codes. We are told that 'a full eighteen months' have elapsed before Dowell writes the novel's epilogue, and at the beginning of this postscript the narrator emphasises above all else, beyond the romantic or the stoical, that his story is a record of human exhaustion:

For, I daresay, all this may sound romantic, but it is tiring, tiring, tiring to have been in the midst of it; to have taken the tickets; to have caught the trains; to have chosen the cabins; to have consulted the purser and the stewards as to diet for the quiescent patient [Nancy] who did nothing but announce her belief in an Omnipotent Deity. This may sound romantic – but it is just a record of fatigue. (*GS*, iv, v, 202)

Dowell is still by his own evidence less than fifty years old, but the months following his departure as a widower for America in September 1913 have preternaturally aged him. 'I don't know. I know nothing. I am very tired', Dowell admits at one point, and elsewhere says:

Of course you have the makings of a situation here, but it is all very humdrum, as far as I am concerned. I should marry Nancy if her reason were ever sufficiently restored to let her appreciate the meaning of the Anglican marriage service. But it is probable that her reason will never be sufficiently restored to let her appreciate the meaning of the Anglican marriage service. Therefore I cannot marry her, according to the law of the land. (*GS*, iv, v, 203–4)

Ford, infrequently praised for the verisimilitude of his fictional speech, has here recorded with a painful accuracy the repetitive deliberateness in thought and expression of a man who has reached the edge of human endurance.

Dowell's final senility, his weary inability to make any moral judgment, was a happy means of avoiding resolution of all the social, sexual and political problems Ford knew to exist in pre-war England, and which he recorded fully in his fiction and essays of this period. Neither the perplexity of the narrator nor the fundamental ahistoricism of the novel's structure encourages us to expect any conclusive response to the cultural problems raised. The 'semiosis' of *The Good Soldier* doesn't permit 'answers that have more than a degree of probability' and certainly no 'answers that carry certitude'.[28] Ford's preoccupation with the limits of omniscient narrative – and Dowell is by the end as divinely knowledgeable as any Victorian narrator – precludes the possibility of *The Good Soldier* being employed as a revolutionary, or even a reformist vehicle. For all his achieved understanding and his sensitivity – and Dowell was sufficiently alert to capture and record Leonora's momentary hesitation before she sat down in the Nauheim restaurant – he is incapable of rendering a coherent review of the history of his circle, or of so ordering events as to generate an inclusive moral significance. Ford has created a world whose only certainty is its lack of a moral architecture. Implicit in such nihilism is the futility of attempting to change a world which cannot even be understood.

The 'drive to neutrality'[29] that characterises *The Good Soldier*, by means of which a limited criticism of conventional social arrangements is subsumed by a formal structure antipathetic to change, was patently useful to a novelist publicly critical of some bourgeois values but unable to discover a viable alternative. There is a wealth of evidence to confirm that such was indeed Ford's dilemma just before the war, and *The Good Soldier* is recognisably an 'objective correlative' of its author's becalmed condition. Yet the social paralysis of which this novel provides such a compelling picture was not confined merely to Ford, the consequence of his marital and political entanglements. On the contrary, the evidence from the history and art of the early twentieth century suggests rather that Ford gave expression to a moral disablement common among the European bourgeoisie of that time. *The Good Soldier* is a novel of such resonance that it's not inappropriate to liken it, in miniature, to Proust's great cycle. If Proust was 'the last great historian of the loves, the society, the intelligence, the diplomacy, the literature and the art of the Heartbreak House of capitalist culture',[30] then Ford's novel assuredly provided an English footnote to that history. The elegant vacuity, the 'strange loss of knowledge. . .in the area of personal relationships'[31] coexisting with a sudden spurt in the physical and psychological sciences, and the deft hypocrisies of that world were rendered with remarkable insight, as Ford, an outsider like Proust, sought to comprehend the alien code of Ashburnham of Branshaw. Most remarkable of all is his picture of the experience of living in a highly formalised, ritual-based society which on the basis of its parasitic privileges attempted to exclude the outside world, the world in which 'there was such a thing as a dollar and. . .a dollar can be extremely desirable if you don't happen to possess one'. (GS, III, iv, 137) Ford's is a memorable portrait of a class which tried to establish a hermetic existence. Even time itself is marginal to *The Good Soldier* as Dowell compresses time past and time present into the timeless world of a memory juggling with the calendar. A life abstracted from time is all that a formal society, lacking the historical imagination, can possibly conceive. The moral ambivalence with which this class and this period have been rendered, far from marring the novel, only serve to confirm the historical verisimilitude of Ford's delineation of a perceptual and moral sightlessness characteristic of its time. *The Good Soldier* presents the world-vision of a class faltering through an epoch of social convulsion.

V

Ford's novel, then, discloses a vital, fruitful tension between a modernist, essentially ahistorical scenario and fiction's traditional energetic concern with the specificities of time and place. While seeking to generalise about the limitations of epistemology, *The Good Soldier* is ballasted by its own precise though invented particularity. Thus while being effective as 'a version of the ways in which a man can know reality', it cannot avoid being at the same time 'a version of reality itself'.[32] Frank Kermode has drawn attention to the danger of modernist art retreating 'into some paradigm, into a timeless and unreal vacuum from which all reality had been pumped', and has argued that *Ulysses* avoided this fate because it 'studies and develops the tension between paradigm and reality, asserts the resistance of fact to fiction, human freedom and unpredictability against plot'.[33] The great mythical superstructure of *Ulysses*, that mesh of Homeric parallels, is grounded upon the novelist's customary interest in the dynamics of the family and the entrancing mundanities of urban life. Similarly the paradigmatic elements in *The Good Soldier* are countermined by another, realistic force: the English novelist's time-honoured interest in the relationship between land and money.

Country houses in fiction 'are places where events prepared elsewhere, continued elsewhere, transiently and intricately occur', their strange irrelevance, their isolation from the main currents of life, being a reflection of the determining economic dimension having shifted from land to money.[34] This analysis is true of *The Good Soldier*, in which almost the only deed of any moment Ashburnham commits in his own house is his self-destruction. Indeed his tragedy can be summarised as his inability to spend all his energies upon the administration of his estate, for while his seignoral values are based on land his wife's more potent energies are cash-centred. As a Philadelphian landowner, Dowell possesses both and is fascinated by both: he relishes alike Edward's traditional loyalties to his tenants and Leonora's pertinacity in salvaging the family fortunes by mortgage, sale and rent. The conflict between these two codes is fundamental to *The Good Soldier*, as it was in English history between 1890 and 1914.

Ford, it is clear, shared with his predecessors, with Defoe, Austen and Dickens, a normal curiosity about money – not the interest of Bennett and Balzac in how money was made, but rather its role as a social lubricant, or abrasive. Throughout his career, from *Mr Fleight* through *Parade's End* to *Henry for Hugh* in the thirties, Ford was alive to the difference wealth made to a man's self-perception and to the way he was seen by others. And so, for all Ford's ambition to create a novel as hard as a brazen casque, he couldn't abandon this materialist preoccupation. Dowell may be a halting judge of ethics, but as narrator Ford has endowed him with a journalist's concern for the exact details of financial transactions. 'The intricate tangle of references and cross-references' to which Ford later referred with some pride[35] may allude to the engrossing chronology of *The Good Soldier*, but it is equally true of that nexus of financial, political, social, emotional, religious and class attitudes that underpins it. Thus it is not coincidental that Edward Ashburnham owns an estate with an income of some £5,000 a year; that he is a Tory, who addresses two public meetings in the month of his death, and whose involvement in the celebrated 'Kilsyte Case' is exploited by his Liberal enemies; that he feels a deep responsibility towards tenant-farmers 'who've been earning money for [him] for centuries'; that he is a sentimentalist, requiring loyalty and admiration from his mistresses; or that he kills himself because Nancy no longer seems to be offering those oblations and also because his wife threatens to confiscate his cheque-book. The point is that *The Good Soldier* is both a technical *tour de force* and, moreover, a novel which places actions such as Edward's suicide within a full context of human behaviour. Dowell allows us to reconstruct the economic determinants of Edward's suicide and with the information he supplies we can discover the full context of the Ashburnham marriage and locate it within a coherent social totality.

Nevertheless one is obliged to write of 'reconstruction' and 'discovery', because, through Dowell, Ford has broken down the history of the Ashburnhams between 1893 and 1914 into a series of discontinuous fragments. By contrast, Tolstoy narrated the career of Levin, whose life has suggestive similarities with Edward's, in a fashion which made obvious the causal connection between his activity as a large, pre-revolutionary landowner and his religious and emotional growth. The classical realist novel took for granted the existence of an explicable social fabric. With *The Good Soldier*, on the other hand, an exegetic effort is required, since Ford, despite his alien's interest in issues of money and class, is unwilling to accept the full implications of this concern. Had Ford patterned his story like the biography or the historical record, it would have been difficult to avoid the conclusion that Edward's death was, at least in part, socially determined. Thus the rearrangement of Dowell's fragments into a coherent chronological narrative might have implied the necessity for a reconstruction of society which neither Ford in 1915, nor that class about which he wrote, was able to accept. Dowell's early admission of the unproductiveness of his circle:

> But upon my word, I don't know how we put in our time. How does one put in one's time? How is it possible to have achieved nine years and to have nothing whatever to show for it? Nothing whatever, you understand. Not so much as a bone penholder, carved to resemble a chessman and with a hole in the top through which you could see four views of Nauheim. And, as for experience, as for knowledge of one's fellow beings – nothing either. (*GS*, i, iv, 41)

was mediated and diluted by a distancing formal structure. Such, in Ford's novel, was the animated tension between 'paradigm' and 'reality'; between, in the society about which he wrote, the reality of distorting inequities and the desire to immortalise the existent structures.

VI

Analysis of *The Good Soldier* brings to the surface a particularly interesting feature of modernist literature: the intricate relationship, within the novels of Joyce, Woolf and
Richardson, between an atemporal formal impulse and
fiction's usual contiguities with a raw material ceaselessly
in motion. Connected and of equal interest is the light the
novel, by its rare shapeliness, throws on the broad critical
debate between 'life' and 'art'. Where does *The Good Soldier*
stand in this debate? Does the novel exhibit those 'clear and
effective relations with reality'[36] demanded of fiction by
critical supporters of the school of 'life'? Is it perhaps merely
a feat of arid technical brilliance?

Certainly notes of dissent have regularly been struck, from
1915 onwards. There have always been readers for whom
The Good Soldier is disqualified by its lack of 'felt life'.
Among such deprecatory comments the most interesting
early example was Theodore Dreiser's *New Republic* notice
in June 1915, in which the American novelist criticised the
novel because, reading it, 'You are never really stirred. You
are never hurt. You are merely told and referred. It is all cold
narrative, never truly poignant.' To Dreiser, the novel was a
tale of missed opportunities, a great theme marred by
'[Ford's] sniffy reverence for conventionalism and the glories
of a fixed [social] condition, . . .fairly representative of that
encrusting formalism which, barnacle-wise, is apparently
overtaking and destroying all that is best in English life'.[37]
Writing at a moment of particular historical crisis – America
was to enter the war in April 1917 – Dreiser mistakes Ford's
record of a society for an *apology*. He assumes that Ford fully
endorsed a conservative conventionalism. *The Good Soldier*,
it is true, doesn't register an unambiguous authorial condemnation. Instead, it performs the more difficult task of making
us aware why, at a particular time and for a particular group,
moral certainty was felt to be inoperative. The absence from
the novel of a clear moral resolution has been the burden of

later critical views. Throughout, the implication has been that Ford lacked a vital sympathy for his characters' troubles; that he had devised a 'devastating game of badminton'[38] solely from delight at the technical potential of the 'game'. 'Life' exists in *The Good Soldier* only for 'art' to work upon in a constant process of rearrangement and impoverishment.

More than one of the questions about *The Good Soldier*'s status as a modernist masterpiece reveal an overt political disagreement between novelist and critic. (Dreiser's review, for example, makes patent his disaffection for the class about which Ford wrote.) It is, therefore, of considerable interest that one of Ford's warmest defenders should have been Granville Hicks, author of a Marxian history of American literature, *The Great Tradition* (1933). In an article on Ford in 1930 Hicks addressed himself to the same problem that had earlier exercised Dreiser, yet Hicks reached very different conclusions:

There was justice in calling it 'the finest French novel in the English language.' With all its technical virtuosity, however, *The Good Soldier* is not merely a 'tour de force'. There is no disproportion between the technical skill and the solidity of the work. As a revelation of life the book is worthy of the technique, and every formal subtlety adds to the accuracy and force of that revelation. With the utmost tenderness Ford pushes deeper and deeper into the minds of his characters, disclosing realms of passion and agony and meanness. Conrad never attempted to present so complex a situation, and James never ventured to explore emotion so intense and volcanic. When the book reaches its terrifying close, one realizes that only such formal perfection as Ford exhibits could bear the weight of this tragedy.[39]

Hicks' essay is of value because it indicates so clearly that around *The Good Soldier* there need be no conflict between values of 'perfection' and 'life'. As Hicks argues,

the choice is unnecessary. Ford's work not only shows that formal excellence may be combined with vitality and vigor; it reminds us that the sole justification of formal excellence is its effect in enhancing the vitality of the work in question.

'Vitality' and 'vigor' may seem odd words to describe a novel about suicides recorded by an enervated inert narrator. Yet what is being demonstrated is the moral and artistic energy implicit, not in the character of Dowell, but in Ford's *invention* of that character. Dowell is capsized on his own perplexity, yet Ford's shaping and patterning of his narrator's introspection asserts the continuance of life. That 'ideal of form' to which *The Good Soldier* stretches doesn't here deny life. Rather, the 'variousness of reality' is warranted by the author's deft choreography. Had Ford himself been as torpid as Dowell or as phlegmatic as Ashburnham, *The Good Soldier* couldn't have been created. The existence of such a coherent picture of incoherence is evidence of its author's lively scepticism even about his own scepticism in 1913 and 1915. 'Don't in any region of thought let any single accepted idea be your final end', Ford had urged a friend in 1913,[40] and *The Good Soldier* is proof of his willingness to look beyond despair. In the matrix of this fiction Ford discovered a way of so fashioning sadness that the crystalline order of that rendering only accentuated its poignancy.

PART THREE

1916–1928

1916–1928

Date	Novels	Prose	Poetry
1916			
1917			
1918			*On Heaven*
1919			
1920			
1921		*Thus to Revisit*	*A House*
1922			
1923	*The Marsden Case*	*Women and Men* *Transatlantic Review*	*Mister Bosphorus*
1924	*Some Do Not . . .* *The Nature of a Crime*	*Transatlantic Review* *Joseph Conrad*	
1925	*No More Parades*		
1926	*A Man Could Stand Up–*	*A Mirror to France*	
1927		*New York is not America* *New York Essays*	*New Poems*
1928	*Last Post* *A Little Less Than Gods*		

5

THE NOVELIST OF RECONSTRUCTION

3–4 Août. L'Allemagne envahit le Luxembourg, lance un ultimatum à la Belgique. Je suis accablé. Je voudrais être mort. Il est
horrible de vivre au milieu de cette humanité démente, et
d'assister, impuissant, à la faillite de la civilisation. Cette guerre
européenne est la plus grande catastrophe de l'histoire, depuis
des siècles, la ruine de nos espoirs les plus saints en la fraternité
humaine.

(3–4 August. Germany invades Luxemburg, gives Belgium an
ultimatum. I am overwhelmed. I should like to be dead. It is
dreadful to live in the midst of this crazy humanity, and to be an
impotent witness to the failure of civilisation. This European war
is the greatest historical tragedy for centuries, the ruin of our most
devout faith in the brotherhood of man.)

Romain Rolland, *Journal des Années de Guerre 1914–1919*

I

The shapeliness of *The Good Soldier* had, in March 1915,
exemplified modernism's claim to be able to build order out
of derangement, for, despite the novel's façade of narrative
irresolution, its deepest impulses had been authoritarian and
assertive. Eight years elapsed between *The Good Soldier* and
his next novel, *The Marsden Case*, during which Ford had
plenty of opportunity to witness at first hand the challenging
disorder of European reality. In a later memoir, *It was the
Nightingale* (1934) Ford was to record how it was revealed
to the soldier in the trenches that

beneath Ordered Life itself was stretched the merest film with,
beneath it, the abysses of Chaos. One had come from the frail
shelters of the Line to a world that was more frail than any canvas
hut. (*IWN*, 49)

113

The war and the revelations of this kind that it brought were indeed the major turning-point of Ford's career, as of so many others of his generation, making it impossible merely to build upon the highly structured *Good Soldier*. Although the latter was demonstrably 'modernist' in its achievement, it didn't offer Ford any potential for later growth along similar lines. It was a novel inherently inimitable, and Ford seemed to acknowledge this when he called *The Good Soldier* his 'auk's egg'. (The last Great Auk had flown in 1844.) D. H. Lawrence recorded in *Kangaroo* how the 'old world ended' in 1915 and, for all its literary radicalism, *The Good Soldier* was, in a sense, too much a part of that razed world to present, after the war, possibilities of confirmation or amplification. It was a consummate achievement, an integral part of this greatness being precisely that it couldn't be duplicated in a changed era, a peacetime world even 'more frail' than the trenches. *The Good Soldier*, then, marked the close of the first half of Ford's career. The years after the Armistice in 1918 were a time of new directions for him, the exploration of new perspectives aptly figured in his personal life by his emigration to France; and by the adoption of a new name, the substitution of the second 'Ford' for his father's 'Hueffer'. (*The Marsden Case*, in May 1923, was the first book to appear from 'Ford Madox Ford', the old name 'Hueffer' appearing only in parenthesis on cover and title-page.)

Circumstances forced silence upon Ford the novelist from 1915 to 1923 – though he continued to write and publish poetry during the war – yet the evidence of his later work suggests that this period of unproductivity was a blessing in disguise. (There was a similar gap in the career of E. M. Forster from *Howards End* (1910) to the early twenties, and in his case too the silence seems to have brought forth a richer later harvest.) Certainly from the traumas of war, of mental and physical collapse, there did emerge, hesitantly in *The Marsden Case* and then more confidently in *Some Do Not...*(1924), a novelist speaking in tones very different from the pre-war Hueffer's. Ford Madox Ford has recorded

how, on his return to London literary circles after the war, he
felt alienated and unsettled, a half-remembered shade from
a distant era, and there is some point in considering his post-
war novels as the work of a writer in most important respects
different from the author of *The Good Soldier*. It was as if
war had effected some kind of 'sea-change' upon Ford. It's
scarcely surprising, though, to discover such far-reaching
changes in Ford's art, for he had lived through a decade
from 1914 to 1924 as momentous as any in Europe since
Napoleon's time.

How did the 'resurrected' Ford, living in this 'new world',
differ from the author of *The Good Soldier*? In the first place,
the titles of his prose between 1920 and 1928 alone suggest
one important strand in his development: essays such as
A Mirror to France (1926), *New York is not America* (1927),
and *New York Essays* (1927); the periodical he edited and
called *Transatlantic Review*. Quite simply, the range of
Ford's interests is now wider. There is a new cosmopolitan-
ism, a new concern for international issues. Harassed and
chastened by war, he now evinces fresh sympathies and
broader receptivities. Ford has now a 'profounder concern
with a world of suffering and crisis on a scale distinct from
the Edwardian problems of luxury and dissolving tradition',
a 'gain in humility and deeper understanding of the general
human plight'. (*Wiley*, 132, 204) War, for all its horror, had
been an educative, humanising experience for Ford, sharpen-
ing rather than dulling his sense of social contradictions. We
sense in Ford's fiction in the twenties a fresh determination,
a new courage and directness in the rendering of human
problems.

In the last months of his life Ford was to comment critically
on *The Good Soldier* being 'rather thin and timid in hand-
ling',[1] and the change in his style suggested by this observation can be illustrated by juxtaposing the last paragraph he
wrote before the war with the opening lines of *Parade's End*.
Here, first, is the conclusion of *The Good Soldier*:

I didn't know what to say. I wanted to say, 'God bless you,' for I also am a sentimentalist. But I thought that perhaps that would not be quite English good form, so I trotted off with the telegram to Leonora. She was quite pleased with it.

And now the opening lines of *Some Do Not. . .*:

The two young men – they were of the English public-official class – sat in the perfectly appointed railway carriage. The leather straps to the windows were of virgin newness; the mirrors beneath the new luggage racks immaculate as if they had reflected very little; the bulging upholstery in its luxuriant, regulated curves was scarlet and yellow in an intricate, minute dragon pattern, the design of a geometrician in Cologne. The compartment smelt faintly, hygienically, of admirable varnish; the train ran as smoothly – Tietjens remembered thinking – as British gilt-edged securities. It travelled fast; yet had it swayed or jolted over the rail-joints, except at the curve before Tonbridge or over the points at Ashford where these eccentricities are expected and allowed for, Macmaster, Tietjens felt certain, would have written to the company. Perhaps he would even have written to *The Times*.

Both paragraphs are perfect in their respective contexts, but placing them side by side does throw into relief some of the fundamental alterations in Ford's fiction between 1914 and 1924.

Both passages are placed by an authorial irony, in which the problematic issue is the nature and working of 'English good form'. Dowell thinks that these conventions would be infringed were he to address an intending suicide, just as Macmaster held that trains 'do not' – to use this novel's controlling verb – jolt except at Tonbridge and Ashford. The irony at work here requires, however, finer discrimination. The irony of *The Good Soldier* is the mournful product of a gap between Dowell's perception of what is proper and the reader's sense that a fuller, more humane response is required in these somewhat unusual circumstances. In *Some Do Not. . .*, on the other hand, Ford's irony is 'dramatic', as his readers perceive that the superficial order of the opening scene in the railway carriage will be shattered by later, public and private horrors of which the two travellers can have no *present* conception. In *The Good Soldier* we can describe the

irony as 'qualitative', in that we place the limitations of
Dowell's response against the possibilities, available at the
same time and documented by Forster and Lawrence, of a
more passional and generous, energetic response. In *Some
Do Not...*, however, an 'historical' irony is operating as
Ford leads us to remark upon the time-bound innocence of
Macmaster and Tietjens. The eyes of these two will only be
opened by the full development of events that are prefigured
faintly in this 'prologue'. (Ominously, the upholstery of this
British carriage was designed in Cologne.)

The differences between these two varieties of irony can
summarise Ford's development across the watershed of the
war. *The Good Soldier* had been built round a series of
'Cubist' variations in the pluperfect tense. The future tense is
notable largely for its absence from the text: the novel's
ironies are lachrymose and static. In *Parade's End*, though,
the irony is a sterner, more masculine mood, to which the
unfolding of the future is intrinsic. Thus, whereas Dowell's
'education' is a product of reminiscence and the re-evaluation
of new information about the *past*, Tietjens' maturation
springs from his experience of a progression of unforeseen
pressures and unexpected affinities.

There is also in Ford's post-war work, and especially in
Parade's End, an opulence and density of verbal texture far
removed from the austerities of the synchronic *Good Soldier*.
Indeed the central impulse behind the latter was the effort
to pare away excrescences, to reduce fiction to its most eco-
nomical form, the result being a model of narrative thrift. In
Parade's End, though, there's a radically different drive. Here
Ford is bent on amplitude, on a leisured, historicist rendering of context and milieu such as he had presented once
before, in his Tudor trilogy. Now, however, it is the present –
or at least, the immediate past – that Ford is vivifying; and
his reconstruction is done with an energy which, in *A Call*
and *The Good Soldier*, had been directed towards formal or
structural exactitudes. Throughout *Parade's End* there's an
affectionate concern with the tangibilities of the natural

world, with men and their relations to such things as, for instance, leather straps, mirrors and bulging upholstery. So dominant had been the sense of memory in *The Good Soldier* that the senses of hearing, touch, sight and smell – all so active in *Parade's End* – had in the earlier novel been virtually defunct. Ford had emerged safely from a deranged world and often seems to be revelling in the very simple pleasure of his own continuing survival. Thus many of the quartet's most vivid scenes are sensuous: the sight of a dawn mist over the Sussex countryside in June; the tackiness of a soldier's congealing blood. The sheer length of so much post-war fiction – of Arnold Zweig's *Trilogy of the Transition,* R. H. Mottram's *Spanish Farm* trilogy, as of *Parade's End* – is but one indication of the novelist's delight in that reprieve granted to all the survivors. Though Zweig, Mottram and Ford are all, in different degrees, critical dissenting novelists, their fiction is united by a certain 'testamentary' quality, the determination to publish a belief in man's power to survive the unspeakable.

The historical solidity of *Parade's End* evident in the meticulous detailed 'camera-work' of the opening paragraph, that repleteness with which Ford situates his action in a spatial and temporal frame; and his fresh interest in international issues, the relationship of Mediterranean and Nordic civilisations, are the constituents of his fiction in the twenties, both of which are united under a different view of the social responsibilities of art. Even before the war, in the pages of *The English Review,* Ford had been thinking about this question, trying to place imaginative literature within the context of a dissolving culture. Now, however, he had first-hand experience of dissolution, and the war provided him with an urgent impulse to validate literature in social terms. The results of Ford's deliberations, his more socially aware aesthetic, were set down in his essays of this period, in *Thus to Revisit, Joseph Conrad* and *A Mirror to France.* Here he contends that art must be both international and popular, for only in this way can a repetition of barbarism be avoided:

'a great, really popular Art, founded on, and expressive of a whole people, is the sole witness of the non-barbarity of a Race'. (*TTR*, 19) Ford had lived through a decade in which the nations of the world had been polarised into two destructive camps, and he was now driven to use his work as a means of uniting states and continents. Art has an important social function in an era of reconstruction, because it is the sole remedy for a 'harassed humanity'. It 'alone can give you knowledge of the hearts, the necessities, the hopes and the fears of your fellow men; and such knowledge alone can guide us through life without disaster'. (*TTR*, 19, 7) The cognitive power of art is a far cry from Ford's pre-war view that even literature could scarcely aspire to illuminate Man's unknowable heart. The nationalism of governments severs: only the internationalism of art can connect. Ford's is a grand design, a vision of the western world united in a 'republic of the Arts and of Pure Thought', 'a region where the clearnesses of Thought and the exactitudes of Art are honoured', a world in which it was the artist's responsibility to communicate with all his audience, across the boundaries of language, class and nation. (*MTF*, 269)

Indeed art's audience, the novelist's distant and solitary readers, is crucial to Ford's post-war aesthetic. Art must be a 'popular' form, he asserts, and everything must be subordinated to the holding of the reader's attention. Symptomatic of this new concern is Ford's attempt to exploit, in the extraordinary Joycean *Mister Bosphorus and the Muses* (1923), the popular art-forms, traditional and modern, of the harlequinade, the music hall, and the silent film. Technique's sole justification, Ford wrote in *Joseph Conrad*, is that it is the only means of keeping a reader's interest. The whole of the novelist's craft, all his armoury of devices, must be directed to grasping and holding the reader – in the ultimate service of art's international concerns. Technique *per se* – Ford calls the word 'dangerous' – must be subservient to these wider artistic purposes, since literature

is a matter of the writer's attitude towards life, and has nothing in the world to do – nothing whatever in the world to do – with whether the lines in which this attitude is put before him be long or short; rhymed or unrhymed; cadenced or interrupted by alliterations or assonances. (*TTR*, 185)

A novelist's style must be clear – 'as clear and as simple as is consonant with the subject treated' – but the novelist should avoid preaching to his readers.[2] Ford's novelist must never utter any views, must never propagandise for any cause, for he holds that man is improved more by being delighted than by reading 'improving' moralistic works. Art's furthest limit is to make man more merciful and understanding, but it cannot reform. Ford's fiction of these years exemplifies the deep humanitarian concerns which he now took to be literature's proper interest, while, at the same time, showing his refusal to employ fiction as a vehicle for explicit proselytism.

Central to Ford's theory and practice in this decade is his ecological preoccupation, for his demand for the maximum clarity in literature is the equivalent to his hatred of environmental waste or extravagance. In both art and in society his call is for frugality. Hence his passion for the civilisation of the south of France is only his admiration for the limpidities of Flaubert and Maupassant writ large and translated into a wider, cultural context. The way of life of the Provençal smallholder – or, rather, Ford's version of such an existence – thus provides a model for artist and citizen alike. Man lives in harmony with Nature, content with his round of pastoral simplicities, proud of his self-sufficiency and spurning the industrialism, big business and 'gilded hotels' of Nordic civilisation. In Ford's view, the Nordic dream, what he calls the 'Monte Carlo' ideal, is a nightmare, 'a tragedy of waste, of brayings, of pimpings, marble, cheap gildings', and in its place Ford would prefer the essential Mediterranean values of 'chivalric generosity, frugality, pure thought and the arts'. (*MTF*, 284, 14) Ford no doubt romanticised France (his comment that 'when a leader of men arises in France he will find men – and that can be said of no other country' is as prophetic of Pétain as of de Gaulle) but such idealism between the wars

involved less distortion of the truth and fewer moral gym-
nastics than the veneration by other English intellectuals
of the Soviet Union under Stalin. (*MTF*, 31) What is certainly beyond doubt is that this structure of values, the
love of husbandry in literature and in life, gave birth in
Parade's End to one of the century's major imaginative
creations.

Earlier, Ford had postulated a historiography of continuing
conflict between national forces within England. Now he
widens his perspective, claiming that the whole course of
western history is a record of the Nordic threats to Mediterranean civilisations. (*MTF*, 112) In the twenties and thirties
Ford envisions the Anglo-American bloc, bloated with
luxuries as a result of its victory in 1918, jeopardising the
frugality and indigence of the Mediterranean littoral in a
further cycle of this historical conflict. But to Ford the
civilisation of Provence offered the only real hope of avoiding
a second holocaust, and his work from 1920 until his death is
an attempt to unite in peace Mediterranean and Nordic, to
substitute the 'realism' of the French for the 'sentimentalism'
of the English and the 'romanticism' of the Germans. Within
this over-arching purpose lie, variously but not inconsistently,
an attack on the standardisation of western food and on the
mass-production of Europe and the U.S.A.; a demand for a
literary style of economy and lucidity; and *Parade's End*'s
impulse away from authoritarianism in the direction of
decentralisation. In Ford's post-war thinking the values of
the metropolitan club give way to those of the rural, self-
sufficient homestead, and the Edwardian ideology of 'honour'
is replaced by the need for ecological harmony. Balance and
concord are the prime impulses behind the second half of
Ford's career. 'In the end', he wrote in the lyrical *Mirror to
France*, 'a civilisation is measured by the proportion of its
citizens that can sit still on grey rocks and think'. (*MTF*, 285)
To increase this fortunate proportion, to democratise the
opportunities for peaceful meditation are the generous ends
of all Ford's writings after the war, just as a widening of

sympathy of this kind is intrinsic to much 'post-modernist' art. Difficulties only arose when Ford tried to set down in fictional terms an activity as bereft of dramatic conflict as quiet cerebration 'on grey rocks'.

One of his visitors has commented on the 'feudal' quality of Ford's private life in the twenties.[3] While this may have been superficially true of his domestic circumstances, the observation has had the harmful effect of encouraging critics to view his work simply as an unchanged expression of his earlier admiration for the Middle Ages. The reality is rather more complex and some place must be found in any serious account of Ford's intellectual development, as it was embodied in his fiction, for – to give only one example – his progressive and public stand towards Irish politics in the twenties.[4] This was scarcely the activity of a medieval hermit. It is always hazardous, of course, to affix a single political or ideological label to so complex an organism as an imaginative artist. (T. S. Eliot's celebrated announcement of his royalism and catholicism can be seen, in part, as an ironic comment on these difficulties.) The danger is always of oversimplification, and, in the period under review here, Ford is not easy to 'pigeonhole'. Thus in 1926 he was claiming that he was fundamentally of the Right:

I have always been contentedly and unobtrusively inclined to the extreme Right in political matters, but. . .I have never considered myself sufficiently intelligent to interfere in the internal politics of my own country. (*MTF*, 101)

This comment, so characteristic of Ford's systematic effort to surround himself in a smokescreen of nonchalance, muffles his vociferous interest, if not 'interference', in Britain's government of Ireland in 1920, and, moreover, is hardly consonant with his remark in the following year, 1927, that he is 'instinct with the sense of the equality of all human beings'. (*NYINA*, 7) We find a similar contradiction between his hatred of militarism in this year – 'militarism is the antithesis of Thought and the Arts, and it is by Thought and the Arts alone that the world can be saved'[5] – and his published love of the British Army in 1926 for 'its efficiency, its solidarity, its construction on a sound basis of psychology', qualities which make it, in Ford's eyes, one of the only two satisfactory institutions in the world. (*MTF*, 101)

Ford's work of the twenties is so replete with paradoxes that, as we tack giddily from left to right, we may be reminded less of anything resembling 'feudalism' and more of the Social Credit movement between the wars. Ford, it appears, made no explicit reference to this group, though his friend Ezra Pound had been a Social Crediter 'since at least 1920', but there is an underlying similarity between C. H. Douglas' thinking and Ford's after 1920.[6] It is this analogy, these broad similarities between patterns of thought and feeling, to which I draw attention, rather than any overt commitment by Ford to Social Credit.

The 'school' was 'founded' by Douglas at the end of the war, and his theories had been published in Orage's *New Age* from 1919 onwards. A by-product of the National Guild movement, Social Credit repudiated doctrines of economic liberalism, the two main planks of its platform being hatred of the existing system of banking and finance, with a concern for the individual as against the monopolistic State. (Ford, of course, had held this second view since the beginning of the century.) Social Credit has scarcely been, outside Alberta, a major political force in the twentieth century, although its monetary theories have far-reaching political and social implications. Douglas rejected both capitalism and socialism, the latter because, in his view, it wouldn't increase the individual's freedom. For the same reason he was always opposed to any central organisation for Social Crediters and, as a consequence, the twenties and thirties were marked by frustration and internecine quarrels among his adherents, some, like Pound, being attracted to Fascism. Ford's own 'factoid' of an international conspiracy of Jewish financiers – the basis of his historical novel of the Napoleonic Wars, *A Little Less Than Gods* – was part of Douglas' thinking too, as was indeed Ford's concern for the rights of the individual and his abhor-

rence of both versions of totalitarianism. More broadly, the
mixture of two extremes in Ford's ideology, his affection for
anarchism alongside his rejection of conventional socialist
panaceas, was duplicated in both Guild Socialism and the
later Social Credit. All three shared a desire for the loosening
of controlling ties, and a belief in both the potential of
creative anomaly – the vitality inherent in disorder is central
to Ford's theory of memoir and biography – and in that
'quickly aroused sympathy with a non-sequential way of
thought which is inherently incapable of maintaining itself
for long'.[7] Ford loathed all post-war governments, economists
and politicians. His remedy, too, was apolitical: the assemblage of 'quiet, decent people' across national barriers to
change public opinion (*MTF*, 233).

In this way Ford's stance on economics and aesthetics
alike can be viewed as reflections of a broadly 'Creditist'
position. His new preoccupation with art's need to communicate widely and internationally; his concern, patent in
the opening of *Parade's End*, that the novel should be more
generally available; the quartet's evidence, both in style and
in comment, of its author's suspicion of monolithic structures,
political or aesthetic; his aversion to didacticism and a moral
impulse that was censorious and centralising: taken together,
these attitudes form a coherent response to the artistic and
cultural problems of reconstruction. In such a response,
whether that of Douglas the economic theorist or of Ford the
novelist, the necessity to stake out an independent position is
clearly fundamental. Hence, as Douglas sought to free himself from allegiance to either capitalism or socialism, Ford as
a writer attempted his own emancipation from what he called
'Established Morality', an impulse symbolised by his decision
to emigrate. Hence in *The Transatlantic Review* Ford be-
moans the subordination of English writers through the ages
to the 'dominant culture':

Living for the artist of England has always meant lip-service to
the Established – to the Established Church for a great portion of
the three hundred years, to Established Social Systems, to

Established Political Parties at various times; and always to Established Morality.[8]

In another, similar observation Ford remarked trenchantly that to be a writer in England after the war was, because of the pressure to conform to the conventional and established, to be like 'a tin of jellied eels that has for years reposed on a country grocer's shelves'. (*NYINA*, 142) By the act of uprooting himself and emigrating to France the 'eel' that was Ford tried to extricate itself from the jelly of an inhibiting society. *Parade's End* is an account, similarly, of Tietjens' sustained attempt to break loose from discredited conventions, to shake off the 'dust'.

II

The Marsden Case was an earlier effort to fashion a man's rebellion and search for independence from a regnant but corrupt culture. Like *Parade's End*, it tells of the triumph of one man, Lord George Marsden, over a neurasthenia induced by the war and by the persecution of his civilian enemies. Though there are no battle scenes, war is nevertheless the novel's central experience, because Ford had understood that the new 'total war' obliterates the line that used to separate Home from Front. War is now just an extension, an intensification of civilian hostilities, and the soldier drawn into the conflict is, as he put it, 'homo duplex', a combatant tortured by thoughts of home, 'a poor fellow whose body is tied in one place, but whose mind and personality brood eternally over another distant locality'. (*IWN*, 197) Thus Jessop, the novel's narrator, reflects that war was not a 'magic and invisible tent' sheltering the soldier from domestic pressures, but an aggravation of those cares: 'round your transparent tent, the old evils, the old heart-breaks and the old cruelties are unceasingly at work'. (*MC*, 305) Still more radical in its social implications was Ford's new grasp of the individual civilian's complicity in, and responsibility for, mass-slaughter. Jessop, again, points to the effect of war upon everyone alive in 1923 – 'the eyes, the ears, the brain and the fibres of every soul today adult have been profoundly seared by those dreadful wickednesses of embattled humanity' – but the novel also infers that domestic strife, sexual and class divisions, had in fact caused the international hostilities. (*MC*, 144) Lawrence was illuminating a similar connection in such stories of the early twenties as 'The Fox' and 'The Ladybird', and in the twelfth chapter of *Kangaroo*, published in the same year as *The Marsden Case*, he analysed the real meaning of the cliché 'civilian war'. Using images that light up the ubiquity of war, Lawrence wrote that London in 1915–16 'perished, perished from being a heart of the world, and became a vortex of broken passions, lusts, hopes, fears, and horrors'.[9] This, precisely, is the subject of *The Marsden Case*, the insidious, jarring violence from July 1914, when the novel opens, to the Armistice; violence as prevalent in a London night-club as in the French trenches.

Ford's reconstruction of madness, of a whole society living on its nerve-ends, is done with great intensity and, as a contemporary reviewer noted, the novel is a 'brilliant and magnificent nightmare'.[10] And yet, for all its vividness, *The Marsden Case* is only a limited success. For one thing, the central plotting of the story around George's attempt to establish that he is Lord Marsden's rightful heir seems contrived and arbitrary. It doesn't grow out of the novel's core as does Tietjens' persecution by London society. As a result, there is something less than inevitable about George's plight, his 'psychological Grand Guignol', an element of unabsorbed melodrama. (*Mizener*, 492) And equally this plight, George's harrowing, is distanced too much by Jessop, Ford's narrator. We are not permitted to share his torture in the way in which we are drawn into the wracked mind of Christopher Tietjens. The latter becomes so large a figure in *Parade's End* that, for all his local quirks, he achieves representative status as a 'type' of all human suffering in those years. George Marsden doesn't impress the reader with this kind of power: his dilemma is too narrowly particular, and it's difficult to generalise outwards from his single torment. Ford, then, failed 'to convince us that these characters and events are representative and revealing of their society'. (*Mizener*, 494) Finally, although Ford creates a powerful sense of this world's ability to torture an individual mentally and physically to suicide, there is a strange lack of connection between the public events and the suffering hero. Improbably, George seems not to change in any important respect, despite all he undergoes, and we find it difficult to believe that his 'high-mindedness', his 'passion for decorum of behaviour' is so immune to external pressures. The anguished consciousness is oddly untouched by social and political reality. Perhaps the root of the trouble lies in Ford's use of Jessop, who, like Dowell, tells the story 'in spots', as it comes back to his mind years later. Yet the potential width and depth of this story, the universality of its implications, require a different narrative form from that employed in *Romance* and *The Good Soldier*. In *Parade's End* Ford discarded his involved narrator in favour of an omniscient detached observer.

With all its flaws, though, *The Marsden Case* is a moving and memorable novel, and, bearing in mind Ford's personal circumstances, a notable achievement. His rendering of the frenetic mood of 1914, 'an accursed year'; the suicide of George's father on 4 August 1914, and his son's attempt to follow him in 1916; the burning of George's lodgings in 1915 and the murder of his German landlady in London – all these are memorable scenes and as emblematic of the period as Lawrence's account of his persecution in Cornwall.

Ford's portrayal, then, of the moral bankruptcy that led to the war and the disillusionment that followed are powerfully effective. Problems begin to arise in *The Marsden Case*, and in *A Little Less Than Gods*, another novel of 'reconstruction', when Ford seeks to move beyond disenchantment and the death of heroism. Faced with a similar problem, D. H. Lawrence built up in *The Plumed Serpent* and *Aaron's Rod* an ideology based on a dominant male culture. Ford wasn't attracted to a solution in these terms, yet the need to formulate some alternative *modus vivendi* is the most pressing problem he faced in this decade. Sceptical, like C. H. Douglas, of the available political solutions, Ford had to discover some substantial creed for his heroes, Marsden and Tietjens, after their abandonment of the politics and culture of the metropolis. Ford wasn't alone in this search. Indeed the search for a new direction was the dominant post-war theme, 'the literature of the early nineteen-twenties offer[ing] various reflections of the efforts to continue living made by those on whom the memories of the war weighed most painfully'.[11] What this literature also indicates is the greater success artists achieved in giving fictional form to their war memories than in building the foundations of a new life in imaginative, or indeed personal terms. In Ford's case, *Parade's End* was his most courageous and sustained attempt to find an answer, to suspend a bridge from the era of destruction to the period of peace. But even here, in this noble achievement, it's symptomatic of the wider issues involved that the quartet's final section, *Last Post*, is the least successful feature of the design. That novel's comparative insubstantiality, when set alongside the three earlier sections, must be viewed in the wider historical context, the complexity of evolving an emergent culture, political or aesthetic, which would appear coherent and solid.

6

PARADE'S END

'Why, on the surface of these blanchëd sands
In characters legible in Orion's belt
I'll write such love and wisdom!'

(Mister Bosphorus and the Muses)

I

The 'love and wisdom' promised at the end of *Mister Bosphorus* are most generously displayed in the quartet of novels that immediately followed, *Parade's End* (1924–8). These novels, *Some Do Not...*, *No More Parades*, *A Man Could Stand Up–* and *Last Post*, map with a fine, humane sympathy their hero's search for a full love-relationship, a journey which provides *Parade's End* with its major narrative thread. 'The rescue into love' of Christopher Tietjens is the theme of Ford's tetralogy as it is of *Middlemarch* and of the contemporaneous *Lady Chatterley's Lover* (1928).[1] In all three novels, 'love' and 'wisdom' are virtually synonymous. Love leads to wisdom, and understanding is unobtainable without emotional fulfilment. The loveless, Casaubon, Chatterley, Sylvia Tietjens, remain benighted. In *The Good Soldier* love had been deceptive and destructive, whereas *Parade's End*'s emphasis on the educative and therapeutic powers of love links it with the mainstream of nineteenth-century fiction – with *Mansfield Park* and *Emma*, with *Far from the Madding Crowd*, with much Dickens and Eliot, and, in the eighteenth century, with *Tom Jones* and *Joseph Andrews*. *The Good Soldier* has been described as a very 'French' novel: *Parade's End* seems to be in a markedly 'English' fictional tradition.

129

Ford's decision to render the war and its aftermath by means of the emotional development of an individual involved modification of the Hulmian aesthetic that had underpinned *The Good Soldier*. Reminiscential and synchronic, the latter had through both form and content denied the possibility of development or improvement. Being epistemological and self-reflexive it had implied a radical pessimism such as Hulme had expressed in his essay 'Romanticism and Classicism'. Now, however, in *Parade's End*, Ford adopts a position which Hulme (who had died in 1917) would have dismissed as 'romantic'. Salvation through love implies a belief in progress and the reality of individual growth. It is based, with its fundamental meliorism, on that 'humanist idealism' denigrated by Hulme. Ford's published comments on *The Good Soldier* had all referred to the text's formal geometry, whereas he glossed *Parade's End* in terms of its content and its didactic purpose. The quartet, Ford wrote in *It was the Nightingale*, was 'a work that should have for its purpose the obviating of all future wars', and the Preface to both *No More Parades* and *A Man Could Stand Up–* had also referred to this overriding aim. (*IWN*, 205) Character and episode in *Parade's End* are fashioned by imperatives that lie outside the boundaries of the text, by the author's desire to construct a work of fiction that will modify human behaviour. In *The Good Soldier*, by contrast, episode and character only echoed and reflected other scenes and motives within the novel itself.

In thus abandoning the fictional purism of *The Good Soldier*, its studied distance from applicability and social purposiveness, *Parade's End* may appear to signal Ford's desertion from the tenets of modernism. Because of its length, its advertised concern with the prevention of further wars, and its generous investment in the 'human substance' of growing characters and their search for regeneration, the quartet may be argued to have betrayed all the technical advances of *The Good Soldier*. The latter's elegance, that quality noted as being so 'French', was actually dependent on a very narrow range of human emotions – jealousy and uncertainty, for the most part – and a limited narrative tone. Ford's range in *Parade's End* is in every respect wider: more characters, more emotional diversity and a narrative that is in turn comic, tragic and farcical. The architecture of the quartet is on a larger scale than that of *The Good Soldier*. But its 'Englishness' involves no abandonment of Ford's commitment to design, no regression to innocent pre-Jamesian modes. Rather, *Parade's End* illustrates a development and enrichment of the strategies employed in *The Good Soldier*, the novelist having added the shape of actual lived history to that elaborate, but autonomous system of balance and counter-balance that had constituted Dowell's narrative. The equation to be solved in *Parade's End* is more complex, involving an extra 'unknown', since the subjective impulses of the central characters must be made congruent with the recorded eddies of historical experience between 1912 and 1920. *Parade's End*, therefore, is not so much an expanded version of *The Good Soldier* as a work with an added, historical dimension. Ford's most sharply original achievement, it is a fiction that tries to weld the sophisticated modernist insights he had perfected in 1915 with the more expansive reportorial functions of a Dickens or Thackeray. As such, it offers valuable evidence that an artist's concern with 'love and wisdom' needn't be accompanied by any relaxation of formal rigour, such as Ford had criticised in Victorian fiction.

II

Ford wrote very clearly about the historical dimensions of the Tietjens novels. 'I wanted the Novelist', he recalled in *It was the Nightingale* (1933), 'to appear in his really proud position as historian of his own time. Proust being dead I could see no one who was doing that.' 'My subject', he continued, 'was the public events of a decade', and 'the world as it culminated in the war.' (*IWN*, 180, 187, 195) He aspired to

write a novel 'in which all the characters should be great
masses of people – or interests', – a phrase that recalls Ford's
fine description of the 'whole human cosmogony' of *Nostromo*
– but he recognises that he is unequipped for this task. Instead, he realised, he would have to 'fall back on the old
device of a world seen through the eyes of a central observer'.
However, the tribulations of this character 'must be sufficient
to carry the reader through his observations of the crumbling
world'. By 'sufficient' Ford meant to stress the need for the
hero to be 'typical' or capable of universal application. The
observer's troubles, Tietjens' disasters, had to be rendered as
representative of the common fate of all the combatants.
The individual had to personify the 'great masses of people
– or interests'. Tietjens was, then, designed to carry the weight
of what Ford saw as the general condition. Ford was thus
setting himself the task of epitomising the activities of large
numbers of people with the same insight he had brought to
the rendering of individual destinies in *The Good Soldier*.
Or, to put this another way, he was attempting to adapt the
techniques of the 'Fifth Queen' trilogy for use on contemporary material. Hence the very different skills he had learnt in
those earlier works were now to be reassembled in *Parade's
End*.

What this means in practice is that the 'affair', the domestic
tribulations of a small circle of people that had produced
the claustrophobic complexities of *The Benefactor*, *A Call*,
The Marsden Case and *The Good Soldier*, here possess an
extra element – felt historical significance. Individual embroilments are now densified in history, but although Ford writes
in *Parade's End* as the 'historian of his own time', he doesn't
need to introduce real figures and incidents in order to
achieve those ends. In *The Fifth Queen*, Henry VIII,
Katharine Howard and Wolsey were all modelled more or
less closely on actual historical figures. In the quartet, Tietjens,
Sylvia and Valentine are Ford's own creations, yet all are
endowed with an acute sense of their own historical roles.
Each of them is aware, particularly at moments of crisis or

decision, that an individual dilemma has a public historic dimension.

Thus Sylvia's realisation in *Last Post* that her games cannot be continued in the changed England of the twenties is charged with a wider cultural emphasis:

Her main bitterness was that they had this peace. She was cutting the painter, but they were going on in this peace; *her world* was waning. It was the fact that her friend Bobbie's husband, Sir Gabriel Blantyre – formerly Bosenheim – was cutting down expenses like a lunatic. In *her world* there was the writing on the wall. Here they could afford to call her a poor bitch – and be in the right of it, as like as not! (*LP*, 309–10: emphasis added)

'Her world', the repeated phrase, carries in this extract a double significance, referring both to Sylvia's fictional 'set' of friends *within* the novel and, as well, to that real historical class *outside* the novel, in England in 1920. Sylvia is both a remarkable fictional character and a personification of major forces in English post-war history.

Similarly, Valentine Wannop's dilemma at the opening of *A Man Could Stand Up–*, when she is wondering whether she should obey the injunctions of her mother and her head-mistress to remain 'nunlike' or commit herself to Christopher, is presented as representative of a wider questioning in post-war Europe of traditional moral sanctions:

It was absurd to think that she could be wanted for that [to give Macmaster callisthenics]! An absurd business. . .There she was, bursting with health, strength, good humour, perfectly *full* of beans – there she was, ready in the cause of order to give Leah Heldenstamm, the large girl, no end of a clump on the side of the jaw or, alternatively, for the sake of all the beanfeastishnesses *in the world* to assist in the amiable discomfiture of the police. There she was in a sort of Nonconformist cloister. Nunlike! Positively nunlike! At the parting of the ways *of the universe*!
She whistled slightly to herself.
'By Jove,' she exclaimed coolly, 'I hope it does not mean an omen that I'm to be – oh, nunlike – for the rest of my career *in the reconstructed world*!' (*AMCSU*, 17: later emphases added)

Once again, *world* has, in Ford's rendering of Valentine's

thoughts, a double meaning, since it refers both to the auto-nomous fictional existence Miss Wannop perceives around her, and to the real historical tensions *Parade's End* mediates. Ford's combination of the roles of modernist novelist and of annalist is thus grounded on the ambiguities, sustained throughout the quartet, of 'world' as a word with double connotations.

The argument that Ford's treatment of his material is internal and psychological, not external and historical, as in *The Forsyte Saga*, is thus founded on a false distinction. What *Parade's End* does is demonstrate the artificiality of that division between 'historical' and 'private', especially during periods of enormous social convulsion. It reveals the congruence between history and the inner life; it 'dramatizes the impact of a historical crisis upon individuals – concretely realized persons who are representative of every level of English society; and the inner life which the author thereby reveals is always consonant with and reflective of the outer world'.[2] The quartet is remarkable for the acuteness of Ford's insight into the political effects of disruption, the end of 'feudalism' and the beginning of the modern world, on his imagined characters. Characters and society continually complement and reinforce one another as historical event and common life are merged. In this respect at least, there is something almost 'Russian' about *Parade's End*, in the way it recalls, say, *On the Eve* and *Fathers and Sons*, or even, in its scale, *Anna Karenina*.

Ford's reputation as a novelist has undeniably been tar-nished by the very success with which in memoir and bio-graphy he practised his own brand of 'impressionism', offering less factual veracity than the truthfulness of mood and personality. His power as a fabulist, that ability to make his readers doubt even the most circumstantial statement, renders the achievement of *Parade's End* even more remark-able. In 1919 the old 'landed interest' sold over a million acres of land and the popular phrase of the day was that 'England was changing hands'. Perhaps no transfer of land

as permanent or as large had occurred since the Tudor dissolution of the monasteries. This indeed is the social convulsion
that *Parade's End* treats with such cogency and verisimilitude. The quartet impresses the reader with a minuteness of
detail and knowledge usually associated in English fiction
with 'regional' novelists – with, say, Hardy or Bennett.
Parade's End is not, in this sense, a regional novel. Nevertheless Ford compels us to believe in the landowners who are
largely his subject with as much confidence as we accord
Constance and Sophia in *The Old Wives' Tale* or Tess and
her wretched family. *Parade's End* seems truthful not as a
result of Ford's intimacy with provincial patterns of behaviour, but because of his understanding of a *class*, the large
rural landowners who work and play in Whitehall and the
West End. Indeed it is precisely because of the absence of
any strong provincial affections in these people – none of
whom spend any great time in their country houses, whose
future is mortgaged to historical uncertainty – that Ford's
characters appear so vulnerable. His subject is the lives of a
class in the very process of deracination, and the value of
Parade's End resides, to a large extent, in Ford's grasp of the
general historical significance of such climactic changes.
Much of his earlier fiction had proved incapable of, and uninterested in, generating this larger cultural relevance. The
problems delineated in *A Call* and *The Benefactor*, for
instance, had seemed too quirkily individual, too eccentric,
too private. Now, however, in the Tietjens quartet, Ford gives
individual lives an enriching typicality through the artist's
power of 'totalisation', the ability, commonly attributed to
Tolstoy, to see a society whole. This is 'the act of grasping
the elements of a culture in their living and changing inter-
relations', 'the capacity to pose personal feelings and public
event, local detail and general vision, in mutually illuminating relation'.[3]

III

Praising *Parade's End* for its historical insights is by no means
a cliché of Ford criticism, for it has frequently been claimed
that the novel's truthfulness as historical record is marred by
Ford's portrayal of his hero, Christopher Tietjens. He is, we
are told, a static character who fails to develop credibly
during the decade spanned by the quartet. Worse, Ford is
accused of having grossly sentimentalised his central figure,
presenting him with 'partisan hyperbole' and with no ironic
detachment. These two charges, separate but related, would,
if sustained, certainly weaken *Parade's End*, if only because
of Tietjens' centrality to three-quarters of the whole design.

The first criticism is perhaps the more difficult to counter,
because our sense of a fictional character's ability to develop
in believable ways is very closely bound up with our experiences during the lengthy process of being immersed in
Parade's End. It's difficult to point to maturation through
brief quotation. Nevertheless, Christopher's momentary
appearance in *Last Post* suggests a lassitude brought on by
everything he has suffered, in war and peace, since the opening of *Some Do Not. . .* in 1912:

Christopher was at the foot of [Mark's] bed. Holding a bicycle
and a lump of wood. Aromatic wood: a chunk sawn from a tree.
His face was white: his eyes stuck out. Blue pebbles. He gazed at
his brother and said:
'Half Groby wall is down. Your bedroom's wrecked. I found
your case of sea-birds thrown on a rubble heap.'
It was as well that one's services were unforgettable!
Valentine was there, panting as if she had been running. She
exclaimed to Christopher:
'You left the prints for Lady Robinson in a jar you gave to
Hudnut the dealer. How could you? Oh, how could you? How
are we going to feed and clothe a child if you do such things?'
He lifted his bicycle wearily round. You could see he was
dreadfully weary, the poor devil. (*LP*, 335)

And, even if *Last Post* is set aside as a flawed postscript, the
Tietjens of the last pages of *A Man Could Stand Up–*, dancing

and drinking with his fellow-soldiers in his stripped house, is a different man, more humane and less seignoral, from the traveller on the train Ford presented in the quartet's opening chapter. Here, by contrast, is the pre-war Tietjens:

Tietjens only caught the Rye train by running alongside it, pitching his enormous kit-bag through the carriage window and swinging on the footboard. Macmaster reflected that if he had done that, half the station would have been yelling, 'Stand away there.'
  As it was Tietjens, a stationmaster was galloping after him to open the carriage door and grinningly to part:
  'Well caught, sir!' for it was a cricketing county. (*SDN*, 28)

The physical energy and aristocratic assurance displayed here have by the time of *Last Post* mellowed. At the conclusion Tietjens is forgetful, for perhaps the first time, and accepts Valentine's rebuke in tacit contrition. Moreover, the important decisions he makes in the second half of *Parade's End* – not to return to the Civil Service, but to live on his wits as an antique-dealer and smallholder; and to live with a woman of inferior social status – these could scarcely have been made by the Tietjens of *Some Do Not*. . . In thinking about himself, Tietjens is certainly aware of changes of this kind, of having been, as an American reviewer put it in 1927, 'educated and humanized by a war which was not at all sporting'.[4]

  The second damaging criticism levelled against Ford is that there is no authorial withdrawal from the hero, of the kind employed with Dowell in *The Good Soldier*. Ford, in this reading, idolised Tietjens, projecting onto him his own frustrated aristocratic fantasies. By contrast, a fellow-novelist, Christopher Isherwood, argued that Ford in reality didn't much like Tietjens, he and Sylvia only providing 'a contrast between two kinds of insanity'.[5] The truth probably lies between these two readings. Certainly there is some evidence, from outside *Parade's End*, that Ford's uncritical early enthusiasm for hounded stiff-lipped Englishmen had waned. By the end of 1922 he was claiming that he had 'arrived at

the stage of finding the gentleman an insupportable pheno-
menon'. (*IWN*, 199) Yet it's also clear that Tietjens was
modelled on a man for whom Ford still had enormous affection; and that he was intended to voice criticisms of English
life Ford fully endorsed. 'His activities', Ford wrote about
Tietjens, 'were most markedly to be in the realm of criticism'. (*IWN*, 198) Broadly speaking, then, Ford seemed to
approve of Tietjens. Indeed he would scarcely have chosen
as a focussing, critical consciousness in a work designed for
'the obviating of all future wars' a man for whom he lacked
all sympathy. The teleology of *Parade's End* demanded a
hero largely, if not absolutely, congenial.

Nevertheless, within such general approbation, Ford
employed a number of means of criticising his own hero, so
that it's an oversimplification to view *Parade's End* as hagio-
graphical. Firstly, several of the other characters in the
quartet criticise Tietjens, most cogently Valentine and
Sylvia. Thus at the very outset of *Some Do Not. . .* Sylvia tells
her mother that her husband has telegraphed her 'because of
that dull display of the English gentleman that I detested. He
gives himself the solemn airs of the Foreign Minister, but
he's only a youngest son at the best.' (*SDN*, 37) This criticism
is largely just, for a gap does exist between Christopher's self-
estimate and the actual modesty of his national importance.
'The solemn airs' Sylvia refers to are in fact part of an un-
attractive theatricality Tietjens doesn't cast off till *Last Post*.

Lacking in hypocrisy, he is still a *poseur*, a man constantly
aware that an 'audience' may imminently appear. Even his
solitariness, as in the hotel at Rye where his heavy drinking
is interrupted by Macmaster, is 'staged', self-conscious. This
aspect of his arrogance is well conveyed in another hotel
scene, this time in Rouen in November 1917. Once more it is
the perceptive Sylvia who brings it to our attention:

In the bluish looking-glass, a few minutes before, she had seen
the agate-blue eyes of her husband, thirty feet away, over arm-
chairs and between the fans of palms. He was standing, holding
a riding-whip, looking rather clumsy in the uniform that did not

suit him. Rather clumsy and worn out, but completely expression-less! He had looked straight into the reflection of her eyes and then looked away. *He moved so that his profile was towards her,* and continued gazing motionless at an elk's head that decorated the space of wall above glazed doors giving into the interior of the hotel. The hotel servant approaching him, he had produced a card and had given it to the servant, uttering three words. She saw his lips move in the three words: Mrs Christopher Tietjens. She said, beneath her breath:

'Damn his chivalry! Oh, God damn his chivalry!' (*NMP*, 386: emphasis added)

Tietjens' chivalry is so self-regarding that it has become brutal; his courtesy so arid as to be uncivil, even when directed towards so imperfect a wife as Sylvia. Tellingly, the latter's criticisms of her husband's lordly woodenness, 'his pompous self-sufficiency', and the fact that 'he's so formal he can't do without all the conventions there are and so truthful he can't use half of them' are observations remark-ably similar to Valentine's. (*SDN*, 38)

Thus in *Some Do Not...* Tietjens' effulgent Toryism is recorded by Ford alongside Miss Wannop's contempt for what she, as a Suffragette and admirer of Rosa Luxemburg, sees as intolerable paternalism:

[Valentine] stopped and said good-naturedly: 'But do, for good-ness' sake, get it over. I'm sorry I was rude to you. But it *is* irritat-ing to have to stand like a stuffed rabbit while a man is acting like a regular Admirable Crichton, and cool and collected, with the English country gentleman air and all.'

Tietjens winced. The young woman had come a little too near the knuckle of his wife's frequent denunciations of himself. (*SDN*, 119)

While it is true that Sylvia is usually rendered with hostility by Ford, the full contexts in which the above comments are embedded mean that we are intended to accept the judg-ments made by the two women. Ford did not allow Tietjens to pass through the quartet uncorrected, for our sympathy for him and acceptance of his critical voice are modified by the responses of his wife, his mistress and, in *Last Post*, his French sister-in-law.

In the 'Dedication' to *A Man Could Stand Up–* Ford had
shrewdly anticipated the later critical argument that he was
too closely attached to Tietjens. He wrote there that Tietjens
'like all of us. . .is neither unprejudiced nor infallible. And
you have here his mental reactions and his reflections –
which are not, *not*, NOT presented as those of the author.'[6]
The triple emphasis underlines the author's anxiety that he
shouldn't be totally identified with his hero, and yet it is clear
that these warnings haven't been heeded by all his readers.
There are several reasons for the mistaken assumption of a
total identity of author with hero. For some readers there
may be an overlap from the known facts and legends of Ford's
life: he often seemed to have behaved like Tietjens. More
interesting, though, is the possible influence of *The Good
Soldier*, many readers' first introduction to Ford. There,
Dowell's narrative role had been so pervasive that we were
hesitant of accepting any character, as it were, 'straight'.
Allowance had continually to be made for possible refraction
or distortion by the narrator. *Parade's End*, though, is a
different kind of fiction, lacking the filter of a Dowell, and
readers can be more confident of accepting the kind of reser-
vations voiced about its hero by Sylvia and Valentine. Some
readers, then, may have approached *Parade's End* expecting
a more problematic ambivalent narrative than the author
intended: the quartet is not surrounded by a haze of moral
obliquity.

Irony does, it is true, exist in *Parade's End*, but it is more
'Victorian' than 'modernist'. Its purpose is not to persuade
us that moral discrimination cannot be exercised, as in
Dowell's totally relativist world, but rather, as in Dickens
and Eliot, to help us see that a character's own view of himself is incomplete. In this way, too, Ford can dissociate himself from some of Tietjens' more pronounced eccentricities
without undermining that character's value as commentator
and censor. In *A Man Could Stand Up–* Ford portrays
Christopher as imagining that he has deteriorated because he
has accepted responsibility for his battalion and has even

relished the thought of the £250 command pay to which he
would thus be entitled:

> It was deterioration. He, Tietjens, was crumpling up morally. He
> had accepted responsibility: he had thought of two hundred and
> fifty pounds with pleasure: now he was competing with a Cockney-
> Celtic Prize man. He was reduced to that level. (*AMCSU*, 96)

Ford intends that we understand *why* the Yorkshire landowner should regard such unexceptionable activities as
'deterioration', but he doesn't want us to agree with Tietjens
at this point. He offers no explicit comment on his hero's
self-deception, yet, within the context of the whole quartet,
what are to Tietjens proofs of moral turpitude are really the
indices of moral growth. For all its technical sophistication,
then, the moral universe here is a good deal less complex and
uncertain than *The Good Soldier*'s. In passages like these
the Toryism of Ford's hero is modified by the novelist's
scrupulousness as an annalist of his own world. It was W. H.
Auden who remarked on the danger of imagining that
because Tietjens is an eccentric 'backwoods' Tory, his
creator must necessarily be a political reactionary or a social
snob. Ford, Auden concluded, 'makes it quite clear that
World War I was a retribution visited upon Western Europe
for the sins and omissions of its ruling class, for which not
only they, but also the innocent conscripted millions on both
sides must suffer'.[7]

IV

Nevertheless, although Christopher Tietjens did develop in
Parade's End, and was there presented critically by Ford, it
is still true that the novelist didn't achieve his aims by means
of a narrowly 'realistic' hero. In an essay on Elizabethan
drama, T. S. Eliot distinguished between a character who
was 'living' and one that was 'true to life':

> A 'living' character is not necessarily 'true to life.' It is a person
> whom we can see and hear, whether he be true or false to human
> nature as we know it. What the creator of character needs is not

so much knowledge of motives as keen sensibility; the dramatist need not understand people, but he must be exceptionally aware of them.[8]

Tietjens is a character who can be seen and heard: he is 'living'. Equally, though, he's not 'true to life' in the sense that, say, Lt Geoffrey Skene, hero of Mottram's *The Spanish Farm* (1924), is. Skene is typical of a young British officer of that class and that period. Tietjens, on the other hand, though credible enough, doesn't possess that kind of sociological representativeness. Both in his self-awareness and in the intractability of his marital life he is in fact atypical, something of a sport, a man who doesn't correspond to any norm. Ford has explained his reasons for creating such a character as the hero of his anti-war quartet. A man 'in lasting tribulation – with a permanent shackle and ball on his leg' was required to lend full weight to what Ford saw as the greatest cruelty of war, its unrelenting power to embroil the combatant in distant domestic worries. (*IWN*, 189) Similarly, his hero had to be an officer of great insight so that his criticism of his class and country should both be lucid and capable of percolating to the top of the war-machine.

Indeed the whole point about *Parade's End* is that it couldn't have enunciated the criticisms Ford intended had its hero been 'sound'. He had to be victimised in peace and in war if Ford was to bring out clearly the cruel injustices of that class at that period. The frequent comparison to Dreyfus is not inapt. Like Hyacinth Robinson in James' *Princess Casamassima* Tietjens must be a significant reflection of the complexities of his own society and neither hero can fulfil this role by being narrowly 'true to life'. Both Hyacinth and Christopher had to be intensely, unusually self-conscious; both had to be uncommonly and largely flawed. In this way, by being larger than, and different from, a strictly realistic 'life', they are employed to canalise and summarise social tensions more comprehensively than could be done by a character as patently life-like and incapable of symbolic insights as Mottram's Skene.

An example of how Ford exploits Tietjens' eccentricities can be found in *No More Parades*. The latter here is in very low water: penniless, physically weak, the pariah of his own class, tormented by his sadistic wife and nursing an apparently hopeless passion. No man would be likely to suffer, let alone survive, such a mass of insoluble problems, and we can therefore say that Ford has 'over-drawn' Tietjens' agonies. And yet the soldiers and officers presented in this novel endure in similar kind, if not in degree. All of them, in the opening scene in the hut near Rouen, are worried, Tietjens about the lateness of a draft, others about the price of a laundry, a queer cow at home, a lost pocket-book. Pte Morgan, whose macabre death so afflicts Tietjens, has a wife who is deceiving him with a boxer; Sylvia Tietjens is rumoured, falsely as it happens, to be sleeping with a General; McKechnie's wife is living in London with an Egyptologist. L/Cpl Girtin is distracted by the need to meet his aged mother, just as Tietjens is exercised by the surprising arrival of his wife in France. In this unit, then, only the quantity of the worries differs from man to man, the quality is common to all:

The evening wore on and on. It astounded Tietjens, looking at one time at his watch, to discover that it was only 21 hrs. 19. He seemed to have been thinking drowsily of his own affairs for ten hours. . .For, in the end, these were his own affairs. . .Money, women, testamentary bothers. Each of these complications from over the Atlantic and *round the world* were his own troubles: *a world in labour*: an army being moved off in the night. Shoved off. Anyhow. And over the top. *A lateral section of the world.* (*NMP*, 326–7: emphases added)

Once again, as so frequently in *Parade's End*, 'world' connotes both the fictional universe and the real world of November 1917. Ford's picture of Tietjens is exaggerated, but not false.[9] He heightens the combatants' problems without essentially distorting them. Ford was less interested in writing of the physical atrocities of war than of its psychological terrors, and these he desired to render as ubiquitous and inescapable.

Sylvia, a brief and unimpressed spectator of war, saw it as a reptile that 'moved and moved, under your eyes dissolving, yet always there. As if you should try to follow one diamond of pattern in the coil of an immense snake that was in irrevocable motion.' (*NMP*, 443) Christopher's appalling mental derangements are intended to show this 'diamond of pattern'; to express war's power of total engrossment, its 'infinitely spreading welter of pain, going away to an eternal horizon of night'. (*NMP*, 444) Although at the beginning of *Parade's End* Tietjens is so closely attached to the loyalties and customs of his own class, by the end of *A Man Could Stand Up*– he has transcended them. He has absorbed those elements in his creation that recall Ford's dreams for himself and his love of Arthur Marwood, and now 'stands in some measure for the unrewarded virtues of personal discipline and endurance in soldiers of lower rank that the war and its perpetual expenditure of human valor had taught Ford to respect'. (*Wiley*, 213) Ford didn't mythicise the war as David Jones did in *In Parenthesis*, with its echoes of *Henry V* and of Anglo-Saxon poetry, but a kind of 'monumental' significance, in both senses of that word, came to be attached to Tietjens. He is Ford's epitaph to the same unsung heroes immortalised by Jones, Owen and Rosenberg.

v

This kind of comprehensive totalising realism, a fiction which includes but moves beyond the strictly 'documentary', may well, as Lukács argued, be 'dependent on the possibility of access to the forces of change in a given moment of history'.[10] Certainly, to take Ford's case, the war enabled him, for the first and last time in his career, to participate in a very minor role at the fulcrum of historical change. There may be a parallel between the effect of war on *Tietjens* – the death of Morgan and the injury to Aranjuez, men for whom he feels responsible, teaching him that Tory aloofness is no longer viable – and the war's effect on *Ford*, humanising him and

widening his vision. If war gave Christopher 'a new vision
and a new dedication', it may have had a similar benevolent
effect on his creator. (*Cassell*, 238) Yet against this progressive
humanistic development in Ford the man has to be set the
artistic problems posed by this particular war, the first 'total
war' and a radically new experience for European man and
the European novelist.

The new immobility of war, the odd settledness of trench
warfare and its lack of any apparent logicality, posed problems to the artist rendering it which had not been met by the
author of, say, *War and Peace*. Walter Benjamin was thinking
of a similar problem when he remarked on the fall in the
value of experience as being one of the effects of the First
War on the mind of western man. Benjamin's comment,
though lengthy, is worth full quotation, because it may have
a bearing on Ford's artistic problems in *Parade's End* –
particularly in *Last Post* – and the solution which he adopted:

With the [First] World War a process began to become apparent
which has not halted since then. Was it not noticeable at the end
of the war that men returned from the battlefield grown silent –
not richer, but poorer in communicable experience? What ten
years later was poured out in the flood of war books was anything
but experience that goes from hand to mouth. And there was
nothing remarkable about that. For never has experience been
contradicted more thoroughly than strategic experience by tactical
warfare, economic experience by inflation, bodily experience by
mechanical warfare, moral experience by those in power.

And now Benjamin describes the experiential effects of the
war in a series of metaphors strikingly similar to those of
Parade's End, which also opens with an elegant journey and
closes with a man lying under the clouds:

A generation that had gone to school on a horse-drawn streetcar
now stood under the open sky in a countryside in which nothing
remained unchanged but the clouds, and beneath these clouds,
in a field of force of destructive torrents and explosions, was the
tiny, fragile human body.[11]

Benjamin is arguing here that the war accelerated a process

which had begun much earlier, and that it effected a crucial diminution in the 'communicability of experience'. For Lukács, periods of such sweeping historical change had been viewed as opportunities for the novelist, touchstones against which the depth and clarity of his vision could be measured. This is how he regarded the Year of Revolutions, 1848. Benjamin, on the other hand, implies that the war of 1914–1918 was an experience quite dissimilar either in quality or quantity from any that had preceded it, and moreover, one that posed cybernetic and semantic problems of a totally new kind for the European novelist. The classic novel of Scott, Balzac and Tolstoy had been so deeply committed to experience's communicability, its publicness, what Benjamin calls 'experience that goes from hand to mouth', that a new fictional mode had to be found to render the private madness of the trenches. Such, at any rate, is Benjamin's hypothesis. If the classic European novels can be defined as being 'questions posed by the novelist about the opportunities for effective action available to a man living in society', how can this fictional form cope with circumstances in which, as Tietjens discovers, the very concept of 'society' is at risk?[12]

Ford's response to the problem of how to treat the 'public events of a decade' so revolutionary was the customary recourse to fiction's central perceiving intelligence. Meditating on his next work in December 1922, as soon as he had arrived in southern France, he realises that he would have to 'fall back on the old device of a world seen through the eyes of a central observer. The tribulations of the central observer must be sufficient to carry the reader through his observations of the crumbling world.' (*IWN*, 195) Already there's a straining incongruity between the chosen narrative mode and the madness of the material to be treated, but Ford's decision at this point, however reluctant, implied that the observer's experiences were of a kind that could be communicated in a basically traditional manner. Most of *Parade's End* is shaped according to these specifications. Through the first three parts of the quartet, as far as the end of *A Man Could Stand Up–*,

on Armistice Day 1918, Tietjens is the novel's organising
nodal consciousness. Thus far it is a novel of mass action with
Tietjens as hub and focus. Christopher himself held that
society was organic and the hero's perception parallels Ford's
decision to employ a synthesising observer as his narrative
mode. The implication in both cases, Ford's and Tietjens', is
that society is comprehensible.

As a result the bulk of *Parade's End* has, despite its time-
shifts and internal monologues, recognisable points of contact
with the classic nineteenth-century novel. Both share a
fidelity to the importance of the 'great exterior turning points
and blows of fate' which Proust, Joyce and Woolf down-
grade.[13] Right up to the end of *A Man Could Stand Up*–
Ford seems confident that events such as the ownership of
Groby and the question of the Single Command of the Allied
armies may be made to yield 'decisive information' about his
subject. Until *Last Post* Ford can design his fiction on the
assumption that life has an order. Indeed had *Parade's End*
concluded at the Armistice scene in Tietjens' house we should
have remarked on its similarity with so many Victorian novels
and how they too end 'with a series of settlements, of new
engagements and formal relationships'.[14]

But there is, of course, a sequel, in which Ford relates the
aftermath of war down to June 1920, and in this fourth novel,
Last Post, our impression is rather of a correspondence between *Parade's End* and the quintessential modern novels, say
Sons and Lovers or *A Portrait of the Artist*, which so frequently end 'with a man going away on his own, having
extricated himself from a dominating situation [here, the
war and Sylvia's hegemony], and found himself in so doing'.[15]
In *Last Post* Ford in fact abandoned narration through the
central observer and substituted several different points of
vision. In consequence it is a radically different novel from
the three earlier ones, in both style and content, and one that,
in the sparsity of its dialogue, seems to exemplify Benjamin's
theory of the new poverty of communicable experience.
One's impression is that fewer words are spoken aloud in

Last Post than in a single chapter of *Some Do Not*. . . Instead it is committed to meditation and reminiscence.

Whereas there had existed contiguity and continuity between the three earlier elements of the quartet, there seems to be a hiatus between these three considered together and the final *Last Post*. The quartet's incrementality is fractured by *Last Post*, which entails some kind of revision, reconsideration, of all that has preceded it. From the standpoint of *Last Post* we look back on *Some Do Not*. . . as being almost an innocent vision. The effect of the concluding novel is to make anachronistic both the world of the earlier parts of the quartet and, crucially, the novelist's way of presenting that world, which, in its deployment of a central observer, was so fundamentally 'old fashioned'. *Last Post* is, therefore, in a double sense, retrospective, firstly because its characters are engaged almost entirely in the act of looking backwards, there being very little action in the present tense; and secondly because it engages the reader in a process of looking back over the novel's eight years and of thinking again about the manner in which he viewed the events of those years. *Last Post* makes us see that *Parade's End* is not only about the derangements caused by the war. It's also concerned with changes in seeing and in rendering the world between 1912 and 1920. Its 'profound imaginative grasp of the effect of the war on the traditional patterns of English life'[16] thus embraces both patterns of essence and patterns of existence, modes of vision and of action. Ford grasped that the war's most permanent legacy, aside from its physical destruction, lay in altering the forms in which man saw, arranged and communicated his own experiences.

It was to this innovation that Ambrose Gordon, in the most eccentric and provocative study of *Parade's End*, was pointing when he wrote that it 'is a great slow novel of change: social, psychological, normative. Above all, it is a novel of qualitative change, a change in the way of seeing things, brought on by – or through – the First World War.' (*Gordon*, 72) It demonstrates Ford's awareness of the inadequacy of earlier realistic models for treating the new privatisation of experience. *Last Post*, then, wasn't a betrayal of Ford's stated commitment to the novelist's role as the recorder of his own times. Instead it provides evidence of a widened definition of the historical novel, which can now include reflections on the changing relationship between fiction and history. The celebrated self-reflexiveness of modernist fictions takes on a wider cultural dimension as the historical novel is enabled to meditate upon its own historicism.

And so *Parade's End* is an astonishingly capacious fiction, successfully embracing the nineteenth-century novel and the post-war novels of sensibility. Placing it fairly and squarely within either genre would oversimplify and diminish it. It properly belongs at the point of historical confluence, but locating the novel here, at the watershed, literary and social, of our own pre-history, when the 'past' was modulating into the 'present', imputes to Ford no act of indecisiveness or opacity. Ford is so faithful to the historical realities of the decade spanned by *Parade's End* that he uses the changing form of the quartet to reveal the historical genesis of modernism itself.

Style and content are intimately allied in *Parade's End*. The changing techniques of the tetralogy, from the omniscient narrative predominant in *Some Do Not . . .* through 'objective' and 'focussed' narratives to the 'interior' narrative of *Last Post*, correspond to the substantive theme of the series as a whole.[17] Thus Tietjens' journey from 'a vestigial sense of community to isolation' is both communicated by, and reflected in these four distinct 'points of view'. *Parade's End* narrates a modulation that is at once both historical and literary, 'the movement of both society and the novel from the nineteenth to the twentieth century'.[18] Mizener's observation that 'the essential subject of *Parade's End* is the inner process by which Christopher and Valentine are gradually transformed from Edwardian to modern people' must be supplemented to the effect that the tetralogy also reflects on the fictional forms available for delineating that transformation. (*Mizener*, 372) This was unmistakably an ambitious project, the largest of Ford's career and as massive as any of his grandfather's civic murals.

VI

Some Do Not... (1924), the first novel of the quartet, is Ford's most striking success in *Parade's End*. It's a sustained polyphonic linking of domestic and national derangements, and its insight into the political reverberations of a misdirected diseased eroticism invites comparison with *The Egoist*, a novel modern before its time, or the best work of D. H. Lawrence. *Some Do Not...* is remembered as a treatment of 'Edwardian' England, but when we return to it we find that only Part One takes place before the war, in June 1912, Part Two in fact being set in August 1917, towards the end of the war. Nevertheless, although it may be strictly inexact to describe it as a fictional record of 'Edwardianism', Ford apparently intended that we should not think of August 1914 as marking the great division between 'peace' and 'war', and the end of the 'Edwardian' age. Certainly the first reviewers of the novel shared with later critics a readiness to accept the accuracy of Ford's unorthodox periodisation, which implies that many of the forms commonly held to be 'Edwardian' survived *after* the outbreak of war and, conversely, that some aspects of the war were apparent before the hostilities began – indeed as early as 1912.

This is no less suggestive than if a later novelist had extended the period we think of as the thirties as far as 1942. And yet although Ford was sometimes, to his disadvantage, guilty of a certain recklessness towards historical fact, in this case he was sharing with his contemporary, Lawrence, the important intuition that war was, for a while, only a continuation of peace. In *Kangaroo* Lawrence places the great change that took place in England in 1915–16, not in August 1914, and in his short stories of this period, in 'The Ladybird',

'The Fox' and 'The Captain's Doll', we find similarly that 'Edwardianism' has survived into the period of hostilities. Likewise, the real stylistic and thematic division in the quartet takes place in November 1917, at the opening of *No More Parades*, with Ford's first description of Tietjens' life in France, even though he had enlisted during the period treated in the earlier novel and had in fact been recuperating from a war wound as early as Part Two of *Some Do Not. . .*

Equally suggestive of Ford's refusal to accept the conventional periodisation is the concluding line of Part One of *Some Do Not. . .* – 'The knacker's cart lumbered round the corner'. Here Ford shows that the arrival of the men from the shambles to collect Mrs Wannop's horse, slaughtered by General Campion's careless driving, anticipates the carnage to come. It's as if Ford's characters were, in June 1912, already experiencing a taste of the insane violence of 1914. The sacrifice of lineality in jumping straight from June 1912 to August 1917 permits Ford to establish the utility of his historical impressionism as a means of demarcating the *felt* boundaries between peace and war. In this way Ford extended the modernist techniques of *The Good Soldier*, time-shift and the non-sequential narrative, so as to make them capable of dealing with a subject-matter previously only amenable to strictly realistic treatment. Ford was indeed 'one of the first novelists to realize the possibilities of the cognitive novel, of the inseparable interaction between the purely technical devices at the writer's command and that external history which makes up an important part of his materials'.[19]

Some Do Not. . . portrays the moral universe of discrete individualism in its death-agonies. By the beginning of the quartet's next novel it will have totally collapsed. At the moment it is still just possible, however, to establish clear moral distinctions, and the novel's binary form reflects such discriminations. *Some Do Not. . .* is indeed built around the moralistic phrase of the title, quoted by Macmaster in the opening chapter:

The gods to each ascribe a differing lot:
Some enter at the portal. Some do not!

Every single character and episode falls into these two cate-
gories, the blessed and the damned.

In Part One Tietjens is still accepted by the ruling class as
a dinner-guest and golf-partner, but his physical isolation of
Part Two is foreshadowed in 1912 by the continual contrasts
between his code of sexual restraint and high society's frequent delinquencies. Tietjens' convention of 'monogamy
and chastity', to which he adheres in his dealings with
Valentine, is betrayed by the sexual hypocrisies of Edith
Duchemin and Vincent Macmaster; by the rancid indiscipline
of Sylvia and her mother; by the businessmen's erotic fantasies about Budapest and their attack on Gertie, the
Suffragette; and by Sandbach's expedition against the feminists. The physical restraint of Tietjens and the Wannops,
lunching frugally, is set against the extravagance of Duchemin, ordering caviar on ice to be sent by train to Sussex for
breakfast. Tietjens' mastery of his horses is twice contrasted
with Campion's lack of control over his car; Valentine's con-
structiveness with the destructiveness of Sylvia.

Some Do Not. . . thus makes a long list of charges against
the 'Edwardian' ruling class, with Ford drawing out the
connections between their lack of emotional stability and
the approaching war. A sharp dramatic irony is present
throughout the novel. The 'twenty tea-trays', a metaphor of
Campion's lethal motor car, will in the next novel be meta-
morphosised into the German shelling of Tietjens' unit. The
extravagant silver service of the Duchemins will be conjured
into the 'candlestick', a metal bar inside a shrapnel shell,
which is to destroy Pte Morgan. Ford's attack on England's
rulers is sharp enough, yet we are also meant to see that,
although Tietjens' values are superior, even these are somewhat incomplete and inauthentic. Valentine Wannop makes
this point to him when she remarks on the falsity of his Tory
paternalism, and how he is a generous man despite his code.
Some Do Not. . . is set at the same period as the conclusion of

The Good Soldier, and returns us to Dowell's persistent question in that novel: 'acting – or, no, not acting?' Just as the railway carriage described on the opening page seems theatrical, stylised and over-perfect, so, similarly, Tietjens' code springs from a straining will imposing itself on a recalcitrant reality. Ford's narrative is sufficiently flexible to enable us to see that the novel's binary distinctions are the product of the hero's oversimplified views. The function of Valentine is to demonstrate that, for all its superiority to what surrounds him, Tietjens' aristocratic idealism is itself in need of modification. She shows us that Tietjens' persistent evocations of the past weaken his code's viability in the present. Ford is now aware of the frailty of nostalgia.

In Part Two of *Some Do Not...* the falsity inherent in Christopher's membership of a corrupt society has reached a critical point, yet the war, now in its third year, has not manufactured social contradictions, only intensified those long in existence. Ford himself remarks authorially that 'it is, in fact, asking for trouble if you are more altruist than the society that surrounds you' and by this time, August 1917, Christopher has cast himself loose. (*SDN*, 211) All contacts have now been broken. He has resigned from his office, protesting against the falsification of statistics to cheat the French; he lives with his wife in virtual silence; his bank returns his cheque for a few shillings; he is alienated from his father and brother, who both believe the slanders circulating about his immorality; he has been disowned by Edith and Macmaster; and finally he is distrusted by the Army for his excessive sympathies with both the French and the Germans. Valentine, too, is strained and alone, now that she has broken with the unscrupulous, self-seeking Macmaster, and is prepared to become Tietjens' mistress. In Part One our view had been confined to Tietjens' perspective. Now, the narrative of *Some Do Not...* is widened to embrace the consciousness of both Tietjens and Miss Wannop, Ford's intention being to heighten our sense of their isolation and reliance upon each other. We wait to see whether they will

seal their commitment before Christopher leaves England,
but although he recognises that there is now no place for him
in established circles, he elects only to pledge himself with a
talismanic parchment. Tietjens is shown as loathing his own
class, but as yet his 'parade' of self-suppression and renunciation prevents him from throwing in his lot with Valentine.
Hence he persists in 'acting', as Dowell put it, in clinging on
to his stubborn nobility in the face of reality.

VII

The contrast at the very beginning of *No More Parades* (1925)
is overpowering, the first scene in the crowded hut near
Rouen exemplifying the 'obsolescence of the gentleman in
war'.[20] This, Keith Douglas maintained, together with 'the
retreat from Mons, the aggregate of new horrors, [and] the
muddling generalship. . .demanded and obtained a new type
of writing to comment on them'. The title of the quartet's
second volume indicates through a resonant metaphor the
collapse of all 'parades', all those social rituals by which a
governing class had reassured itself of its hegemony. Between
the end of *Some Do Not. . .* and the beginning of *No More
Parades* the old world, sustained by social, military and
sexual 'parades', had disintegrated, and Ford responded to
the necessity for a different formal expression of the 'new
world' that succeeded it. The opening two paragraphs of *No
More Parades*, describing the hut behind the lines, can be
contrasted with the stateliness, in manner and in matter, of
the quartet's first paragraph, the railway carriage of *Some Do
Not. . .*

   This is the first page of *No More Parades*, our first intuition
that the old world has finally collapsed:

When you came in, the space was desultory, rectangular, warm
after the drip of the winter night, and transfused with a brown-
orange dust that was light. It was shaped like the house a child
draws. Three groups of brown limbs spotted with brass took dim
high-lights from shafts that came from a bucket pierced with
holes, filled with incandescent coke and covered in with a sheet of

iron in the shape of a tunnel. Two men, as if hierarchically smaller, crouched on the floor beside the brazier; four, two at each end of the hut, drooped over tables in attitudes of extreme indifference. From the eaves above the parallelogram of black that was the doorway fell intermittent drippings of collected moisture, persistent, with glasslike intervals of musical sound. The two men squatting on their heels over the brazier – they had been miners – began to talk in a low sing-song of dialect, hardly audible. It went on and on, monotonously, without animation. It was as if one told the other long, long stories to which his companion manifested his comprehension or sympathy with animal grunts. . .

An immense tea-tray, august, its voice filling the black circle of the horizon, thundered to the ground. Numerous pieces of sheet-iron said, 'Pack. Pack. Pack.' In a minute the clay floor of the hut shook, the drums of ears were pressed inwards, solid noise showered about the universe, enormous echoes pushed these men – to the right, to the left, or down towards the tables – and crackling like that of flames among vast underwood became the settled condition of the night. Catching the light from the brazier as the head leaned over, the lips of one of the two men on the floor were incredibly red and full and went on talking and talking. (*NMP*, 295)

A crucially important development has taken place since the end of *Some Do Not*. . . In part, the setting and the characters themselves are quite dissimilar, for the crudeness of the hut's furnishings and Tietjens' closeness to two ex-colliers have no parallel with anything in the earlier novel. Perhaps more noticeable, however, is the changed style of this passage, the new manner in which people and places are now being rendered. The railway carriage at the opening of the quartet had been described in a series of associations with a world, stable and unquestioned, that both surrounded the compartment and, in a sense, supported it. The three images that impinged on Tietjens' mind – of the German designer of the upholstery, of British 'gilts' as a simile for the train's reliability, and of a letter to *The Times* should the train jolt unexpectedly – implied the existence of national and class harmony. The very externality of these three pictures implied a community of experience and response, shared between character, author and reader.

The hut near Rouen, however, is not presented in the same way. Once again the perceiving consciousness, the point of view, is Tietjens', but he now responds to his surroundings privately and subjectively, noting the pattern of shapes, sounds and colours whose only reality lies within the mind of the beholder. The 'minute dragon pattern' of the pre-war cushions would have existed without Tietjens' presence, whereas 'the parallelogram of black that was the doorway' is only Tietjens' response, his impression, and there is nothing external to him to verify this image. In *Some Do Not...* Man had built his environment, Nature had been harnessed to Man's control. Now, though, Man has shrunk and has no rational power over his surroundings. The railway carriage had been 'perfectly appointed', but the hut's space is 'desultory', illogical, arbitrary. The frontiers between the individual, nature and reason have been obliterated. Nobody in *No More Parades* (which is all set in France) seems to have any space or time. Campion the General, Sylvia the civilian, Tietjens the young officer, and the unidentified soldiers are all living crowded, stressful, hurried lives. The phrase 'catching the light from the brazier as the head leaned over' leaves it uncertain whether the 'head' is the soldier's or the brazier's. Soldier's 'brown limbs', as in a Picasso or a Braque, have been separated from their trunks. Man's humanity, even his organicism, is perpetually threatened.

'The world was foundering', Tietjens thinks at one moment in *No More Parades*. (*NMP*, 364) Henri Barbusse's response to this experience was the horrifying realism of *Le Feu* (1916), but *Parade's End* doesn't often seek to arouse such physical disgust – perhaps only with Morgan's death and Aranjuez' loss of an eye. Ford's repudiation of realism, after having frequently employed it in *Some Do Not...*, was an equally effective expression of the horror of war, and of the 'new world' to which both Douglas and Walter Benjamin alluded. Realism is the register of a world in which the boundaries between Man and both his organic and inorganic environment are clear and non-problematic. Christopher's inability to perceive his situation in November 1917 'realistically', and his adoption, instead, of the 'impressionism' of the paragraphs quoted shows the impotence of his old code. In *Some Do Not...* he had 'adopted a habit of behaviour that he considered to be the best in the world for the normal life', while also admitting that his 'peculiarly English habit of self-suppression...puts the Englishman at a great disadvantage in moments of unusual stresses'. (*SDN*, 183) Between 1912 and 1917 Tietjens had some success in reordering the world to make it fit his own views, but his parade of Tory rectitude has no place in an environment perpetually full of 'unusual stresses'. Tietjens' philosophy as well as his body is under bombardment at the beginning of *No More Parades*.

After the inferno of unremitting mental pressure Tietjens has a luminous vision, an 'epiphany'. During Campion's inspection of his cookhouse the General orders the pepper canisters to be opened:

To Tietjens this was like the sudden bursting out of the regimental quick step, as after a funeral with military honours the band and drums march away, back to barracks. (*NMP*, 504)

There will, he perceives, now be no more 'parades' of renunciation and self-suppression. The war, which he has only been able to apprehend and communicate through the subjectivity of his own impressions, has taught him the value of the individual, irrespective of class or birth. Tietjens sees his 'draft' as individual human beings

Each man a man with a backbone, knees, breeches, braces, a rifle, a home, passions, fornications, drunks, pals, some scheme of the universe, corns, inherited diseases, a greengrocer's business, a milk-walk, a paper-stall, brats, a slut of a wife. (*NMP*, 301)

His vision of the precious individuality of others enables him to recognise that his future allegiance must be to his own private needs, not to any anachronistic abstract code. The experience of shared suffering has taught him that his obsessive fidelity to his 'public school's ethical system' has been 'adolescent'. (*NMP*, 494) *Parade's End* shows the decisive historical moment when the 'acting' of *The Good Soldier*, the deceptions of a whole class, had to stop. The latter novel, 'plus all that the War implied gives us *Parade's End*: immensely complex personal misery plus the shattering of all the externals of the order that had sustained the poise of gentlemen'.[21]

Parade's End, then, is a novel acutely sensitive to changes in class-consciousness, the ways people saw themselves and each other, as well as objective political developments between 1912 and 1920. *Some Do Not. . .* and *No More Parades*, the first two segments of Ford's historical record, convey his impression of the different phases in these changes. Their unique value as an account of the revolution 'in the British social structure' lies in Ford's deployment of 'style as vision', a congruity between the objective historical movements – from certitude to agnosticism, peace to war – and the manner in which such developments were perceived in, and mediated through a 'typical' human consciousness.[22] The sustained realism of *Le Feu, The Spanish Farm Trilogy* and Arnold Zweig's *Trilogy* chronicled modulations of the first kind. Ford's use, though, of a much wider range of techniques enables him to show us, from the inside as it were, why the changes in the way in which Tietjens *perceived* events inevitably entailed the hero's abandonment of 'parade'.

VIII

Tietjens' authentic and untheatrical sense of human community is born in *No More Parades* out of his relationship with Pte Morgan and the Canadian, L/Cpl Girtin. With her usual percipience Sylvia grasps the implications, which are social and in the widest sense political, of war as the great leveller of class distinctions. She hates the democratisation of which her husband is a part, that now he will speak to anyone, irrespective of class and nationality, that he, once so marmoreal, is tormented by the death of a former miner:

She had never seen Tietjens put his head together with any soul before: he was the lonely buffalo...Now! Anyone: any fatuous staff officer, whom at home he would never so much as have spoken to: any trustworthy, beer-sodden sergeant, any street-urchin dressed up as orderly. (*NMP*, 443)

The quartet's third volume, *A Man Could Stand Up–* (1926), shows Tietjens applying what he has learnt of his kinship with the unprivileged to his own life as a soldier and as a lover. Divided into three parts, Part One presents Valentine's uncertainty on Armistice Day as to Tietjens' feelings for her. Part Two, Christopher's experience under fire seven months earlier, when the Germans threatened a decisive break-through, both answers Valentine's question – for plainly he is obsessed with her – and explains his later decision to join her, in Part Three, a few hours after the Armistice. Once more, Ford's formal dispositions, the juxtaposition of Valentine's thoughts in the first moments of peace with the officer's experience during the nadir of the war, the point of view being divided between the civilian teacher and the soldier, bring home the new power of total war to spill over into the lives of non-combatants.

Another interesting aspect of the form of *A Man Could Stand Up–* is that there's now a close correspondence between fiction's elapsed time and the time taken by the reader to follow these same events and thoughts. With each succeeding novel a shorter period has been 'covered', and, assuming that our reading speed is roughly constant throughout the four texts, this means that the relation between 'real' time and fictive time is changing markedly.[23] In *Some Do Not...* five years elapse: in *No More Parades* two days. Now, in *A Man Could Stand Up–*, there's an approximate parity between the two kinds of time, the characters' experiences and our reading of them. In *Last Post*, indeed, real time is probably longer than fictive time. The point of closest corre-spondence between art's time and life's occurs in Part Two of *A Man Could Stand Up–*, where Section One opens (on page 46) some 45 minutes before the German barrage is expected, this attack beginning on page 102. Fifty-six pages, then, describe Tietjens' thoughts and actions during these 45 minutes. Ford's juggling with time's two forms – one a *donnée*, the other created by the writer alone – underlines the removal of authenticity from the public world and its lodgment instead in the private and subjective. In *Some Do Not. . .* human value had apparently been located in a matrix of public events. Now, though, the external world can offer no touchstone to either Christopher or Valentine. They find themselves within themselves.

Such self-discovery is indeed the theme of *A Man Could Stand Up–*, as Tietjens and Miss Wannop attempt to discover how, in the words of the former's sergeant, 'a man could stand hup on an 'ill'. (*AMCSU*, 72) Both are seeking to free themselves from conventions largely discredited by all the events that have taken place since they first walked together in June 1912. For Valentine imprisonment lies in the morality of her headmistress urging her to continue chaste and 'nun-like'. She frees herself by the decision to spend Armistice Day with Tietjens, who is discredited socially and may even be deranged. The latter had made his decision earlier when, in April 1918, he had been faced with the breakdown of his superior, an alcoholic colonel. (In the chronology of these two personal crises Ford exemplifies war's power of accelerating, for the combatant, problems which the civilian only has to face at the end of the war.) Tietjens' pre-war code had urged self-effacement. Will he now, in his colonel's enforced absence, have the courage to accept the 'moral responsibility' of command? (*AMCSU*, 88) Like Valentine, who will accept personal responsibility for her own life, Christopher, toughened by war, succeeds in asserting himself, abandoning the Tory 'parade' of renunciation. A crucial element in this decision is his feeling of comradeship with the rest of his unit, that promiscuity which so disgusts Sylvia:

He was bound to do his best for that unit. That poor b——y unit. And for the poor b——y knock-about comedians to whom he had lately promised tickets for Drury Lane at Christmas. . .
An immense sense of those grimy, shuffling, grouching, dirty-

nosed pantomime-supers came over him and an intense desire to give them a bit of luck. (*AMCSU*, 92–3)

With the British Army threatened by a massive German advance, Tietjens assumes command.

The counterpart of Tietjens' new self-confidence as an officer is his firm decision to try to win Miss Wannop as soon as the war is over. His 'passionate desire to command that battalion' is as strong as his need for the girl. His military obsession with the lines of communication between units is akin to his love of her clarity, her 'exact mind, . . . impatience of solecisms and facile generalizations'. (*AMCSU*, 111, 107) Tietjens' assumption of command is paralleled by his decision to abdicate from Groby and live with Valentine. They will 'stand up' together, asserting the independence of their lives from restricting and discredited codes. Just as isolation in London has matured Valentine, so for Christopher

The war had made a man of him! It had coarsened him and hardened him. There was no other way to look at it. It had made him reach a point at which he would no longer stand unbearable things. . .today *the world* changed. Feudalism was finished; its last vestiges were gone. It held no place for him. (*AMCSU*, 171: emphasis added)

As so often in *Parade's End* moments of personal insights are accompanied by understanding of the wider contexts of individual decisions. Tietjens records this change in his own life, and its accordance with developments in the world outside him, of which he is also a part.

Throughout *Parade's End* Ford invests his modernist techniques with this kind of historical significance. Another example is Ford's highly impressionistic rendering of the incident in which Tietjens is entombed with L/Cpl Duckett, a man who interests him because of an uncanny physical resemblance to Valentine. Their being buried together, by an accident of war, assumes a kind of symbolic reverberation. Here is Ford's narration of the episode, seen through Tietjens' eyes:

He was looking at Aranjuez from a considerable height. He was

enjoying a considerable view. Aranjuez's face had a rapt expression – like that of a man composing poetry. Long dollops of liquid
mud surrounded them in the air. Like black pancakes being
tossed. He thought: 'Thank God I did not write to her. We are
being blown up!' The earth turned like a weary hippopotamus. It
settled down slowly over the face of Lance-Corporal Duckett,
who lay on his side, and went on in a slow wave.

It was slow, slow, slow. . .like a slowed-down movie. The earth
manoeuvred for an infinite time. He remained suspended in space.
As if he were suspended as he had wanted to be in front of that
coxscomb in whitewash. Coincidence! (*AMCSU*, 140)

In this remarkable passage Ford's impressionism is engaged
in rendering the sensations of a man shot into the air and
then buried under a mound of liquid earth. So strikingly
successful is the passage that it takes on parabolic meaning,
with Tietjens' rescue of himself, then his assistance in retriev-
ing Duckett, a military version of what happens in private
life between Tietjens and Valentine. Here, Tietjens first frees
himself from a choking social incubus before assisting
Valentine in her liberation. Thus Ford's language operates
on two levels: the impression, immensely vivid, of an incident
in the war also serves as a heightened summary of a lengthy
personal, psychological development. War is neither a
glorious transcendence nor a bestial degradation of nor-
mality. Rather, it is an intensification and clarification of
certain human traits also visible in peacetime.

IX

The title of the concluding *Last Post* (1928) refers to the
buglecall sounded at the end of military funerals, and these
represent the 'parade' of misplaced loyalties Tietjens and
Valentine had discarded on Armistice Day. It stands apart
from the rest of the Tietjens series, in that its right to inclusion in *Parade's End* has been questioned. Indeed its most
extreme critics, Graham Greene being the foremost, argue
for its exclusion from the series, and it was omitted from the
Bodley Head edition of *Parade's End*. The arguments

advanced against *Last Post* deserve the most careful consideration, but perhaps Ford was right to balance his comments in favour, finally, of *Last Post*'s inclusion in *Parade's End*.[24]

Samuel Hynes, one of the shrewdest of Ford's critics, argued that *Last Post* was 'unhistorical', whereas the rest of *Parade's End* was a faithful cultural record. Ford, he claimed, strayed out of history into a timeless 'pastoral romance'.[25] Hynes maintained carefully that *Last Post* should be regarded as a kind of 'optional extra', an accessory that the frugal reader could refuse to pay for. In the most narrow and literal sense this argument is correct, for *Last Post* does lack that visible structure of a verifiable public reality. Nevertheless, in the larger view, it is the very lack of an external historical dimension that is, paradoxically, the clearest evidence of Ford's fundamental loyalty to the course of history. As Malcolm Bradbury has argued, *Parade's End* treats history so fully and so respectfully that *Last Post* cannot have the earlier novels' overt commitment to the public world of military or metropolitan politics, just because this world has been demonstrated as meaningless, not viable.[26]

Nevertheless, the veracity with which *Last Post* records that large cultural shift from a public to a private morality, the novel's value as an historical *document*, may not necessarily make it an effective *novel*. The question at issue really is whether *Last Post* is an effective rendering of the lives that Tietjens and Valentine had elected to live in *A Man Could Stand Up–*. There they had chosen to move from a 'traditional' to a 'consequential' morality. The former 'imposes upon the individual a repetition of similar patterns of behaviour' in obedience to ancient pieties, those 'parades' which are gradually evacuated of meaning as the quartet progresses. Consequential morality, on the other hand, 'involves a detailed study of particular situations, a series of choices which vary according to circumstances'.[27] *A Man Could Stand Up–* certainly hadn't promised any relaxation of moral strenuousness for the future. Indeed the new location of moral decision within the individual, instead of in the rubric of class or sect, would rather imply an intensification of the moral life, in which each question, each issue would have to be debated afresh. Yet it is just this moral and experiential vitality which is noticeably absent from *Last Post*, a novel markedly free of tension, uncertainty and moral conflict. Sylvia's surprise is the reader's too. 'It did not seem possible', Mrs Tietjens felt, 'that Christopher should settle down into tranquil devotion to brother and mistress after the years of emotion she had given him'. (*LP*, 293) Calm seems too easily won in *Last Post*; aspiration too smoothly transformed into achievement.

Tietjens' new occupation cannot really explain *Last Post*'s moral enervation, for there is no evidence that the private lives of furniture dealers and housewives are any less rich than those of landowning soldiers and school-mistresses. More significant is the change in location, from the crowded urban settings – and even those wartime scenes in the fields of France were closer to urban than to rural rhythms – to the sparsely populated Sussex countryside. Much of the novel, like the bulk of Ford's essays of this period, records, as in the passage that follows, the satisfactions available to a self-sufficient small-holder:

She [Marie Léonie, Tietjens' sister-in-law] went into the dark, warm, odorous depths of the hen-house-stable shed, the horse-box being divided off from the hen half by wire netting, nest-boxes, blankets extended on use-poles. She had to bend down to get into the hen half. The cracks of light between the uprights of the walls blinked at her. She carried the bowl of tepid water gingerly and thrust her hand into the warm hay hollows. The eggs were fever-heat or thereabouts; she turned them and sprinkled in the tepid water; thirteen, fourteen, fourteen, eleven – that hen was a breaker! – and fifteen. She emptied out the tepid water and from other nests took out egg after egg. The acquisition gratified her. (*LP*, 197)

This passage could be mistaken for the work of D. H. Lawrence – Miriam on her family's farm in *Sons and Lovers*, perhaps – but whereas in Lawrence's work this kind of writing, the detailed, affectionate evocation of simplicity, accompanies, even verifies, a full moral life, in *Last Post* the loving record of these rituals is pressed into duty as a *substitute* for the narration of moral struggle. Without any artistic justification in the earlier part of the quartet, such actions as the exercising of an old mare, the cutting of a hedge or the bottling of cider have suddenly been invested with a magic power to cure that social malaise so well analysed earlier. In the attention allocated to them they even threaten to dwarf the major human events of *Last Post* – Sylvia's visit to Christopher's retreat, leading to her decision to cease tormenting him, and the death of Mark Tietjens. Ford is asking us to accept that the tensions endemic to the relationship of Christopher and Valentine can be spirited away by their rural residence. Too much weight is being placed on the virtue of the countryside.

The earlier volumes in *Parade's End* had been built on the contradictions between man-as-individual and man-as-social being. However, now that Ford, faithful to historical reality, has demonstrated how this contradiction has been erased, he is left with the problem of imparting some significant vitality and purposefulness to the retirement of Christopher and Valentine. It is true that there is a continuing feud between the Tietjens brothers over Groby, but this struggle significantly is silent. Valentine describes it as a 'long chess-game' in which the brothers move their 'pieces' mutely. (*LP*, 319) Gesture indeed has replaced the verbalised conflicts of the earlier novels. In thus displacing the word – and so exemplifying Benjamin's theory of the incommunicability of modern experience – *Last Post* was reaching outwards to the frontiers of fiction itself. The problem is one of how to express the nihilistic, 'post-verbal' insights that were the legacy of the war – to Christopher, and especially to Mark, who had gone so far as to take a vow of silence – in a medium, fictional prose, so dependent on verbal textures. Certainly they could not be mediated through the device of the articulate central observer, employed in the previous volumes, and so the

novelist adopted the strategy of dividing *Last Post* among
several points of view: those of Mark and his wife, Valentine,
Sylvia, Christopher's son, and, briefly, his employees. The
inevitable consequence of this plurality of vision was a certain
diffuseness, the absence of that powerful, lucid focal-point
provided earlier by Christopher.

Ford, though, was by no means alone during the twenties
in trying to discover a new fictional structure to replace what
the war and its experiential consequences had made anachronistic. Indeed this search for new forms was the overriding
problem for the literature of that decade:

The feeling of surveying an existence without essence, a continuum without a structure, runs deep in the art [of the twenties]
and gives it a sense of internal strain – a certain terminal quality
in the writing which reveals that it is attempting to reach towards
the limits of language, the ultimate possibilities of form, the
extreme of an aesthetic order beyond time and history.[28]

Last Post is a further illustration of this tension, and its
artistic imperfections are finally indistinguishable from its
value as a cultural and historic record.

Ford's commitment there to values now called 'ecological',
the need for man to locate his life within natural rhythms
which he had attempted to destroy between 1914 and 1918,
was his attempt, one among many, to introduce some meaning into a demented world. Our disappointment with *Last
Post* doesn't result from any belief that Ford's philosophy
was mistaken, but from a suspicion that he was, in Lawrence's
metaphor, placing his thumb on the scales. In the preceding
novels human behaviour had emerged, as if naturally, from
the world the novelist had invented and set in motion. Now,
though, Ford seems to be imposing a structure of meaning
that has not germinated from the characters and their own
lives. It's strangely ironic that Ford's philosophy of the 'small
producer', the need for the individual to achieve economic
self-sufficiency and independence from large political and
commercial forces, should have made the allusive *Last Post*,
not the trenchant *Some Do Not...*, the most tendentious of

the quartet. The epilogue to *Parade's End* has customarily been seen as suffering from a lack of direction, from Ford's flight into 'romance'. On the contrary, its weakness is rather that, unlike the rest of the series, it is too nakedly preceptive in its desire to eulogise a way of life that in spirit is closer to Social Credit than to either of the period's extremisms, Fascism or communism.

Last Post, finally, marks a turning-point in Ford's career. For a decade between 1915 and 1926, in *The Good Soldier* and the first three sections of *Parade's End*, he had chosen to 'include the barbarity and immerse himself in it'. He had submitted to the 'destructive element' and had constructed from it a handful of major innovative novels.[29] Now, and for the remainder of his life, he will stand back to condemn it. For this willed isolation a price must be paid.

PART FOUR

1929–1939

1929–1939

Date	Novels	Prose	Poetry
1929	*No Enemy*	*The English Novel*	
1930			
1931	*When the Wicked Man*	*Return to Yesterday*	
1932			
1933	*The Rash Act*	*It was the Nightingale*	
1934	*Henry for Hugh*		
1935		*Provence*	
1936	*Vive Le Roy*		*Collected Poems*
1937		*Great Trade Route*	
1938		*Mightier than the Sword*	
		The March of Literature	

7

FORD'S LAST NOVELS: 'THE SMALL PRODUCER'

Sadly, the four novels of Ford's last years are beyond reclamation, though his criticism, *The English Novel* (1929) in particular, and his memoirs are still worth reading and are evidence of no loss of acumen or stamina. Ford's last book, *The March of Literature* (1938), was indeed, as Greene noted, positively 'Wellsian' in its scope and energy.[1] At one point in this remarkable survey of world literature from Babylon to the present there's a comment by Ford which may offer one clue to the weakness of his fiction in this decade. Discussing the poetry of the medieval troubadours and their creation of a substantial body of verse out of the slightest material, Ford digresses to the wider implications of that achievement. His argument is that the work of the minnesingers approached the ideal of all writers, 'absolute imaginative literature, using the word "absolute" in the sense that it is used by musicians'. Without stopping to prove that this is really the goal of all writers, Ford goes on to comment in terms that are plainly personal, claiming that

if you could read the secrets of the hearts of writers, you would find that every one of them in the end, in the spirit either of weariness or of aversion, craves enormously to write versified or cadenced words that shall have beauty and be almost without significance. You get tired of having to tell stories or to treat of subjects; the thought of words set in due order and of unchanging meaning seems to you intolerably fatiguing. You long to express yourself by means of pure sound as the musician can impress you and as nothing else can impress you, by a fugue that consists of nothing but notes. The one follows and mingles with the other but the whole has no meaning whatever. It depends solely on those sounds to influence your moods of the moment or such of your deeper emotions as may permanently affect your disposition. (*MOL*, 301)

Ford then finds a modern example of this quasi-musical technique in James Joyce, the true inheritor of the troubadours and a novelist 'whose content is of relatively little importance, the excitement in reading him coming almost entirely from his skill in juggling words as a juggler will play with many gilt balls at once'. (*MOL*, 302)

Ford's claim in this passage that musicality was the ambition of all verbal art, and his praise of the troubadours for having approximated to this condition mean that he was, in a sense, returning full-circle to the earliest influence, that of his father, for Francis Hueffer, as a lover of Provençal poetry and a distinguished music-critic, had combined both these ideals. Ford's admiration here for a verbal art 'without significance', of 'no meaning', and his aversion to 'stories', 'subjects', 'words set in due order', certainly marks a decisive break from his earlier respect for the art of Flaubert, Maupassant and James. These writers had appealed to him because of their full commitment to a fiction of meaning and human significance. Now, though, Ford sounds tired of the struggle with the obstinacy of language which had exercised him since his first meeting with Conrad in 1898. Certainly his argument here has an obvious connection with his career over the preceding forty years, that long devotion to 'stories' and 'subjects' having reached its climax in *Parade's End*. As late as 1929, when he published that excellent critical survey, *The English Novel*, Ford had been faithful to the novel's 'significance' and lineality, to fiction's importance as a mentor, remarking then that it was the novelist's aim to give his reader 'a better view of the complicated predicaments that surround him'. (*EN*, 21) In the first chapter of *The English Novel*, revealingly entitled 'Function', Ford had been at pains to stress the usefulness of fiction as the only medium for showing life whole. Thus in 1929 Ford had still believed in the novel's kinship with historical and sociological modes, whereas his comment in *The March of Literature* advertises his abandonment of that position. Now he aligns all the verbal arts with the non-verbal form of music.

Plainly, then, there was an important shift in Ford's thinking about the craft of fiction during the last decade of his life, and the results of this revaluation were discernible in the four novels he published during this period: *The Rash Act* (1933) and *Henry for Hugh* (1934), two parts of a proposed trilogy; *When the Wicked Man* (1931); and *Vive Le Roy* (1936). In all four works Ford is much less concerned with a tight plot and the delineation of firm characters in a coherent setting. And, as setting and characterisation become less stable, so elements of myth and romance, themes of. metamorphosis and rebirth, move to the fore. If Tietjens is thought of as Ford's 'Lear', these late novels recall *Cymbeline* and *Winter's Tale*. Yet alongside this modulation from 'novel' to 'romance' goes a vestigial interest in what Ford called 'subjects'. Thus the unfinished trilogy was plainly affected by the economic depression of the inter-war years. (*The Rash Act* was published nine days before Roosevelt closed the Banks.) Similarly *Vive Le Roy* is a response of some kind to the succession of French political crises which culminated in the fall of Daladier in February 1934. They do have their roots in contemporary history and Ford's last novels aren't really comparable with the 'fugal' *Finnegans Wake*. (Ford had the *Wake* in mind when he praised Joyce for his 'musicality', for although it wasn't published till 1939 Ford was familiar enough with the prototype, *Work in Progress*.) The weakness of these late novels can't, then, be ascribed to their lack of any important subject-matter. Nor can they simply be dismissed with the 'formalist' argument that Ford was unable to perfect the kind of non-linear, musical notation he admired in *Work in Progress* – which he had published as a supplement to the April 1924 number of *Transatlantic Review*. It's more likely that there was a conflict within Ford himself, as, on the one hand, he attempted to free himself, under the influence of *Finnegans Wake*, from fiction's historicism,

while, on the other, remaining absorbed in the task of trying
to explore contemporary realities through the form of the
novel. Some of this tension has been glimpsed earlier in *Last
Post*, where Ford found it hard to reconcile the pressure of
'words set in due order', that would round off the 'story' of
Christopher Tietjens, with his interest in the larger fugal
rhythms of birth and death.

Outside his fiction, though, many of Ford's energies were
certainly devoted to a commentary upon the world around,
his views being set out most fully in *Provence* and *Great
Trade Route*. At the heart of these books lies Ford's belief
that communities of small producers were the panacea for
economic disaster and for the polarisation of ideologies
between Fascism and communism. The small producer is
defined in *Great Trade Route* as

the man supporting himself and his family from his plot of ground
and by the work of his hands. . .the man who with a certain
knowledge of various crafts can set his hand to most kinds of work
that go to the maintenance of humble existences. . .above all, he
can produce and teach his family to produce good food according
to the seasons. . .[and] keep his household supplied independent
of the flux of currencies and the tides of world supplies – and. . .
have a surplus for his neighbours. He is the insurance premium of
his race. In short – a Man. (*GTR*, 188–9)

Since these words were first written in 1937 many events
have combined to reinforce our sense of the importance of
economic self-sufficiency and the immorality of waste. In
particular the 'energy crisis' of the seventies and the current
notion of 'spaceship earth' have made Ford's doctrines less
bizarre than they must have seemed forty years ago. And,
for all their weaknesses, *Provence* and *Great Trade Route*
also possess a certain Horatian charm, which is, in part, even
a function of the books' implausibilities. We can share what
Graham Greene, writing of *Provence*, called Ford's 'hilarious
depression', only because of the difficulty of attending
seriously to his philosophy.[2] Thus, although several of Ford's
darker imaginings have already come to pass, the two books

are full of local indifferences to fact and coherent argument.
For example, the dependence of his small communities upon
a sophisticated urban society seems to have escaped his attention: his communalists will, inexplicably, be able to enjoy
movies and cars made in a mysterious elsewhere. Similarly,
centres of political and economic power do exist in Ford's
utopia, but he doesn't attend to the question of who will
control such resources. Finally, as Greene again has noted,
the awkward facts that Hitler came from the *south* of Germany and that Italy was the first nation to break the post-war
peace hardly accord with Ford's confidence that the world
will be renewed from the southern shores of Europe. His
Provençal heaven was built upon the shakiest of foundations.

None of this would matter very much if Ford's beliefs had
inspired any major imaginative literature, in the way that
Lawrence's 'Dark Gods', Yeats' 'Byzantium' or the agrarian
simplicities of Eliot had creative results. But in Ford's case
his philosophy was barren: he wrote no fiction of major importance after *Parade's End*. The explanation for this sterility
doesn't lie in the improbability of his social criticism, for, as
the work of his contemporaries indicates, literature isn't
dependent upon a coherent and plausible ideology. Yet whatever we think about the politics of Yeats or Lawrence, we
cannot ignore the weight of feeling behind their private
myth-making. Superficially, too, *Provence* and *Great Trade
Route* would appear to be deeply felt responses to the era
of crisis. Ford's friend Douglas Goldring found in them
evidence of Ford's admiration for the working class, while
a contemporary reviewer discovered a 'passionate hatred
of cruelty and injustice, [a] profound sympathy with humanity'.[3]

However, on closer inspection it is precisely passion and
deep sympathy which is missing from all Ford's work in the
thirties. Thus the inaccuracies of detail and even of proposal
in *Provence* and *Great Trade Route* could be overlooked had
Ford there maintained a sense of perspective. Instead we

find that beneath his loathing of mechanisation and nationalism lie only the urges of the gourmet, so that the sole reference to 'the crisis' in *Provence* is seen in terms of its effect on
Tarascon cookery. Reality is trivialised when in the same
book Ford suggests that 'there is no hope for us unless we
reform the cooking at least of our rulers'. (*PROV*, 71) There
were larger problems in the thirties than the diet of the ruling
class. Similarly, Ford's claim that both Lenin and Stalin
supported his 'small producer' philosophy ignores their other,
more pressing claims on his attention. (*GTR*, 78–9) External
reality, the world of mass unemployment and genocide, only
impinges on Ford insofar as it can throw into relief the
compensatory delights of the Mediterranean littoral.

Ford's philosophy in these years was founded on 'the
gourmandisation of politics', the flattening of all ideological
conflicts into the question of the cultivation, preparation and
consumption of food. Yet Ford hadn't elected to ridicule the
problems of Europe as a 'front' for any covert support of
Fascism. On this count Ford's record, unlike some of his contemporary writers, is unblemished. (He publicly dissociated
himself from Franco and said about Hitler that he hoped his
end 'and soon – may be a long stay in a cage in the Tier-
garten of some small South German town'.[4] It is, then, a
serious oversimplification to claim that Ford's prejudices
'were tending toward fascism in politics'.[5] He had in fact
been much more authoritarian in the years immediately
before the war.

The truth is rather that Ford's hatred embraced *all* politicians and the whole spectrum of available systems in the
1930s. Consequently his ideal of communities of rural small-
holders living in ecological frugality was less an alternative
to, or even a rationalisation of the bestialities of Hitler and
Stalin than a refuge, a sanctuary from them. 'Aversion' and
'weariness', the two words he had used to describe the cause
of the novelist's retreat from 'significance', were exactly the
impulse behind Ford's social criticism of this period. The
comment by a contemporary that Ford and Janice Biala

'seemed to inhabit a closed world' (*Mizener*, 425) is immensely revealing here, for it corresponds to our feeling that all Ford's later writings, his social philosophy and his novels, were hermetically sealed from any contact with a living reality of exertion and disappointment. It was as if he wrote from a cocoon. Caroline Gordon's remark is also cognate with the metaphor Ford himself chose to describe art in *It was the Nightingale*. 'One's art', he wrote there, 'is a small enclosed garden within whose high walls one moves administering certain manures and certain treatments in order to get certain effects...say of saxifrages against granite.' (*IWN*, 127) The kitchen and the garden were the node of Ford's life and art after *Parade's End*, but beyond the 'high walls' lay strife and cruelty. Beyond them, too, existed the 'subjects' and 'stories' he had treated in *The Good Soldier* and the Tietjens novels, which were now being abandoned in favour of an art of 'pure sound'. Ford's life in his 'closed world' is, then, closely allied to the changes in his aesthetic and to his social beliefs. In all three areas the destructive element from which he had fashioned *Parade's End* was distanced by barriers behind which he cultivated the myth of an agrarian communalism and a fiction of improbability and incoherence. The myths of salvation woven by Yeats and Lawrence may have been unsalubrious, but they never lacked purposefulness or vitality. By contrast, Ford's work of this decade seems consistently deoxygenated.

Vive Le Roy (1936) exemplifies the difficulty of creating fiction in a 'walled garden'. The novel's insubstantiality, its air of willed fortuitousness, proves that the construction of narrative requires skills different from those involved in the juxtaposition of saxifrage and granite. The novel may be as ornamental as a flower-bed, but it lacks any solidity. Set in modern France during a Civil War between Royalists and Communists, *Vive Le Roy* tells how a courier from the New York Communist Party, Walter Leroy, is kidnapped by the Royalists and substituted for their dead king in order to stabilise the regime after the socialists' defeat. The Royalists are led by the benevolent de la Penthièvre and aim to establish France as a nation 'of rich peasant communities loosely linked under a central government presided over by an absolute monarch'. (*VLR*, 243) They are opposed from two sides – by the reactionaries, *les camelots du roi*, under the leadership of Meung, and by the Communists of M. Arzipanopov, a figure whose very name exemplifies Ford's confusion of ideology with gastronomy. There are one or two good episodes in *Vive Le Roy*, as there are in all the late novels – the scene in which the Communists, mistaking Leroy for the hated king, machine-gun his car; and the secret meeting of Leroy and his mistress in the vaults of an old Parisian church – but the novel as a whole is marred by its basic implausibilities. It's not credible that the likeable Leroy should suddenly abandon his 'humanitarian form of Communism' to cooperate with his Royalist captors. (*VLR*, 245) Nor does Ford trouble to explain how the Royalists will win over their recent opponents, of Left and of Right, and graft a pre-industrial organisation onto a twentieth-century, mechanised state. Process, political and personal development, which had been so firmly embodied in the first three volumes of *Parade's End* is scantily treated in all Ford's late novels.

Vive Le Roy, then, lacks any coherent centre, for it cannot be taken seriously either as a political novel or as a detective story. Ford admired the modern *roman policier*, especially Simenon's work,[6] and a Simenon novel is indeed used in *Vive Le Roy* to conceal the dollars Leroy is importing from New York. Yet Ford's novel lacks the tight spring of suspense developed in the best detective stories. At one point it even appears that Ford is using *Vive Le Roy* to parody Conrad's political fiction, for the improbable Arzipanopov carries a bomb in his pocket. But even as parody *Vive Le Roy* is limp – it was a form the versatile Ford never mastered – and it seems distinctly odd that Ford could have hoped to extract comic material from events as important as the Stavisky Scandal, the violent clashes on the Paris streets between Left and Right, or the General Strike of February 12, 1934.

Plainly these were what had 'inspired' Ford, though the manner of their fictional treatment suggests that Ford didn't quite believe in what was happening in France at that time. Malraux's *L'Espoir*, for example, was an energetic and serious response to contemporary history, whereas Ford offers us a pantomimic version of reality, diminishing and denaturing the world and even passing up the chance to develop his own communalist solutions in fictional terms. *Vive Le Roy*, then, is a failure, but a failure of a different kind from, say, *The Benefactor* or *A Call*, for in them could be seen an outline of what Ford had been attempting. With *Vive Le Roy*, and the other three late novels, it's very difficult to make out what Ford was aiming to achieve. All of them lack cohesiveness, dramatic intensity or narrative responsibility.

Nevertheless, analysis of the failure of these novels must be accompanied by recognition of the parallels between their *weaknesses* and what Ford felt to be the *strengths* of his agrarian utopia. The leisurely meanderings condemned in the novels are indeed analogous to that life of creative leisure Ford adumbrates in *Provence* and *Great Trade Route*. Here, in Ford's imagined worlds, his small producers would finish their work in field and vineyard and use the bulk of their time, all their afternoons and evenings 'and most of the winter months for the movies, the theatres, the concert halls, the churches, the night clubs, the dancing floors. . .for field sports, hitch-hiking, for distant travel. Or even for the Arts'. (*GTR*, 194) All this may be impossibly idealistic, but it's not far from the spirit of randomness and haphazardness characteristic of the *form* of his fiction in the thirties. There's no point in trying to salvage this fiction, yet it's worth noting that there is a real problem of fictional aesthetics in trying to embody the rhythms of creative langour in the form of the novel, with all its teleological assumptions.

Between *Last Post* and his death in 1939 Ford was concerned to advocate a very different kind of social order from that which had already led to one major war and was, he feared, going to produce a second. What he desired in its place was a community based on traditional observance and on political and religious stabilities; homogeneous rather than fissiparous, rural rather than urban. This ideal is close to Ferdinand Tonnies' *Gemeinschaft* social order, in which

men tend to function through traditional status arrangements, and to live by certain willing renunciations – by ideologies that encourage them to adjust to their lot, restrain excessive aspiration, and fulfil themselves through inherited roles, patterns of conduct, and a cohesive sense of community. They act and know one another through a series of face-to-face contacts, spread through various types of social occasion (work and religion, home and family). They share a more or less common culture or body of values, and have more need of religion than sociology.[7]

All this is strikingly like the kind of life Ford had designed for Tietjens and Valentine in *Last Post*, and which he had amplified in *Provence* and *Great Trade Route*. Its political implausibility is of secondary interest to the fact that a culture of this type had never articulated itself through the medium of the novel. *Gemeinschaft* societies have, rather, been celebrated in different artistic modes: those of the dance or of music, or, as with the Homeric epics and the Anglo-Saxon *Beowulf*, in the form of a highly stylised, formulaic poetry. Indeed in the conventional histories of western fiction the European novel is seen as a part of a widespread cultural revulsion from the *gemeinschaft* societies of feudalism. Certainly English fiction, from Defoe, Fielding and Richardson mediated an 'open' society, whose characteristic features weren't renunciation and restraint, but an aggressive mobility, aspiration, consumption and display.

At some stage in the late twenties Ford evidently decided that societies built on these principles of individualistic advancement and capitalist productivity, Max Weber's 'Protestant' cultures, were bankrupt. Like Lawrence, Ford searched for an alternative world, and found his particular solution in an idealised version of the life of the Provençal smallholder. The central unresolved artistic problem was bound up in the tension between the novel as a genre and the kind of life the fiction celebrated. Already this stress had been marked in *Parade's End*, where the historicist form of the first three volumes was unsuitable for rendering the communal and seasonal rhythms of *Last Post*. In the thirties, as Ford experimented with a verbal form that would possess the absolute freedom of music, these problems intensified, so that it's hardly surprising that his two travelogues should be superior to his fiction. In the rambling topographical essay Ford had the leisure to back-track, digress or stop for meditation. Even though these two books may be inaccurate and oversimplified, their form, the traveller's monologue, permitted Ford to capture something of the spirit of the world he was imagining, where the rhythms of work and leisure, in John Vaizey's words, 'were dictated by the seasons and the weather, and which reflected a ritual interpretation of life, with fiestas and fasts, high days and low days'.[8] However, when these cycles were given a narrative form they appeared only slack and enervated.

Ford, like Woolf and Lawrence, was searching for an extension of fiction that would lead the novel away from its sociological roots and in the direction of music or ritual. In Ford's case the exploration was in vain, but it does provide evidence of his refusal ever to remain satisfied with an achieved perfection. Thus after the Tudor trilogy he was never to return with any seriousness to the historical novel, nor did he attempt to write a novel like *The Good Soldier* merely to repeat that success. Notterdam, the hero of *When the Wicked Man*, has some similarity with Christopher Tietjens and this late novel could have been no more than a recapitulation of the theme of the victim hounded by his family and society. As such, *When the Wicked Man* might have proved a better novel than the one he actually wrote, but Ford was always ready to sacrifice success to exploration and experiment.

When he was buried in Deauville Cemetery in 1939, only three friends attended the funeral: by moving boldly onwards after *Parade's End* Ford had lost the audience the Tietjens novels had secured him. At his death he left unfinished a novel about the Leftist intelligentsia of the thirties. Its working title, 'Left Turn', is an appropriate memorial to a novelist who had spent his life espousing new directions for fiction, and in two works had led by example.

8

THE SHAPE OF AN ACHIEVEMENT

Despite the publication of several critical studies since 1961, as well as a massive biography, the stature of Ford Madox Ford remains disputable. On the one hand, his two best novels, *The Good Soldier* and *Parade's End*, now command substantial academic respect as works that have helped shape the way in which we perceive English culture in the first quarter of the century. On the other hand, though, their creator only merits passing references in a recent encyclopaedic survey of 'Modernism', a volume that includes quite full discussions of Joyce, Woolf and Conrad.[1] In an earlier generation it was perhaps the unevenness of Ford's private life, the personal and literary enmities he aroused, that worked against him. Now that these ripples have stilled maybe it's the unevenness of his *œuvre* that prevents the establishment of an assured reputation as a major modern novelist. Certainly the two outstanding works are surrounded by more than seventy texts, the majority long out of print. The importance of Ford's few successful novels, together with the innovative theories that, in the shadow of Gustave Flaubert and in the company of Joseph Conrad, he advanced at the turn of the century, have been decisively outweighed by the large undistinguished mass of his canon.

The cumulative effect of recent studies of the Ford–Conrad collaboration has been to question the older view that the partnership was grossly unequal; that Ford was merely valuable as an amanuensis to the great novelist and an improver of Conrad's broken English. Demonstrably Ford brought more to the collaboration than his skills as secretary and translator. Moreover, his kind of impressionism, which sought to render visual phenomena as a modern man would see them, was very different from Conrad's devotion to a symbolic, iconographical representation. One critic has even argued that in terms of their impact on modern fiction it is Ford, rather than the more celebrated Conrad, 'who must be seen as the more influential writer'.[2] Ford certainly had little interest in a slavishly literal rendering of the external world, the liberties he took with facts being the source of much of the hostility he aroused, and even when writing in non-fictional genres his approach was 'novelistic'. 'In a funda-mental and consistent way, everything he wrote was fiction.' (*Stang*, 130) Ford's impressionism, his determination to ren-der the impression made by fact on the mind rather than the literal truth, is as potent in the memoirs, essays and criticism as in the novels.

This recognition of Ford's importance as a theorist of modern fiction, as a harbinger of many later subjectivist experimentations, still leaves unsolved the curious problem of his unsettled reputation. If his theories were so boldly innovative and his practice in five texts so assured, why doesn't he now stand alongside the modern masters? Ford himself patently aspired to be affiliated with them, with James, Conrad and the modernists, and in these writers he invested a lifetime's admiration and affection. Yet the regu-larity with which he betrayed their austere ideals for fiction by publishing work that appeared to ignore both the theories he shared and had helped formulate, and the practice (*Nostromo*, *What Maisie Knew*) he had publicly applauded surely distinguishes Ford as a fundamentally different breed of novelist. His canon has been aptly described as 'the inces-sant outpourings of a polygraph',[3] and polygraphy was deeply antipathetic to the chaste prudential ideals of modernism. The economic pressures on Ford to publish incessantly were doubtless sharp enough – Mizener has documented them – but the argument that these forced him to produce too many 'pot-boilers' doesn't quite dispel the suspicion that his prolificacy had causes deeper than financial embarrassment. Economy and thrift were tenets central to the aesthetics of James and Conrad, and these Ford practised outstandingly in *The Good Soldier*. Nevertheless, the nature of his canon, the sheer bulk of his published work, the variety of topics to which he addressed himself and the plurality of modes adopted – the memoir, art-criticism, travelogue, children's books, the founded journals, as well as poetry and fiction – all this heterogeneity hints that Ford's creative energies were basically centrifugal. It suggests too that he might have written in this same manner, diffusely and prodigally, even had he been blessed with economic independence. The notion that all these books 'are in reality one gigantic book', each one a variation on the central theme, 'the problems of getting the modern world into focus, of acquiring historical perspective in a quickly changing world', is doubtless both attractive and useful in equipping the reader with a map to guide him through the maze of streets and side-streets that constitute Ford's legacy to us. (*Stang*, 6, 44) However, we still need to think about why Ford's preoccupation with continuity and tradition necessitated so many reworkings.

In a very early book, the biography of his grandfather the painter, Ford had begun to try to establish his place at the end of a long line of family innovators, traced back as far as Dr John Brown, a radical physician and contemporary of Austen and Scott. Thus even before his first meeting with Conrad in 1898 Ford was bent on marking himself as a potential revolutionary. Yet the record of his published work is curiously contradictory, for it suggests that his true affinities lay more with the prolific polemical authors of an earlier generation, with Ruskin or Carlyle, than with those radical contemporaries, James or Conrad, who above all valued introspection and self-denial, specialisation and reticence. Ford's attitude to the great Victorians was indeed always ambivalent, for, although they discomforted him, he never lost an acute sense that it was to the nineteenth century that he really belonged. Perhaps Ford was trying to combine two incompatible aesthetics – a modernist view of *art* committing him to self-effacement and withdrawal away from the text, alongside a Victorian notion of the *artist*'s duty as seer, prophet, teacher, commentator. The former belief helped him produce *Parade's End* and *The Good Soldier*, whereas the Victorian allegiance would account for the plurality and breadth of his *œuvre*.

The centrality of self in all Ford's work, irrespective of subject matter – that is, our inability ever quite to forget the presence of Ford the individual – distinguishes him from Conrad or James, and aligns him with Ruskin or Carlyle, Dickens or George Eliot. We can read the whole of *Nostromo* without being pressed to think about the relations between the text and the personality of the author whom we've met in the biographies of Karl or Baines. Conrad's own beliefs are diffused and refracted by the text. The 'Author's Note' and Conrad's comment there that 'My principal authority for the history of Costaguana is, of course, my venerated friend, the late Don José Avellanos' is the first of many attempts at authorial dissociation, the displacement of 'authority' away from Conrad himself.

Nostromo, then, lacks that compelling personal dimension always close to the surface of a Ford text. Graham Greene remarked upon our 'sense of Ford's involvement' in *The Good Soldier*. Here and in *Parade's End* Ford's presence behind or alongside Dowell, Ashburnham or Tietjens never departs from the text. Ford had no real ambition to withdraw, no sense of *literary* privacy, and, though he frequently acknowledged his debt to Flaubert, no ability to replicate the latter's self-abnegation. Ford certainly endorsed Flaubert's theory that the work was paramount, the author unimportant, but he never managed to practise the 'discipline', the 'perpetual sacrifice' that, as Flaubert wrote to George Sand, were necessary to authorial withdrawal. He couldn't match Flaubert's radical modesty, the consistent suppression of self. Ford's memoirs demonstrate that his rarefied upbringing among artists and musicians had implanted a very early self-consciousness. He was uncomfortably aware of having been born into 'a dynasty of highly-gifted celebrities' and his work suggests that he could never forget this pedigree.[4] As a result of this premature self-consciousness Ford always strikes us as a theatrical figure, a man ever aware of himself and the reverberations he 'produces' on those around him.

This is a trait of Christopher's character which, as we have seen, Ford caught very well in *Parade's End* (pp. 138–9, above). Ford was always successful in his portrayals of acute, studied self-consciousness, and the devices it employed to attract and maintain the observer's attention. Tietjens carrying a riding-whip and placing himself next to the stuffed animal-head is in this context exactly right, for he had been 'ridden' nearly to death by his wife's persecution. The novelist equipped Tietjens with his own theatrical sense of the perfect 'blocking' of a scene.

Similarly effective is Ford's account in *Return to Yesterday* of the casualness he affected in 1898 for his first encounter with Joseph Conrad:

Conrad came round the corner of the house. I was doing something at the open fireplace in the house-end. He was in advance of Mr Garnett who had gone inside, I suppose, to find me. Conrad stood looking at the view. His hands were in the pockets of his reefer-coat, the thumbs sticking out. His black, torpedo beard pointed at the horizon. He placed a monocle in his eye. Then he caught sight of me. I was very untidy, in my working clothes. He started back a little. I said: 'I'm Hueffer.' He had taken me for the gardener. (*RTY*, 52)

There's a strong impression here of artifice, of choreography, and all the novelist's heroes – Katharine Howard, Ashburnham, as well as Tietjens – were also fine actors, masters of gesture, pose and timing, through whom Ford demonstrated an understanding of the nature of theatricality and self-consciousness.

His own life, likewise, is a record of gestures struck and positions taken up. Even in his privacy and unguardedness he was prepared to meet a camera or an interviewer. His eccentricity was part of the public figure's sense of occasion, and observers noted these traits in Ford when he was still young and unknown. Olive Garnett recorded in her diary how her mother had called one day on Ford Madox Brown to see his latest painting. Ford, his grandson, would have been eighteen at this time. The visitor had asked the old man if he were going to begin another cartoon:

> Mr Brown said 'Yes, I see no reason why I should not begin, but my grandson Ford says that I must design a frontispiece for his novel, & that he can't wait, so I suppose I had better begin sketching it out tonight.' The frame of the picture is of wood covered with gilt Japanese paper so the people who did not know what to say admired it, which amused Ford immensely. He... *stood like an iceberg in the middle of the room & behaved with great ceremony.*[5]

Olive Garnett's view of the young novelist pre-empting the centre of the stage and compelling notice anticipates Ford's portrait of Tietjens' theatricality in the novel written thirty years later. Neither James nor Conrad was the epitome of modesty, but their conceits don't impinge upon their fiction as Ford's constantly did. Like the iceberg in the drawing-room, Ford is always a felt presence in his fiction. This determination to dominate, the preoccupation with establishing his own character, with 'making an impression', the inability to displace or camouflage his private obsessions, is closely connected with the prolixity and plurality of his output. It was as if he had to 'have his say' on everything.

Such egoism, which perhaps hid a deep unconfidence, the unease of an immigrant's son, is now only of concern in so far as it affected the novels. In the fictional techniques employed, *The Good Soldier* and *Parade's End* may be two, very different, monuments of modernism. They represent, respectively, the aggressive and the assimilative strains in the movement. Yet they are successful not because Ford there managed any Flaubertian self-effacement, but rather because he found a way of expressing through them the tensions of his own life

different values, absolutist, idealist, and unfashionable.
During the same period, between about 1910 and 1927,
Forster and Lawrence were also active in criticising the
sexual and economic hegemony, yet they differed essentially
from Ford in being able to draw sustaining values from outside the dominant culture – from the Schlegel sisters or from
Birkin. Ford, though, employed parodistic versions of the
ruling class itself as a means of delineating the moral inertia
of the powerful.

This method is exemplified in the conversation between
General Campion and Sylvia Tietjens in *No More Parades*,
where Campion is interrogating the dishonoured wife about
her husband's principles:

'. . .But what, then, is it that Christopher has said?. . .Hang it all:
what *is* at the bottom of that fellow's mind?. . .'
    'He desires,' Sylvia said, and she had no idea when she said it,
'to model himself upon Our Lord. . .'
    The general leant back in the sofa. He said almost indulgently:
'Who's that. . .Our *Lord?*'
    Sylvia said:
    'Upon Our Lord Jesus Christ. . .'
He sprang to his feet as if she had stabbed him with a hat-pin.
    'Our. . .' he exclaimed. 'Good God!. . .I always knew he had a
screw loose. . .But. . .' He said briskly: 'Give all his goods to the
poor!. . .But He wasn't a. . .not a socialist! What was it He said:
Render unto Caesar. . .It wouldn't be necessary to drum Him out
of the army. . .' He said: 'Good Lord!. . .Good Lord!. . .Of course
his poor dear mother was a little. . .But, hang it!. . .The Wannop
girl!. . .' Extreme discomfort overcame him. . .Tietjens was half-
way across from the inner room, coming towards them. (*NMP*, 417)

This episode, a scene of magnificent high comedy, demonstrates that the values of a Christian civilisation, which
Campion purports to be defending against German 'barbarism', really reside in Christopher, the pariah of the establishment. Ford's tactics, then, were hyperbolic: he drew stylised,
exaggerated pictures of the dominant class in order to portray
its moral bankruptcy. As Walter Benjamin remarked of
Baudelaire, Ford was a 'secret agent' of the social and political order – a 'mole' – destroying from within, rather than, as

Forster and Lawrence did, from without.[10] By overstating
the chivalric disinterestedness of his harried heroes Ford
recorded the self-interest of the rulers.

Ford's style of perception and notation is, then, frankly
non-mimetic, metaphorical. His methods of characterisation
– of himself and of his fictional creations – are close to those
of the caricaturist. His novels weren't intended as precise
renderings of the external world of the realists. Ford's
memoirs, too, portray the past as he himself saw it, in preference to any objective photographic version. His weakest
novels are ineffective just because they seem so private,
quirky and lacking in any public reverberations. We have no
means of 'naturalizing' *Mr Apollo* or *The New Humpty-
Dumpty* because we can't discern how these two texts might
be set against any real world.[11] Here Ford had invested so
heavily in the depiction of extreme and violent mental states
that when these failed to resonate, the reader has nothing
else on which to fall back. On the other hand, his indubitably
major work, *The Good Soldier* and *Parade's End*, succeeds
because the embattled mental conditions there presented
epitomised certain sectional or national neuroses of the time.
It was, in other words, no accident that *The Good Soldier*
coincided with a period of acute pre-war crisis for a particular
class, nor that the Tietjens cycle, likewise, depicted an
abnormally dangerous national emergency. In both instances,
Ford's eccentric, highly subjective vision overlapped more
widely held structures of feeling and experience.

The relative infrequency with which Ford managed to
create novels of such permanence – though most novelists of
any age would be content to have written *The Good Soldier*
or *Parade's End* – may, then, be attributed to the kind of
novelist he was, rather than to the personal vicissitudes of his
life, to the marital entanglements and persistent insolvency
documented by Mizener. Ford in truth was an 'expressionist'
artist in his revulsion from science – the single subject of which
he invariably claimed ignorance – and the triumphs of the
bourgeois state. He saw the Germany created by Bismarck

as a nightmare of the modern world, and feared England was rushing down a parallel slope, propelled by the Fabians and Social Imperialists satirised in *The Inheritors*. In revulsion Ford turned inwards and made his own feelings – particularly the notion of a pristine honour defending itself against intrigue, calumny and pragmatism – the true subject-matter of his work. His cavalier attitude towards facts and history was a part of this movement inwards, away from the external world. Such expressionist subjectivity, however, often ran counter to the deepest impulses and conventions of Ford's preferred form, for, of all genres the novel is most closely affiliated with the history Ford was rejecting: 'the notions of narrative, of character, and of formal unity in fiction are all congruent with the system of concepts making up the Western idea of history'.[12] Ford's unsuccessful novels disturbed fiction's intimacy with history, while his handful of major works resulted from an ability to project his inner visions and link them with historical developments. Thus the nightmares of Ashburnham in 1914 and of Tietjens between 1912 and 1920 were expressive of the widespread convulsions of that era. German expressionism was deeply implicated in war, revolution and cultural crisis. Similarly it was no co-incidence that Ford's lasting achievements as an expressionist novelist were also the product of a decade of acute public upheaval. His best work required historical crises to validate the novelist's inner disjunctions.

NOTES

1. The early years

1 The main source that I have used for Ford's life is *Mizener*.
2 Letter from Conrad to Ford of November 1898, cited in *Mizener*, p. 18.
3 Preface to *The Nigger of the 'Narcissus'*, reprinted in M. D. Zabel, ed., *The Portable Conrad* (New York, 1968), p. 707.
4 *Ibid.*, p. 706.
5 H. Stuart Hughes, *Consciousness and Society: The Reorientation of European Social Thought, 1890–1930* (New York, 1958), p. 37.
6 Zabel, *Conrad*, p. 707 (italics added).
7 Hughes, *Consciousness and Society*, p. 66.
8 Zabel, *Conrad*, p. 708.
9 'Editor's Introduction', Zabel, *Conrad*, p. 8.
10 Hugh Kenner, 'Conrad and Ford', *Shenandoah*, iii (Summer 1952), 50–5, cited in *Harvey*, pp. 449–50.
11 Frederick R. Karl, 'Conrad, Ford, and the novel', *Midway*, x, ii (Autumn 1969), 23.
12 Zabel, *Conrad*, p. 705 (italics added).
13 *Ibid.*, p. 706.
14 Hugh Kenner, 'Remember that I have remembered', *Hudson Review*, iii (Winter 1951), 602–11. This offers a serviceable summary of their views on fiction.
15 Zabel, *Conrad*, p. 705.
16 *Ibid.*, p. 706.
17 Beatrice Webb, *Our Partnership* (London, 1948), p. 222.
18 *Ibid.*, p. 84.
19 *Ibid.*, p. 107.
20 *Ibid.*, p. 299.
21 *Ibid.*, p. 117.
22 Richard Shannon, *The Crisis of Imperialism 1865–1915* (London, 1974), p. 142.
23 Robert J. Scally, *The Origins of the Lloyd George Coalition* (Princeton, 1975), p. 16.
24 Bernard Semmel, *Imperialism and Social Reform: English Social–Imperial Thought 1895–1914* (London, 1960), p. 63 (italics added).
25 Shannon, *Imperialism*, p. 251.

26 M. M. Mahood, 'Conrad and the Duke of Brabant', 4. Paper delivered to the Second International Conference of Conrad Scholars, University of London: September 1972.
27 Shannon, *Imperialism*, p. 315.
28 Scally, *Lloyd George Coalition*, p. 9.
29 *Ibid.*, p. 4.
30 *Independent*, LIII (31 October 1901), cited in *Harvey*, p. 281.
31 Scally, *Lloyd George Coalition*, p. 12.
32 Shannon, *Imperialism*, pp. 269, 276.
33 H. G. Wells, *The New Machiavelli* (Harmondsworth, 1966), p. 112.
34 Hughes, *Consciousness and Society*, pp. 358–9.
35 Articles by Graham and Hobson from the Left were offset by Arthur Marwood's definition of the 'tory utopia', in which every employee would be given £400 p.a. and a plot of land: *ER*, I, i (December 1908), 159; *GTR*, pp. 407–8.
36 Anon, 'Ford as others saw him', *The Times Literary Supplement*, 3662 (5 May 1972), 519.
37 *RTY*, p. 80 has a comment on London's poor. On Ford and Lawrence, see John Beer, 'Ford's impression of the Lawrences', *The Times Literary Supplement*, 3662 (5 May 1972), 520: 'the general impression which is given [in *RTY* is] of the breadth of thought and discussion in some English provincial areas during the years before the First World War'. On the culture of Lawrence and Eastwood, see also Donald Davie, 'Dissent in the present century', *The Times Literary Supplement*, 3899 (3 December 1976), 1519–20.

2. The 'Fifth Queen' trilogy

1 I am drawing here on Frank Kermode's valuable discussion of *The Good Soldier* in 'Novels: recognition and deception', *Critical Inquiry*, I (September 1974), 103–21.
2 Douglas Goldring, *The Last Pre-Raphaelite: A Record of the Life and Writings of Ford Madox Ford* (London, 1948), p. 114.
3 'Introduction', *The Bodley Head Ford Madox Ford* (London, 1962), p. 10.
4 Avrom Fleishman, *The English Historical Novel: Walter Scott to Virginia Woolf* (Baltimore, 1971), p. 210.
5 M. D. Zabel, *Craft and Character in Modern Fiction* (London, 1957), p. 254.
6 Frank Kermode, *The Sense of an Ending* (New York, 1967), p. 112.
7 Georg Lukács, *The Historical Novel* (Harmondsworth, 1969), p. 197.
8 Irving Howe, *Politics and the Novel* (New York, 1967), p. 25.
9 Fleishman, *English Historical Novel*, p. 211.
10 George Plekhanov, *The Role of the Individual in History* (New York, 1940), p. 41.
11 Marx and Engels, *The Communist Manifesto* (Harmondsworth, 1967), p. 82.
12 Georg Lukács, *Studies in European Realism* (London, 1950), p. 145.

13　Samuel Hynes, 'Ford and the spirit of romance', *Modern Fiction Studies*, IX, i (Spring 1963), 22.

14　Cited in Goldring, *Last Pre-Raphaelite*, p. 137.

3. Georgian pessimism

1　G. D. H. Cole and R. Postgate, *The Common People, 1746–1946* (London, 1949), p. 450.

2　David Thomson, *England in the Nineteenth Century, 1815–1914* (Harmondsworth, 1951), ch. IX.

3　L. Stevenson, *Yesterday and After* (New York, 1967), p. 78. (Volume XI of E. A. Baker, *A History of the English Novel*.)

4　In a letter of November 1909 Lawrence had written that *CALL* 'has more art than life': *Harvey*, p. 549. Bennett, in a very intelligent review, had admired the novel's fairy-tale qualities, but found it unrealistic: 'I consider "A Call" to be profoundly and hopelessly untrue to life. It treats of the lazy rich. . .Mr Hueffer endows these persons with a comprehensive fineness of perception, and a skill in verbal expression, which it is absolutely impossible that they, living the life they do live, could possess. . .But regard "A Call" as an original kind of fairy tale, and it is about perfect'. *New Age*, VI (17 March 1910), cited in *Harvey*, p. 303. The whole review is conveniently reprinted in Frank MacShane, ed., *Ford Madox Ford: The Critical Heritage* (London, 1972), pp. 33–5.

5　Richard Shannon, *The Crisis of Imperialism 1865–1915* (London, 1974), p. 447.

6　*Ibid.*

7　H. Stuart Hughes, *Consciousness and Society: The Reorientation of European Social Thought 1890–1930* (New York, 1958), p. 365.

8　H. G. Wells, *The New Machiavelli* (Harmondsworth, 1966), p. 39.

9　*Ibid.*, p. 205.

10　*Ibid.*, p. 387.

11　*Ibid.*, p. 267.

12　Bernard Bergonzi, 'Before 1914: Writers and the threat of war', *Critical Quarterly*, VI, ii (Summer 1964), 126–34.

13　Shannon, *Imperialism*, p. 272.

14　*Ibid.*, p. 279.

15　'Literary Portraits – XVIII: Mr A. G. Gardiner and "Pillars of Society" ', *Outlook*, XXXIII (10 January 1914), 46–7, cited in *Harvey*, p. 182.

16　*Outlook*, XXXIII (30 May 1914), 751–2, cited in *Harvey*, p. 190.

17　Robert J. Scally, *The Origins of the Lloyd George Coalition* (Princeton, 1975), p. 245.

18　*Outlook*, XXXIV (29 August 1914), 270–1, cited in *Harvey*, pp. 199–200.

19　*Outlook*, XXXIV (19 September 1914), 367–8, cited in *Harvey*, p. 201.

20　Beatrice Webb, *Our Partnership* (London, 1948), p. 97.

21　Richard Burdon Haldane, *An Autobiography* (London, 1929), pp. 212–13.

22　*Outlook*, XXXV (2 January 1915), 14–15, and XXXV (9 January 1915), 46–7, cited in *Harvey*, p. 203.

23 Douglas Goldring, *The Last Pre-Raphaelite – A Record of the Life and Writings of Ford Madox Ford* (London, 1948), p. 202.

24 Leon Trotsky, *Literature and Revolution* (New York, 1957), p. 45.

25 Richard M. Ludwig, ed., *Letters of Ford Madox Ford* (Princeton, 1965), p. 287. The letter is dated February 1938.

4. *'The Good Soldier'*

1 John Berger, *G* (Harmondsworth, 1973), p. 40.

2 Richard Shannon, *The Crisis of Imperialism 1865–1915* (London, 1974), pp. 269, 276–7.

3 'Literary Portraits – xx: Mr Gilbert Cannan and "Old Mole"', *Outlook*, xxxiii (24 January 1914), 110–11, cited in *Harvey*, p. 183.

4 David Lodge, *The Modes of Modern Writing* (London, 1977), pp. 75–7, 81, 84–5 and 91–3.

5 'Literary Portraits – xx', *Harvey*, p. 183.

6 Stuart Hampshire, 'Joyce and Vico: the middle way', *New York Review of Books*, xx, xvi (18 October 1973), 8–21.

7 Mark Schorer, *'The Good Soldier*: a tale of passion', *The World We Imagine* (London, 1969), pp. 97–104.

8 Joseph Frank, 'Spatial form in modern literature', *Sewanee Review*, liii, ii (Spring 1945), 221–40; liii, iii (Summer 1945), 433–56; liii, iv (Autumn 1945), 643–53. For a reply to Frank, see Walter Sutton, 'The literary image and the reader', *Journal of Aesthetics and Art Criticism*, xvi, i (1957–8), 112–23. Frank has recently made another contribution to the debate he began in 1945, offering an amplification and defence of his original essay in 'Spatial form: an answer to the critics', *Critical Inquiry*, iv, ii (Winter 1977), 231–52.

9 Frank, 'Spatial form', 653.

10 *Ibid.*

11 Malcolm Bradbury, *The Social Context of Modern English Literature* (Oxford, 1971), pp. 104–5.

12 Bernard Bergonzi, 'Thoughts on the personality explosion', *Innovations* (London, 1968), p. 186. It is interesting to note how many critics describe *The Good Soldier* in plastic and visualist metaphors, as a 'kaleidoscope', 'a relentless spiral', 'a hall of mirrors', and an 'intellectual construct. . .in a literary mathematics': Walter Allen, *The English Novel* (Harmondsworth, 1958), p. 329; *Meixner*, p. 151; Schorer, 'A tale of passion', p. 98; *Wiley*, p. 78.

13 'Literary portraits – xxxvi: Les Jeunes and "Des Imagistes"', *Outlook*, xxxiii (16 May 1914), 682–3 (emphasis added), cited in *Harvey*, p. 189.

14 William C. Wees, *Vorticism and the English Avant-Garde* (Manchester, 1972), pp. 177, 190, 191.

15 Frank Kermode, *The Sense of an Ending* (New York, 1967), p. 123. Kermode offers a fuller treatment in 'Novels: recognition and deception', *Critical Inquiry*, i (September 1974), 103–21.

16 Wylie Sypher, *Loss of the Self in Modern Literature and Art* (New York, 1962), pp. 62, 62–3. I am also indebted to Sypher's *Rococo to*

Cubism in Art and Literature (New York, 1960), and to John Berger, 'The moment of Cubism', *Selected Essays and Articles* (Harmondsworth, 1972).

17 Berger, 'Cubism', p. 150.
18 Schorer, 'A tale of passion', p. 104; Sypher, *Rococo*, p. 269.
19 Kermode, 'Novels: recognition and deception', 111. For an alternative, more 'traditional' reading, see Denis Donoghue, 'A reply to Frank Kermode', *Critical Inquiry*, i (December 1974), 447–52.
20 Sypher, *Rococo*, p. 306.
21 Bernard Bergonzi, *The Situation of the Novel* (London, 1970), p. 132.
22 Geoffrey Wagner, 'Ford Madox Ford: the honest Edwardian', *Essays in Criticism*, xvii (January 1967), 75–88.
23 *Letters of Henry James*, ed. Percy Lubbock, 2 vols (New York, 1920), vol. ii, 384. Letter dated 14 August 1914.
24 Stephen Spender, *The Destructive Element* (London, 1937), p. 14.
25 H. Stuart Hughes, *Consciousness and Society: The Reorientation of European Social Thought, 1890–1930* (New York, 1958), p. 338.
26 Samuel Hynes, 'The epistemology of *The Good Soldier*', *Sewanee Review*, lxix (Spring 1961), 225–35.
27 L. W. Jones, 'The quality of sadness in Ford's *The Good Soldier*', *English Literature in Transition*, xiii, iv (1970), 296–302.
28 J. Wiesenfarth, 'Criticism and the semiosis of *The Good Soldier*', *Modern Fiction Studies*, ix, i (Spring 1963), 39–49.
29 I borrow the phrase from Terry Eagleton's discussion of Conrad in *Exiles and Emigrés: Studies in Modern Literature* (London, 1970).
30 Edmund Wilson, *Axel's Castle* (London, 1961), p. 154.
31 E. B. Burgum, *The Novel and the World's Dilemma* (New York, 1947), pp. 39–40.
32 Hynes, 'Epistemology', 225–35.
33 Kermode, *The Sense of an Ending*, p. 113.
34 Raymond Williams, *The Country and the City* (London, 1973), p. 249.
35 'Dedicatory letter to Stella Ford', written for a later edition of *The Good Soldier* on 9 January 1927. The letter is included in the recent paperback edition of *The Good Soldier* (Harmondsworth, 1972).
36 Lionel Trilling, *The Liberal Imagination* (London, 1951), p. 270.
37 Dreiser's review is reprinted in Frank MacShane, ed., *Ford Madox Ford: The Critical Heritage* (London, 1972), pp. 47–51.
38 V. S. Pritchett, 'The Good Soldier', *New Statesman* (5 May 1972), 599.
39 Hicks' notice, like Dreiser's, is reprinted in MacShane, *Critical Heritage*, pp. 194–204. It was first published in *Bookman*, lxxii (December 1930), 364–70, under the title 'Ford Madox Ford – a neglected contemporary'.
40 Letter addressed to Mrs Lucy Masterman in Richard M. Ludwig, ed., *Letters of Ford Madox Ford* (Princeton, 1965), p. 54.

5. The novelist of reconstruction

1 R. M. Ludwig, ed., *Letters of Ford Madox Ford* (Princeton, 1965), p. 295. The letter was dated June 1938.
2 *Transatlantic Review*, ii, iv (October 1924), 398.
3 Alec Waugh, cited in Douglas Goldring, *The Last Pre-Raphaelite – A Record of the Life and Writings of Ford Madox Ford* (London, 1948), p. 218.
4 Margaret Cole has attested to Ford's love of freedom and how in 1920 he was directing 'a propaganda campaign against the Black-and-Tans and the English occupation of Ireland': *Growing Up Into Revolution* (London, 1949), pp. 82–3. Douglas Goldring, too, wrote of Ford's passionate reaction to Irish atrocities and of his leading part in producing a writers' manifesto: *Odd Man Out: The Autobiography of a 'Propaganda Novelist'* (London, 1935), p. 209. See further, *Harvey*, pp. 500, 523–4.
5 'Preparedness', *New York Herald Tribune Magazine* (6 November 1927), 18, cited in *Harvey*, p. 248.
6 John I. Finlay, *Social Credit: The English Origins* (Montreal, 1972), p. 174. For a discussion of Pound and Social Credit, see Hugh Kenner, *The Pound Era* (London, 1972), pp. 407–13.
7 Finlay, *Social Credit*, p. 254.
8 *Transatlantic Review*, ii, i (July 1924), 69.
9 D. H. Lawrence, *Kangaroo* (Harmondsworth, 1950), p. 240.
10 *The Times Literary Supplement* (10 May 1923), 320, cited in *Harvey*, p. 339.
11 Bernard Bergonzi, *Heroes' Twilight: A Study of the Literature of the Great War* (London, 1965), p. 144.

6. 'Parade's End'

1 Both the phrase and the illustrations are taken from Barbara Hardy, *The Appropriate Form* (London, 1964).
2 George Core, 'Ordered life and the abysses of chaos: *Parade's End*', *Southern Review*, viii, iii (July 1972), 527.
3 Terry Eagleton, *Exiles and Emigrés: Studies in Modern Literature* (London, 1970), pp. 10, fn. 1, and 189.
4 Clifton P. Fadiman, Review of *The Good Soldier*, *Nation*, cxxiv (20 April 1927), 451–2, cited in *Harvey*, p. 372.
5 Review of *Parade's End*, *Tomorrow*, x (November 1950), 53–5, cited in *Harvey*, pp. 445–6.
6 *A Man Could Stand Up–* (Harmondsworth, 1948), p. 12. The various Dedications were not reprinted in the New American Library edition.
7 W. H. Auden, 'Il faut payer', *Mid-Century*, xxii (February 1961), 3–10, cited in *Harvey*, p. 467.
8 The passage is invoked by Dr Leavis in his essay on *Nostromo* in *The Great Tradition* (Harmondsworth, 1966), p. 216.
9 Bernard Bergonzi, *Heroes' Twilight: A Study of the Literature of the Great War* (London, 1965), p. 177.

10 Fredric Jameson, *Marxism and Form* (Princeton, 1971), p. 204. Jameson is attributing this view to Lukács' reading of Balzac and Tolstoy.
11 Walter Benjamin, *Illuminations*, ed. Hannah Arendt (London, 1970), p. 84.
12 Jean Duvignaud, *The Sociology of Art* (London, 1972), p. 122.
13 Erich Auerbach, *Mimesis: The Representation of Reality in Western Literature* (Princeton, 1953), p. 547.
14 Raymond Williams, *The Long Revolution* (London, 1961), p. 286.
15 *Ibid.*
16 Bergonzi, *Heroes' Twilight*, p. 176.
17 James M. Heldman, 'The last Victorian novel: technique and theme in *Parade's End*', *Twentieth Century Literature*, xviii (October 1972), 271–84.
18 *Ibid.*, 283.
19 John McCormick, *Catastrophe and Imagination* (London, 1957), p. 220.
20 Keith Douglas, 'Poets in this war', [? May 1943] *The Times Literary Supplement*, 3608 (23 April 1971), 478.
21 Hugh Kenner, 'Remember that I have remembered', *Hudson Review*, iii (Winter 1951), 602–11, cited in *Harvey*, p. 448.
22 Burton Rascoe, Review of *No More Parades*, *Arts and Decoration*, xxiv (February 1926), 57, cited in Frank MacShane, ed., *Ford Madox Ford: The Critical Heritage* (London, 1972), p. 100.
23 Actually many readers would find the largely 'realistic' *Some Do Not . . .* quicker to read than *Last Post*.
24 *Last Post* had been in Ford's mind in 1924–5, when, in the Preface to *No More Parades*, he had written of his wish to show Tietjens 'in process of being re-constructed'. Similarly, the Preface to *A Man Could Stand Up* – states quite plainly that a final part is to follow. This is contradicted by his important letter to Pinker of August 1930, in which he also suggested the title *Parade's End*. Here he stated, 'I strongly wish to omit the *Last Post* from the edition. I do not like the book and have never liked it and always [*sic*] intended the series to end with *A Man Could Stand Up*': *Letters of Ford Madox Ford*, ed. Richard M. Ludwig (Princeton, 1965), pp. 196–7. However, in an earlier letter, of November 1927, he had described *Last Post* as 'the last of the Tietjens series' (*ibid.*, p. 174), and five years later, *after* the disclaimer to Pinker, he is writing about the 'Tietjens tetralogy [*sic*]' (*ibid.*, p. 208).
25 Samuel Hynes, 'Ford Madox Ford: three dedicatory letters to *Parade's End* with commentary and notes', *Modern Fiction Studies*, xvi, iv (Winter 1970), 515–28.
26 Malcolm Bradbury, *Possibilities: Essays on the State of the Novel* (London, 1973), p. 138.
27 The terms and definitions are taken from C. B. Cox, *The Free Spirit* (London, 1963), p. 10.
28 Bradbury, *Possibilities*, p. 90.
29 Malcolm Bradbury, *The Social Context of Modern English Literature* (Oxford, 1971), p. 97.

7. Ford's last novels

1 Graham Greene, Review of *The March of Literature*, *Spectator*, CLXIII (17 November 1939), cited in *Harvey*, p. 429.

2 Graham Greene, Review of *Provence*, *London Mercury*, XXXIX (December 1938), 217–18, cited in *Harvey*, p. 422.

3 Douglas Goldring, *South Lodge* (London, 1943), pp. 220–1; A. G. Macdonnell, Review of *Great Trade Route*, *Observer* (17 January 1937), 4, cited in *Harvey*, p. 409.

4 *Harvey*, p. 100; *Provence*, p. 332; Douglas Goldring, *The Last Pre-Raphaelite – A Record of the Life and Writings of Ford Madox Ford* (London, 1948), p. 271.

5 Lionel Stevenson, *Yesterday and After* (New York, 1967), p. 86; the comment was made about *Vive Le Roy*.

6 *Mightier than the Sword*, p. 95; *The March of Literature*, p. 759.

7 The account is taken from Malcolm Bradbury, *The Social Context of Modern English Literature* (Oxford, 1971), p. 9.

8 John Vaizey, *Revolutions of Our Time: Capitalism* (London, 1971), p. 97.

8. The shape of an achievement

1 Malcolm Bradbury and James McFarlane, eds., *Pelican Guides to European Literature: Modernism 1890–1930* (Harmondsworth, 1976).

2 Lawrence Thornton, 'Deux bonshommes distincts: Conrad, Ford, and the visual arts', *Conradiana*, VIII (1976), 11.

3 M. D. Zabel, *Craft and Character in Modern Fiction* (London, 1957), p. 259.

4 Douglas Goldring, *The Last Pre-Raphaelite: A Record of the Life and Writings of Ford Madox Ford* (London, 1948), p. 18.

5 Thomas C. Moser, 'From Olive Garnett's diary: impressions of Ford Madox Ford and his friends, 1890–1906', *Texas Studies in Literature and Language*, XVI, iii (Fall 1974), 516 (italics added).

6 Bernard Bergonzi, *The Turn of a Century: Essays on Victorian and Modern English Literature* (London, 1973), p. 145.

7 Terry Eagleton, *Exiles and Emigrés: Studies in Modern Literature* (London, 1970), p. 15.

8 *Ibid.*, p. 18.

9 'Literary Portraits – LV: Trimalchio', *Outlook*, XXXIV (26 September 1914), 399–400, cited in *Harvey*, p. 202. A lengthy extract was cited and discussed in Chapter 3, p. 77, above.

10 Walter Benjamin, *Charles Baudelaire: A Lyric Poet in the Era of High Capitalism* (London, 1973), p. 104, fn. 1.

11 I take the concept of 'naturalization' from Jonathan Culler, *Structuralist Poetics* (London, 1975), ch. VII.

12 J. Hillis Miller, 'Narrative and history', *English Literary History*, XLI, iii (Fall 1974), 461.

BIBLIOGRAPHY

Primary sources

There is no 'Collected Edition' of Ford's works, and only a handful are regularly in print. Many were published in both America and Britain; and by a large variety of publishers. The lists below, which are based on Harvey's *Bibliography*, indicate details of first American edition, first British edition, edition referred to in this study wherever this is not the first British Edition. Place of publication, unless stated, is New York or London. Superscript numerals refer to the notes at the end of this section.

Title	American edition	British edition	Edition used
Ford Madox Brown, A Record of his Life and Work		Longman's Green, 1896	
The Cinque Ports, A Historical and Descriptive Record		Blackwood, 1900	
The Inheritors, An Extravagant Story	McClure, Phillips, 1901	Heinemann, 1901	N.Y.: Doubleday, Page, 1924
Rossetti, A Critical Essay on his Art	Dutton, 1902	Duckworth, 1902	N.Y.: Rand, McNally, 1915
Romance, A Novel	McClure, Phillips, 1904	Smith, Elder, 1903	N.Y.: Doubleday, Page, 1924
The Soul of London, A Survey of a Modern City		Alston Rivers, 1905	
The Benefactor, A Tale of a Small Circle		Brown, Langham, 1905	
Hans Holbein the Younger, A Critical Monograph	Dutton, 1905	Duckworth, 1905	Chicago: Rand, McNally, 1914
The Fifth Queen, And How She Came to Court		Alston Rivers, 1906	London: Bodley Head, 1962

Title	American edition	British edition	Edition used
The Heart of the Country, A Survey of a Modern Land		Alston Rivers, 1906	
Privy Seal, His Last Venture		Alston Rivers, 1907	London: Bodley Head, 1962
England and the English, An Interpretation[1]	McClure, Phillips, 1907		N.Y.: McClure, Phillips, 1907
An English Girl, A Romance		Methuen, 1907	
The Pre-Raphaelite Brotherhood, A Critical Monograph	Dutton, 1907	Duckworth, 1907	
The Spirit of the People, An Analysis of the English Mind		Alston Rivers, 1907	
The Fifth Queen Crowned, A Romance		Eveleigh Nash, 1908	London: Bodley Head, 1962
Mr Apollo, A Just Possible Story		Methuen, 1908	
The 'Half-Moon', A Romance of the Old World and the New	Doubleday, Page, 1909	Eveleigh Nash, 1909	N.Y.: Doubleday, Page, 1909
A Call, The Tale of Two Passions		Chatto and Windus, 1910	
The Portrait		Methuen, 1910	
Ancient Lights and Certain New Reflections, Being the Memories of a Young Man	Harper, 1911[2]	Chapman and Hall, 1911	
Ladies Whose Bright Eyes, A Romance		Constable, 1911	
The Critical Attitude		Duckworth, 1911	London: Duckworth, 1915
The Panel, A Sheer Comedy	Bobbs-Merrill, 1913[3]	Constable, 1912	
The New Humpty-Dumpty[4]	John Lane, 1912	John Lane, 1912	

Title	*American edition*	*British edition*	*Edition used*
Mr Fleight		Howard Latimer, 1913	
Collected Poems		Max Goschen, 1914[5]	London: Martin Secker, 1916
Henry James, A Critical Study		Martin Secker, 1913 [6]	
The Good Soldier, A Tale of Passion	John Lane, 1915	John Lane, 1915	London: Bodley Head, 1962[7]
When Blood is their Argument, An Analysis of Prussian Culture		Hodder and Stoughton, 1915	
Between St Dennis and St George, A Sketch of Three Civilisations		Hodder and Stoughton, 1915	
On Heaven and Poems Written On Active Service		John Lane, 1918	
Thus to Revisit, Some Reminiscences		Chapman and Hall, 1921	
The Marsden Case, A Romance		Duckworth, 1923[8]	
Women and Men		Paris: Three Mountains Press, 1923	
Mister Bosphorus and the Muses, Or a Short History of Poetry in Britain, Variety Entertainment in Four Acts		Duckworth, 1923	
Some Do Not . . ., A Novel	T. Seltzer, 1924	Duckworth, 1924	N.Y.: New American Library, 1964[9]
The Nature of a Crime[10]	Doubleday, Page, 1924	Duckworth, 1924	N.Y.: Doubleday, Page, 1924
Joseph Conrad, A Personal Remembrance	Boston: Little, Brown, 1924	Duckworth, 1924	

Title	American edition	British edition	Edition used
No More Parades, A Novel	Boni, 1925	Duckworth, 1925	N.Y.: New American Library, 1964[9]
A Mirror to France		Duckworth, 1926	
A Man Could Stand Up–, A Novel	Boni, 1926	Duckworth, 1926	N.Y.: New American Library, 1965[9]
New Poems	Rudge, 1927		N.Y.: Rudge, 1927
New York is not America	Boni, 1927	Duckworth, 1927	
New York Essays	Rudge, 1927		N.Y.: Rudge, 1927
Last Post[11]	Literary Guild, 1928	Duckworth, 1928	N.Y.: New American Library, 1965[9]
A Little Less Than Gods, A Romance	Viking, 1928	Duckworth, 1928	
The English Novel from the Earliest Days to the Death of Joseph Conrad	Philadelphia: Lippincott, 1929	Constable, 1930	
Reminiscences 1894–1914, Return to Yesterday	Liveright, 1932	Gollancz, 1931	N.Y.: Liveright, 1932
When the Wicked Man	Liveright, 1931	Cape, 1932	
The Rash Act, A Novel	Long and Smith, 1933	Cape, 1933	
It was the Nightingale	Philadelphia: Lippincott, 1933	Heinemann, 1934	
Provence, From Minstrels to the Machine[12]	Philadelphia: Lippincott, 1935	Allen and Unwin, 1938	
Vive Le Roy, A Novel	Philadelphia: Lippincott, 1936	Allen and Unwin, 1937	
Great Trade Route	O.U.P., 1937	Allen and Unwin, 1937	
Mightier than the Sword, Memories and Criticisms[13]	Houghton Mifflin, 1937	Allen and Unwin, 1938	
The March of Literature from Confucius to Modern Times	Dial Press, 1938	Allen and Unwin, 1939	London: Allen and Unwin, 1947

Notes

1 A republication in one volume of *The Soul of London, The Heart of the Country,* and *The Spirit of the People.*
2 Published in America as *Memories and Impressions, A Study in Atmospheres.*
3 Published in America as *Ring for Nancy, A Sheer Comedy,* being a revised and expanded version of *The Panel.*
4 Published under the pseudonym of 'Daniel Chaucer'.
5 Actually published in 1913 and postdated.
6 Actually published in 1914.
7 Reprinted Harmondsworth: Penguin, 1972.
8 First book with name 'Ford Madox Ford' to appear on the title-page.
9 Reprinted in one volume, *Parade's End* (New York: Vintage, 1979).
10 First published in *The English Review,* 1909.
11 Published in America under the title of *The Last Post.*
12 Reprinted New York: Ecco Press, 1979.
13 Published in America as *Portraits From Life, Memories and Criticisms.*

Secondary sources

Place of publication is London, unless otherwise stated.

Bibliographies

David Dow Harvey, *Ford Madox Ford 1873–1939, A Bibliography of Works and Criticism* (Princeton, 1962)
Modern Fiction Studies, IX, i (Spring 1963), 94–100.
English Literature in Transition

Collections and anthologies

The Bodley Head Ford Madox Ford (5 vols., 1962–71)
    Vol. I, *The Good Soldier; Selected Memories; Poems*
    Vol. II, *The Fifth Queen Trilogy*
    Vol. III, *Some Do Not. . .*
    Vol. IV, *No More Parades; A Man Could Stand Up–*
    Vol. V, *Memories and Impressions,* ed. Michael Killigrew (reprinted Harmondsworth, 1979)
Critical Writings of Ford Madox Ford, ed. Frank MacShane (Lincoln, Nebraska, 1964)
Letters of Ford Madox Ford, ed. Richard M. Ludwig (Princeton, 1965)
Selected Poems, ed. Basil Bunting (Cambridge, Mass., 1972)

Books and articles on Ford

This selected bibliography may be supplemented by Harvey's lengthy annotated bibliography (1962), and, for criticism published thereafter, by the regular listings in *English Literature in Transition*. Works listed in *Harvey* have not been included below, except where I have found them particularly illuminating.

Andreach, R. J., *The Slain and Resurrected God: Conrad, Ford and the Christian Myth* (New York, 1970)

Annan, Noel, 'Champion of Bohemia', *New York Review of Books*, XVI, xi (17 June 1971), 17–18

Anon., 'Ford as others saw him', *The Times Literary Supplement*, 3662 (5 May 1972), 519–20

Aswell, D., 'The saddest storyteller in Ford's *The Good Soldier*', *College Language Association Journal*, XIV, ii (December 1970), 187–96

Auden, W. H., 'Il faut payer', *Mid-Century*, XXII (February 1961), 3–10

Baernstein, J.-A., 'Image, identity and insight in *The Good Soldier*', *Critique: Studies in Modern Fiction*, IX, i (1966), 19–42

Barnes, D. R., 'Ford and the "Slaughtered Saints": a new reading of *The Good Soldier*', *Modern Fiction Studies*, XIV, ii (Summer 1968), 157–70

Beer, John, 'Ford's impression of the Lawrences', *The Times Literary Supplement*, 3662 (5 May 1972), 520

Bergonzi, B., 'The reputation of Ford Madox Ford', *The Turn of a Century: Essays on Victorian and Modern English Literature* (1973), pp. 139–46

Bornhauser, F., 'Ford as art critic', *Shenandoah*, IV (Spring 1953), 51–9

Borowitz, H. O., 'The paint beneath the prose: Ford Madox Ford's Pre-Raphaelite ancestry', *Modern Fiction Studies*, XXI (1975), 483–98

Bort, B. D., '*The Good Soldier*: comedy or tragedy?' *Twentieth Century Literature*, XII (January 1967), 194–202

Bradbury, Malcolm, 'The English Review', *London Magazine*, V (August 1958), 46–57

Possibilities: Essays on the State of the Novel (1973), ch. VII

'The denuded place: war and form in *Parade's End* and *USA*', H. Klein, ed., *The First World War in Fiction* (1976), pp. 193–209

Braybrooke, N., 'The walrus and the windmill: a study of Ford Madox Ford', *Sewanee Review*, LXXIV (Autumn 1966), 810–31

'Fiction's long shadow: *The Good Soldier*', *Contemporary Review*, 209 (November 1966), 261–4

'Ford Madox Ford: the writing windmill', *Month*, CCXXVI (October 1968), 186–96

Brebach, R. T., 'The making of *Romance*, Part Fifth', *Conradiana*, VI (1974), 171–81

Brown, C., 'Marlow and Dowell', *Philological Quarterly*, LVI, i (Winter 1977), 136–40

Cassell, R. A., *Ford Madox Ford – a Study of his Novels* (Baltimore, 1961)

'Images of collapse and reconstruction: Ford's vision of society', *English Literature in Transition*, XIX (1976), 265–82

'The two Sorrells of Ford Madox Ford', *Modern Philology*, LIX (November 1961), 114–21

ed., *Ford Madox Ford – Modern Judgments* (1962)

Cohen, Mary, '*The Good Soldier*: outworn codes', *Studies in the Novel*, V, iii (Fall 1973), 284–97

Core, George, 'Ordered life and the abysses of chaos: *Parade's End*', *Southern Review*, VIII, iii (July 1972), 520–32

Cox, James T., 'Ford's passion for Provence', *English Literary History*, XXVIII (December 1961), 383–98

'The finest French novel in the English language', *Modern Fiction Studies*, IX, i (Spring 1963), 79–93

Dekoven, Marianne, 'Valentine Wannop and thematic structure in Ford Madox Ford's *Parade's End*', *English Literature in Transition*, XX, ii (1977), 56–68

Delbaere-Garant, J., ' "Who shall inherit England?" A comparison between *Howards End, Parade's End* and *Unconditional Surrender*', *English Studies*, L (February 1969), 101–5

Donoghue, Denis, 'A reply to Frank Kermode', *Critical Inquiry*, I (December 1974), 447–52

Esslinger, P. M., 'A theory and three experiments: the failure of the Conrad–Ford collaboration', *Western Humanities Review*, XXII, ii (Spring 1972), 59–67

Firebaugh, J. J., 'Tietjens and the tradition', *Pacific Spectator*, VI (Winter 1952), 23–32

Gabbay, L. R., 'The four square coterie: a comparison of Ford Madox Ford and Henry James', *Studies in the Novel*, VI, iv (Winter 1974), 439–53

Goldring, Douglas, *South Lodge* (1943)

The Last Pre-Raphaelite: A Record of the Life and Writings of Ford Madox Ford (1948)

Gordon, Ambrose, *The Invisible Tent: The War Novels of Ford Madox Ford* (Austin, 1964)

Gordon, Caroline, 'The Elephant', *Sewanee Review*, LXXIV (Autumn 1966), 854–71

Gose, Elliott B., 'Reality to romance: a study of Ford's *Parade's End*', *College English*, XVII (May 1956), 445–50

'The strange irregular rhythm: an analysis of *The Good Soldier*', *Publications of the Modern Language Association*, LXII (June 1957), 494–509

Grainger, J. H., 'A presentment of Englishry', *Contemporary Review*, 213 (September 1968), 151–6

Green, Robert, 'Ford Madox Ford's *The Inheritors:* a conservative response to Social Imperialism', *English Literature in Transition*, XXII, i (1979), 50–61

'*The Good Soldier*: the politics of agnosticism', *Modernist Studies*, III (1980)

Griffith, M., 'A double reading of *Parade's End*', *Modern Fiction Studies*, IX, i (Spring 1963), 25–38

Hanzo, T. A., 'Downward to darkness', *Sewanee Review*, LXXIV (Autumn 1966), 833–55

Harvey, D. D., '*Pro Patria Mori*: the neglect of Ford's novels in England', *Modern Fiction Studies*, IX, i (Spring 1963), 3–16

Heldman, J. M., 'The last Victorian novel: technique and theme in *Parade's End*', *Twentieth Century Literature*, XVIII (October 1972), 271–84

Henighan, T. J., 'Mr Bransdon: a Ford lampoon of Conrad?', *American Notes and Queries*, viii (September 1969), 3–5; *ibid.* (October 1969), 20–2

'Tietjens transformed: A reading of *Parade's End*', *English Literature in Transition*, xv, ii (1972), 144–57

Higdon, D. L., 'The Conrad–Ford collaboration', *Conradiana*, vi (1974), 155–6

Hill, A. G., 'The literary career of Ford Madox Ford', *Critical Quarterly*, v (Winter 1963), 369–79

Hoffmann, Charles, *Ford Madox Ford* (New York, 1967)

' "The Life and Times of Henry VIII": an original for Ford Madox Ford's Fifth Queen trilogy', *Notes and Queries*, xiv (July 1967), 248–50

Homberger, Eric, 'Pound, Ford and "Prose": The making of a modern poet', *Journal of American Studies*, v, iii (December 1971), 281–92

Howarth, Herbert, 'Hewlett and Ford among Renaissance women', *Journal of Modern Literature*, v, i (1976), 79–88

Hungiville, M., ' "The last happy time": Ford Madox Ford in America', *Journal of Modern Literature*, vi (1977), 209–21

Huntley, H. R., *The Alien Protagonist of Ford Madox Ford* (Chapel Hill, 1970)

Hynes, Samuel, 'The epistemology of *The Good Soldier*', *Sewanee Review*, lxix (Spring 1961), 225–35

'The conscious artist', *The Times Literary Supplement*, 3146 (15 June 1962), 437–9

'Ford and the spirit of romance', *Modern Fiction Studies*, ix, i (Spring 1963), 17–24

'Ford Madox Ford: three dedicatory letters to *Parade's End* with commentary and notes', *Modern Fiction Studies*, xvi, iv (Winter 1970), 515–28

'Conrad and Ford: two Rye revolutionists', *Edwardian Occasions* (1972), pp. 48–53

Jacobs, Carol, '*The* (too) *Good Soldier*: "a real story" ', *Glyph 3: Johns Hopkins Textual Studies* (Baltimore, 1978), pp. 32–51

Johnson, A. S., 'Narrative form in *The Good Soldier*', *Critique: Studies in Modern Fiction*, xi, ii (1968), 70–80

Jones, L. W., 'The quality of sadness in Ford's *The Good Soldier*', *English Literature in Transition*, xiii, iv (1970), 296–302

Karl, F. R., 'Conrad, Ford, and the novel', *Midway*, x, ii (Autumn 1969), 17–34

Kashner, Rita J., 'Tietjens' education: Ford Madox Ford's tetralogy', *Critical Quarterly*, viii (Summer 1966), 150–63

Kazin, Alfred, 'Ford's modern romance', *New York Review of Books*, xxvi, xviii (22 November 1979), 31–2

Kennedy, Alan, 'Tietjens' travels: *Parade's End* as comedy', *Twentieth Century Literature*, xvi (April 1970), 85–95

Kenner, Hugh, 'Remember that I have remembered', *Hudson Review*, iii (Winter 1951), 602–11

'Conrad and Ford', *Shenandoah*, iii (Summer 1952), 50–5

Kermode, Frank, 'Novels: recognition and deception', *Critical Inquiry*, I (September 1974), 103–21

Laughlin, C., 'Ford's corrections to *The March of Literature*', *Book Collector*, XXVI (Spring 1977), 107–8

Leer, Norman, *The Limited Hero* (Michigan, 1966)

Lehan, Richard, 'Ford Madox Ford and the absurd: *The Good Soldier*', *Texas Studies in Literature and Language*, v, ii (Summer 1963), 219–31

Lentz, Vern B., 'Ford's good narrator', *Studies in the Novel*, v, iv (Winter 1973), 483–90

Leverence, J., 'Carlos Drake and Ford Madox Ford', *Lost Generation Journal*, IV, ii (1976), 9

Levin, G., 'Character and myth in Ford's *Parade's End*', *Journal of Modern Literature*, I, ii (1970–1), 183–96

Lid, Richard W., *Ford Madox Ford – The Essence of his Art* (Berkeley, 1964)

Loeb, Harold, 'Ford Madox Ford's *The Good Soldier*: a critical reminiscence', *The Carleton Miscellany*, VI (Spring 1965), 27–41

Macauley, R., 'A moveable myth', *Encounter*, XXIII, iii (September 1964), 56–8

McFate, Patricia and Golden, Bruce, '*The Good Soldier*: A tragedy of self-deception', *Modern Fiction Studies*, IX, i (Spring 1963), 50–60

McLaughlin, A. V., 'Dowell's doubt: the tragic flaw in *The Good Soldier*', *Horizontes*, XXV (1974), 17–18

McLaughlin, M. B., 'Adjusting the lens for *The Good Soldier*', *English Record*, XXII, iii (Spring 1972), 41–8

MacShane, Frank, 'The English Review', *South Atlantic Quarterly*, LX (Summer 1961), 311–20

The Life and Work of Ford Madox Ford (1965)

ed., *Ford Madox Ford: The critical heritage* (1972)

Martin, J. J., 'Edward Garnett and Conrad's reshaping of time', *Conradiana*, VI, ii (1974), 89–105

Meixner, John A., *Ford Madox Ford's Novels – A Critical Study* (Minneapolis, 1962)

'Ford and Conrad', *Conradiana*, VI (1974), 157–69

Meyer, Bernard C., *Joseph Conrad: A Psychoanalytic Biography* (Princeton, 1967), ch. VII

Mizener, Arthur, 'Ford Madox Ford', *Contemporary Literature*, IX, iii (Summer 1968), 442–8

The Saddest Story – A Biography of Ford Madox Ford (New York, 1971)

Mohay, B., 'Ford Madox Ford's contribution to the theory of the novel', *Hungarian Studies in English*, VIII (December 1974), 57–68

Moser, Thomas C., 'Towards *The Good Soldier* – discovery of a sexual theme', *Daedalus*, LXXXII (Spring 1963), 312–25

'Conrad, Marwood, and Ford: biographical speculations on the genesis of *The Good Soldier*', *Mosaic*, VIII, i (Fall 1974), 217–27

'From Olive Garnett's diary: impressions of Ford Madox Ford and his friends, 1890–1906', *Texas Studies in Literature and Language*, XVI, iii (Fall 1974), 511–34

'Conrad, Ford, and the sources of *Chance*', *Conradiana*, vii (1975), 207–24

'Conrad and *The Good Soldier*', N. Sherry, ed., *Joseph Conrad: A Commemoration* (1976), pp. 174–82

Mosher, Harold F., 'Wayne Booth and the failure of rhetoric in *The Good Soldier*', *Caliban*, iv (1969), 49–52

Ohmann, Carol, *Ford Madox Ford – from Appentice to Craftsman* (Middletown, 1964)

Poli, Bernard, *Ford Madox Ford and the Transatlantic Review* (Syracuse, 1967)

Pritchett, V. S., 'The Good Soldier', *New Statesman* (5 May 1972), 599–600

Rodway, Allan, 'Unhappily ever after: on Ford Madox Ford', *Encounter*, xxxix, vi (December 1972), 66–70

Rose, C., '*Romance* and the maiden archetype', *Conradiana*, vi (1974), 183–8

Schorer, Mark, '*The Good Soldier*: a tale of passion', *The World We Imagine* (1969), pp. 97–104

Schow, H. Wayne, 'Ironic structure in *The Good Soldier*', *English Literature in Transition*, xviii, iii (1975), 203–11

Secor, Marie, 'Violet Hunt, novelist: a reintroduction', *English Literature in Transition*, xix, i (1976), 25–34

Seiden, Melvin, 'Ford Madox Ford and his tetralogy', *London Magazine*, vi (August 1959), 45–55

'Persecution and paranoia in *Parade's End*', *Criticism*, viii (Summer 1966), 246–61

Siemens, Reynold, 'The juxtaposition of composed renderings in Ford's *The Good Soldier*', *Humanities Association Bulletin*, xxiii, iii (Summer 1972), 44–9

Smith, Grover, *Ford Madox Ford* (New York, 1972)

Solomon, Eric, 'From Christ in Flanders to *Catch 22*: An approach to war fiction', *Texas Studies in Literature and Language*, xi (1969), 851–66

Spear, H. D., 'The accuracy of impressions: kaleidoscopic viewpoints in *The Good Soldier*', *Durham University Journal*, lxx (June 1978), 149–53

Stang, S. J., 'A reading of Ford's *The Good Soldier*', *Modern Language Quarterly*, xxx, iv (December 1969), 545–63

Ford Madox Ford (New York, 1977)

Stevenson, Lionel, *Yesterday and After* (New York, 1967), pp. 73–87

Sullivan, Z. T., 'Civilization and its darkness: Conrad's *Heart of Darkness* and Ford's *The Good Soldier*', *Conradiana*, viii (1976), 110–20

Swinden, Patrick, *Unofficial Selves: Character in the Novel from Dickens to the Present Day* (1973), ch. v

Tanner, T., 'A saint of literature', *Encounter*, xxv, v (November 1965), 71–8

Thornton, L., 'Escaping the impasse: criticism and the mitosis of *The Good Soldier*', *Modern Fiction Studies*, xxi (1975), 237–41

'Ford Madox Ford and *The Great Gatsby*', *Fitzgerald–Hemingway Annual* (1975), 57–74

' "Deux bonshommes distincts": Conrad, Ford, and the visual arts', *Conradiana*, vIII (1976), 3–12

Tytell, J., 'The Jamesian Legacy in *The Good Soldier*', *Studies in the Novel*, III, iv (Winter 1971), 365–73

Vidan, Ivo, 'Rehearsal for *Nostromo*', *Studia Romanica et Anglica*, XII (December 1961), 9–16

'Ford's interpretation of Conrad's technique', N. Sherry, ed., *Joseph Conrad: A Commemoration* (1976), pp. 183–93

Wagner, Geoffrey, 'Ford Madox Ford: the honest Edwardian', *Essays in Criticism*, XVII (January 1967), 75–88

Walter, E. V., 'The political sense of Ford Madox Ford', *New Republic*, CXXXIV, xiii (26 March 1956), 17–19

Webb, Igor, 'Marriage and sex in the novels of Ford Madox Ford', *Modern Fiction Studies*, XXIII (1977–8), 586–92

Webb, Max, 'Ford Madox Ford and the Baton Rouge Writers' Conference', *Southern Review*, x, iv (October 1974), 892–903

Whitlow, Roger, 'Ford Madox Ford and William Golding: function and technique in the novel', *CEA Critic*, XXXIX, iii (1977), 21–5

Wiesenfarth, J., 'Criticism and the semiosis of *The Good Soldier*', *Modern Fiction Studies*, IX, i (Spring 1963), 39–49

Wiley, Paul L., *Novelist of Three Worlds – Ford Madox Ford* (Syracuse, 1962)

'Two tales of passion', *Conradiana*, VI (1974), 189–95

Winegarten, Renee, 'Ford Madox Ford – Zionist', *Midstream*, XII (August–September 1966), 71–5

Young, Kenneth, *Ford Madox Ford* (1956)

Zabel, M. D., *Craft and Character in Modern Fiction* (1957)

INDEX

Ashley, Sir William, 75
Attlee, Clement, 84
Auden, W. H., 141
Austen, Jane, 105, 185
  Emma, 129
  Mansfield Park, 129

Balfour, Arthur, Earl of, 14, 15, 16,
  21, 22, 29, 30, 39, 40, 63
Balzac, Honoré de, 105, 146
Barbusse, Henri
  Le Feu, 156, 158
Baudelaire, Charles, 193
Beckett, Samuel, 99
  Endgame, 100
  Waiting for Godot, 100
Belloc, Hilaire, 42
Benjamin, Walter, 156, 193
Bennett, Arnold, 59, 60, 68, 69, 85,
  105, 135
  The Old Wives' Tale, 87, 135,
  189–90, 191
Beowulf, 180
Berger, John, 92
  G, 80
Bergonzi, Bernard, 66, 90, 93
Bergson, Henri, 8
Beveridge, William, Baron, 84
Biala, Janice, 176–7
Bismarck, Otto von, 75, 76, 194
Blythe, Ronald
  Akenfield, 189
Bradbury, Malcolm, 163
Braque, Georges, 156
Brontë, Charlotte
  Wuthering Heights, 94
Brown, Ford Madox, 4, 23, 38, 63,
  188
Brown, John, 185

Carlyle, Thomas, 185, 186

Cassell, Richard A., 5, 145
Chamberlain, Joseph, 14, 15, 16, 17,
  20, 21, 22, 29, 40
Chesterton, G. K., 42
Churchill, Randolph, 16
Conrad, Jessie, 11
Conrad, Joseph, x, 4, 5–13, 20, 25,
  26, 28, 34, 35, 36, 49, 50, 84,
  96, 172, 178, 183–92 *passim*
  Almayer's Folly, 6
  An Outcast of the Islands, 6
  Heart of Darkness, 11–12, 17, 20,
  23
  Lord Jim, 10, 97
  Nostromo, 10, 23, 36, 38, 132, 184,
  186
  The Nigger of the 'Narcissus', 6–8,
  10–11
Cromwell, Thomas, 42, 43–6, 47
Cunningham, William, 75

Daladier, Edouard, 173
Darwin, Charles, 40
Defoe, Daniel, x, 34, 105, 180
Dickens, Charles, 35, 105, 131, 186
  Bleak House, 92
Douglas, C. H., ix, 123, 124, 128,
  156
Dreiser, Theodore, 107, 108
Durkheim, Emile, 8

Eagleton, Terry, 190–1
Eliot, George, 66, 186
  Middlemarch, 129
Eliot, T. S., 41, 88, 89, 122, 175,
  189, 190, 191
  Criterion, 31, 141–2
Epstein, Jacob, 90

Fielding, Henry, 180
  Joseph Andrews, 129
  Tom Jones, 129

215

Flaubert, Gustave, xi, 68, 120, 172, 183, 186, 189
Madame Bovary, 9
Fleishman, Avrom, 47
Flint, F. S., 34
Ford, Ford Madox
A Call, xi, 34, 49, 56–62 *passim*, 69, 117, 132, 135, 179
A Little Less Than Gods, xi, 40, 123, 127
A Man Could Stand Up–, 129, 130, 133–4, 136–7, 140–1, 144, 146–7, 159–62, 163–4
A Mirror to France, 115, 118, 121
An English Girl, 28
Ancient Lights, x, 62–7 *passim*, 72
Between St Dennis and St George, 62, 74, 75
England and the English, 59, 64, 80
Ford Madox Brown, 5–6
Great Trade Route, x, 174, 175–6, 179, 180, 189
Henry for Hugh, 105, 173
Henry James, x, 8, 62, 70–2, 82
It was the Nightingale, 113, 130, 131–2, 177
Joseph Conrad, 11, 118, 119
Ladies Whose Bright Eyes, 37, 40, 53, 54, 55, 73
Last Post, 128, 129, 133, 136, 138, 139, 147, 148, 149, 159, 162–7, 174, 179, 180, 181
'Left Turn', 182
Mightier than the Sword, x, 31
Mr Apollo, 29, 194
Mister Bosphorus and the Muses, 119, 129
Mr Fleight, 49, 54, 55, 56, 57, 65, 82, 105
New York Essays, 115
New York is not America, 115
No More Parades, 129, 130, 143, 151, 154–7, 159, 198
Parade's End, xi, 10, 24, 28, 39, 40, 50, 81, 92, 100, 105, 115, 117–18, 121–8 *passim*, 129–67, 172, 175, 177–88 *passim*, 192, 194
Privy Seal, 33, 44
Provence, x, 174, 175–6, 179, 180, 189
Return to Yesterday, 8, 187

Romance, 5, 10, 11, 15, 28, 50, 62, 127
'Seraphina', 5, 6
Some Do Not . . ., 114–17, 129, 136, 137, 138, 139, 148, 149, 150–60, 166–7
The Benefactor, 28, 29, 34, 42, 132, 135, 179
The Brown Owl, 4
The Cinque Ports, 12–13, 21, 63
The Critical Attitude, x, 62, 66–72 *passim*, 82
The English Novel, 171, 172
The English Review, 3, 9, 27, 29, 30, 31, 63, 66, 69, 72, 76, 79, 118
The Feather, 4
The Fifth Queen, 33, 38, 49, 92, 132–3
The Fifth Queen Crowned, 33, 37, 45, 46, 60
The Good Soldier, xi, 10, 33–6 *passim*, 41, 49–78 *passim*, 80–109, 137, 140, 141, 151, 153, 167, 177, 181–8 *passim*, 192, 194
The Half-Moon, 40, 50
The Inheritors, xi, 10, 11, 13–26, 27, 28, 29, 39, 42, 43, 50, 62, 70, 74, 75, 76, 93, 195
The March of Literature, x, 9, 39–40, 171–2, 173
The Marsden Case, xi, 113, 114, 125–8, 132
The New Humpty-Dumpty, 49, 53, 55, 56, 61, 65, 194
The Panel, 54–5
The Portrait, 40, 54, 55
The Queen Who Flew, 4
The Rash Act, 173
The Shifting of the Fire, 5, 6
The Soul of London, 25
The Spirit of the People, 41, 43
The Transatlantic Review, 3, 115, 124–5, 173
Thus to Revisit, 118–20
Vive Le Roy, xi, 173, 177–9
When Blood is their Argument, 44, 62, 74–7
When the Wicked Man, 173, 181
Forster, E. M., 46, 57, 68, 97, 190, 193
Howards End, 98, 114

Franco, Francisco, 176
Frank, Joseph, 88, 89
Freud, Sigmund, 8

Galsworthy, John, 46, 49, 68, 69, 85, 189
   The Forsyte Saga, 134
Garnett, Edward, 6
Garnett, Olive, 188
Gaudier-Brzeska, Henri, 90
Gaulle, Charles de, 120
Gide, André, 30, 62, 92–3
   Nouvelle Revue Française, 30
Gladstone, W. E., 16
Goldring, Douglas, 37, 78, 175
Gordon, Ambrose, 94, 148
Gordon, Caroline, 177
Graham, R. B. Cunninghame, 30, 73
Greene, Graham, 37, 162, 171, 174, 175, 186

Haldane, R. B., 75, 76
Hampshire, Stuart, 87
Hardy, Thomas, 98, 135
   Desperate Remedies, 5
   Far from the Madding Crowd, 129
   Jude the Obscure, 98
   Tess of the D'Urbervilles, 135
Harvey, D. D., xii
Hay, Ian, 83
Hegel, G. W. F., 40
Henley, 6
Henry VIII, King, 42, 45, 192
Hewlett, Maurice
   The Queen's Quair, 35
Hicks, Granville
   The Great Tradition, 108
Hitler, Adolf, 175, 176
Hobson, J. A., 20, 73
Hoffmann, Charles, 94
Holbein, Hans, 37, 43
Howard, Katharine, 42–7, 48
Howe, Irving, 47
Hueffer, Ford Madox, 77, 80, 192
Hueffer, Francis, 3, 4, 172
Hughes, H. Stuart, 97
Hulme, T. E., 41, 49, 66, 69, 70, 75, 83, 88, 189
   'Romanticism and Classicism', 130
Hynes, Samuel, 163

Ionesco, Eugene, 99

James, Henry, 7, 10, 26, 49, 70–2, 94–6, 172, 183–92 *passim*
   Princess Casamassima, 142
   What Maisie Knew, 7, 93, 184
Jones, David
   In Parenthesis, 144
Joyce, James, 68, 84, 89, 107, 147, 172, 183, 189, 190
   A Portrait of the Artist, 68, 147
   Finnegans Wake, 173
   Ulysses, 104
   Work in Progress, 173

Kermode, Frank, 33, 91, 92, 104

Law, A. Bonar, 69, 83, 97
Lawrence, D. H., 31–2, 34, 60, 63, 150, 177, 180, 181, 193
   Aaron's Rod, 127
   Kangaroo, 114, 150
   Lady Chatterley's Lover, 129
   short stories, 150–1
   Sons and Lovers, 147, 164
   The Plumed Serpent, 127
   The Rainbow, 98
   The White Peacock, 59
Leavis, F. R.
   Scrutiny, 31
Lenin, V. I., 20
Leopold, King of the Belgians, 16, 20
Lewis, P. Wyndham, 41
   Blast, 90, 91
Lloyd George, David, 62, 64, 73, 83
Lodge, David, 85
Lukács, Georg, x, 48, 144, 146
Luxemburg, Rosa, 20

Mackinder, William, 20
MacShane, Frank, xii
Mallock, W. H., 73
Malraux, André
   L'Espoir, 179
Mann, Thomas, 62
Marinetti, Filippo, 90
Marx, Karl, 48
Masterman, J. H. B., 19
   Condition of England, 19, 29, 67, 69
Maupassant, Guy de, 9, 120, 172
Meredith, George
   The Egoist, 150
Milner, Alfred, Viscount, 17, 20

Mizener, Arthur, xii, 5, 126, 127, 149, 150, 184, 194
Morris, William, 4, 63
Mottram, R. H.
  Spanish Farm trilogy, 118, 142, 158

New Republic, 107, 108
Nicolson, Nigel,
  Portrait of a Marriage, 60

Orage, A. R., 123
Outlook, 72–4
Owen, Wilfred, 74, 144

Pater, Walter, 7, 22
Pétain, Philippe, 120
Picasso, Pablo, 156
Pound, Ezra, 34, 41, 83, 89, 123
Proust, Marcel, 62, 89, 103, 147

Ragged-Trousered Philanthropists, The (Tressell), 94
Richardson, Dorothy, 84, 107
Richardson, Samuel, 180
Rolland, Romain, 113
Rosebery, Archibald, Earl of, 17, 18, 22, 164
Rosenberg, Isaac, 144
Rossetti, Gabriel, 4, 63, 191
Ruskin, John, 185, 186

'Saki', 57
Salisbury, Robert Cecil, Marquis of, 14, 16, 20, 63, 84
Sand, George, 186
Schopenhauer, Arthur, 3
Schorer, Mark, 88
Scott, Sir Walter, 35, 84, 146, 185
Shakespeare, William
  Cymbeline, 173
  Henry V, 144
  The Winter's Tale, 173
Shannon, Richard, 67
Shelley, P. B., 7

Sidney, Sir Philip, 7
Simenon, Georges, 178
Spender, Stephen, 96–7
Stalin, Joseph, 176
Stang, S. J., 184, 185
Stendhal, 9
Sturt, George
  The Wheelwright's Shop, 189
Sypher, Wylie, 91, 92–3

Taine, Hippolyte, 40
Tennyson, Alfred, Lord, 66
Thackeray, W. M., 35, 131
Thomson, David, 57
Throckmorton, 43, 44
Tolstoy, Count Leo, 106, 146
  Anna Karenina, 134
  War and Peace, 145
Tonnies, Ferdinand, 180
Trotsky, Leo, 78
Turgenev, Ivan, 9

Vaizey, John, 181

Wagner, Geoffrey, 93
Webb, Beatrice, 14, 17, 26
  Our Partnership, 26, 84
Webb, Beatrice and Sidney, 12–13, 16, 20, 23, 30
Weber, Max, 180
Wells, H. G., 19, 68, 85, 189–90, 191
  Ann Veronica, 98
  The New Machiavelli, 27, 29, 65, 83, 84
  The Time Machine, 25
Wiley, Paul L., 115, 144
Woolf, Leonard
  Beginning Again, 63
Woolf, Virginia, 68, 84, 107, 147, 181, 183

Yeats, W. B., 5, 41, 177, 190
  'Byzantium', 175

Zweig, Arnold
  Trilogy of the Transition, 118, 158